JCE
99.95

WITHDRAWN
from
EASTERN FLORIDA STATE COLLEGE LIBRARIES

D1474527

Seven Steps to a Successful Business Plan

Seven Steps
to a
Successful
Business Plan

Al Coke

AMACOM
American Management Association

New York • Atlanta • Brussels • Buenos Aires • Chicago • London • Mexico City
San Francisco • Shanghai • Tokyo • Toronto • Washington, D.C.

Special discounts on bulk quantities of AMACOM books are available to corporations, professional associations, and other organizations. For details, contact Special Sales Department, AMACOM, a division of American Management Association, 1601 Broadway, New York, NY 10019. Tel.: 212-903-8316. Fax: 212-903-8083. Web site: www. amacombooks.org

This publication is designed to provide accurate and authoritative information in regard to the subject matter covered. It is sold with the understanding that the publisher is not engaged in rendering legal, accounting, or other professional service. If legal advice or other expert assistance is required, the services of a competent professional person should be sought.

Library of Congress Cataloging-in-Publication Data

Coke, Al.
    Seven steps to a successful business plan / Al Coke.
        p. cm.
    Includes bibliographical references and index.
    ISBN 0-8144-0648-3
    1. Business planning. 2. Strategic planning. 3. Success in business.
I. Title.

HD30.28 .C6422 2001
658.4'012—dc21

                                                    2001033579

©2002 Alfred M. Coke
All rights reserved.
Printed in the United States of America.

This publication may not be reproduced,
stored in a retrieval system,
or transmitted in whole or in part,
in any form or by any means, electronic,
mechanical, photocopying, recording, or otherwise,
without the prior written permission of AMACOM,
a division of American Management Association,
1601 Broadway, New York, NY 10019.

Printing number

10 9 8 7 6 5 4 3 2 1

Contents

1 How to Create a Compelling Company Story That Inspires Employees to Excel   1

2 The Practical Guidelines for Building a Business Plan in Five Pages

9 Structuring Your Story: How to Develop an Organizational Plan   243

11 Contingency Planning: How to Prepare for the Unexpected

12 Implementing and Sustaining Your Business Plan

List of Figures

CHAPTER 1

CHAPTER 2

CHAPTER 3

Chapter 11

Chapter 12

How This Book Can Help You Develop a Powerful Business Plan That Works

This book gives you a proven method to help ensure your company's success. Organizations fail to accomplish their goals for one simple reason: The management story being told is incomplete, inaccurate, and incongruent. This book cuts past the traditional problems of planning and provides management with a documented method of building a simplified business plan that works. You'll learn how to tell a story that is inclusive of employees and empowers them to participate in the company success.

THE FIVE CRITICAL INGREDIENTS OF A SUCCESSFUL BUSINESS PLAN

There are five conditions critical to successfully building a powerful, executable business plan. You must:

1. Simplify definitions and use words in plain business language.
2. Clearly demonstrate the relationships among planning elements.
3. Successfully link the connections between your strategic, operational, organizational, resources, and contingency plans.
4. Incorporate all functions into a single planning model.
5. Achieve total employee involvement by taking the business plan to all levels.

I wrote this book for you as a manager, someone who is the steward of any organization, be it large or small. The concepts of business apply no matter whether you are an entrepreneur or a manager for a well-established, publicly traded company. Companies are organizations, no matter what their size, type, or product. This means you must have an integrated business plan no matter who you are or what you do. Business planning is important whether you are a start-up company in e-business or working on a multinational planning team. This book gives you a place to start, a system to make sense of the confusion around planning, and a model to build a complete package.

WHY THE TRADITIONAL PLANNING MODELS FOR BUILDING A BUSINESS PLAN DON'T WORK

I can contribute to your success by sharing a method of business planning based on an approach that's different from the dry, traditional numbers method. My experience is that you are currently using one of three approaches to business planning: traditional, piecemeal, or one with a deflected focus.

The Traditional Approach: Good Intentions, Dismal Results

A large number of published works and many management consultants simply say the same thing. They are replays of the same themes of setting the vision, establishing goals, and getting employee buy-in. Had the traditional approach of forming a planning team and producing a document been successful, there would be no need for this book.

The traditional planning approach fails because the required parts are not integrated, the results are boring, and the process is not completed throughout the company. These three faults create a deadly waste of company time, money, and talent. While the intentions are good, the results are dismal. That is why traditional planning appears to have management teams simply going through the motions over and over again with each yearly plan.

The Piecemeal Approach: No Way to Fit the Pieces Together

This book gives you all the elements of the business plan and shows you how to fit them together. Most businesses think they are planning when in fact they are going about it in a piecemeal fashion. Company presidents need to see a simple but complete picture that tells them how to be successful. Everyone needs to understand the relationship between strategic goals and next week's tasks. Employees need to understand the annual targets and how they apply to their performance. Objectives need to be tied to accountability and responsibility. In a piecemeal approach I've found management teams that do not understand the interactive relationships of the parts and pieces of planning.

This book gives you the tools you need for designing a fully integrated business plan for your company. A business plan is simple on the one hand yet sophisticated on the other (see Appendix A). You must be able to present that simplicity and complexity simultaneously. The picture you create must encompass both the short- and long-term views. It must be strategic yet contain details of the daily requirements. The concept must include verification of where you are today as well as documentation of where you intend to take the business. Finally, it must serve as a reference tool for your employees and management as they conduct business.

This book creates a vehicle for bonding among your team. What better way to become a team than to deal with real business issues in an orderly, professional fashion? And finally, this book helps you create a condition for full participation in the plan, not the traditional "let's get it over with" attitude. Once you get your team on the same page, there will be no serious blocks in your planning process.

The Deflected Focus Approach: Falling Short of Your Company's Real Needs

Planning models and theories that approach faddish status usually prove to fall short of achieving business success. They don't present a complete process, resembling more bits and pieces of processes rather than a unified, logical pathway to the future. They deflect from the true needs of planners to tell a story in business terms. For example, hundreds of millions of dollars have been spent on reengineering efforts, Total Quality Management (TQM), and the balanced scorecard, all with minimum overall return. These activities may be good as specific tools, but they cannot substitute for a completely integrated planning model. Unfortunately, companies attempt shortcuts with these overpromised tools and get fragmented success. Only by using a complete planning cycle and applying appropriate tools at appropriate times can you ever achieve the full force of the business plan.

THE THREE UNIQUE FEATURES OF THIS BOOK THAT WILL HELP YOU ACHIEVE YOUR BUSINESS PLAN GOALS

There is a fourth option that overcomes the problems with traditional, piecemeal, or deflected business planning. This planning process puts energy and emotion back into the company. It energizes the workforce by tapping into employees' purpose and passion. The model encourages the use of intellectual capital and promotes the empowerment of people to take responsibility for accomplishing agreed-on, realistic goals. The planning process forces examination of how work is done with the idea of eliminating unnecessary and wasted efforts that translate to lost profits.

This book will help you find a sensible starting point, illustrate the value of the parts and pieces of an integrated planning model, and build a case so logical that you cannot avoid writing a business plan. I'm going to be appealing to your most basic business sense and show you how to be successful in setting goals and reaching your vision.

Your Management Story

This book centers on your management story. I like the concept of story because it conveys meaning in the simplest possible way. We live, love, and entertain through storytelling. Today you may have bits and pieces of the story, but is it believable, consistent, and authentic? Is the story being told in a way that your employees understand, buy into, and implement with minimum loss of work effort? A central message throughout this book is the need to have all the parts and pieces connected in such a way that they reinforce each other. In short, they must hang together in a way that forms a story of hope, passion, and opportunity for success.

The Concept of backPlanning*

Another unique element of this book is the concept of backPlanning. This requires the company to define where it wants to be and then work backward from that point. This forces management to put a stake in the ground about where they intend to take the company. The normal fear of vagueness often associated with vision-based planning is eliminated because backPlanning also stresses forward execution. This means the strategic goals are converted to short-term, practical, operational activities. You will see the connection between your daily requirements and where you want to take the company.

The 5-Page Business Plan

The traditional business plan does not meet the needs of real-world managers. They need a simple, effective tool that is easy-to-read, portable, and keys them into what needs to get done. My planning tool gives you a concise, functional plan in five pages. I have been extremely successful helping many companies build powerful plans using the 5-Page Business Plan format. Simple plans are popular from executives down to operators because they are convenient, concise, and user-friendly. Use this book to help you consolidate your complete business plan into five pages.

HOW TO CONVERT YOUR GOALS INTO PRACTICAL BUSINESS BEHAVIOR

Over the years I have met and worked with thousands of managers as a consultant and trainer. So many of you have told me of the need to convert vague, esoteric, and often unrealistic planning into something concrete and doable. I heard you. Business planning is of no value unless it can be connected to next year's daily activities.

---

* backPlanning is a registered trademark of Al Coke & Associates, International.

There is a way to make the connection between the desired end state or vision and the existing present state or mission. Those connections are illustrated in this model and they stem from a basic principle in my planning approach: Everything you do on a daily basis must contribute in some way to your strategic goals. The reverse is also true. Your goals must be converted to practical, daily behavior.

A critical point raised in my many discussions with managers is the failure of planning to reach all levels. That failure is directly attributed to the planning model, the planning documentation, and the lack of planning accountability. Typically, planning is a three-day conference held at a resort. There's a lot of build up, hoopla, and fanfare. Promises are made knowing they will be broken. Numbers are bantered about as if they actually mean something. Tough talk is heard about roles, responsibilities, and accountability. The session ends with a charge by the president "to go out and do good." Two weeks later the budget people tell you the plan is invalid because it can't be financed. The salespeople react to the numbers as unrealistic. The manufacturing folks tell you they cannot sustain the production levels. The information technology (IT) people need a complete hardware/software upgrade that requires millions of dollars. And so on and so on. Lengthy modifications are pieced into the master plan, distorting what was initially thought to be a viable, integrated solution. This delays the plan for months. I've witnessed companies still trying to get their plan together in the fall for the existing year.

Even with no staff distortion, at best, feeble attempts are made to roll the modified plan to the company. The norm is to move one level below top management before the plan loses its momentum. The planning effort is set aside, diluted, or ignored. That type of management behavior is unacceptable. To change it requires a change in the planning framework. Built into the backPlanning model is a mechanism requiring the plan to be communicated to every employee at every level. The mechanism has a built-in safeguard for performance accountability. The model will not work unless these steps are included.

Finally, as your consultant, I heard your concerns about the failures of planning to meet your real-time business needs. This book brings to life the planning process by explaining how business works in the most practical sense. Its value is that it forms a communications vehicle to reach every person in your company and tells them about the urgency of all parties honoring the plan. It defines success as well as failure.

This book will help make planning work for you. The steps are well researched, tested, and documented. It requires you to get your management story together, develop a clear direction, establish a concise, fully integrated business plan, and then implement the plan with methodical accountability. The next chapters outline exactly how that is to be done.

THE KEY QUESTIONS: THE BUSINESS PLAN SELF-TEST

To help identify problems with the development and application of a powerful business plan, complete the following self-test of ten questions. This simple exercise will bring to focus indications of your state of planning. If you are not satisfied with the answers, begin the planning process now.

1. When was the last time you read your company business plan?

2. How would you describe your existing planning process?

3. How complete is your business plan?

4. How satisfied are you with both the planning process and the product?

5. Would you be willing to invest in a new model of planning?

6. What internal or external forces would hinder your developing an integrated business plan?

7. Take a walk around your company and ask for a copy of your business plan. How many copies can you find?

8. Ask employees a simple question: "Where are we going with this company?"

9. Ask your management team, "How satisfied are you with our planning process?"

10. Ask anyone, "Have you ever read a complete business plan for this company?"

1

How to Create a Compelling Company Story That Inspires Employees to Excel

This chapter introduces the concept of a company story and shows you how to analyze your story against an established business growth line. You will learn to create a company story, use selected elements of your story to create organizational energy fields, and recognize the three stages of a company's life cycle. You will practice writing your company story and learn how to shift your story to prevent stagnation or failure.

THE COMPANY STORY: THE "SINGLE MOST POWERFUL WEAPON" IN PREPARING A BUSINESS PLAN

> *"And I suggest, further, that it is stories of identity—narratives that help individuals think about and feel who they are, where they come from, and where they are headed—that constitute the single most powerful weapon in the leader's literary arsenal."*   —Howard Gardner[1]

I can think of no statement more powerful in setting the stage for describing the concept of story than the one by Howard Gardner. Originally I read his book *Leading Minds: An Anatomy of Leadership* to find a piece missing from my leadership models and subsequent leadership seminars. His work is convincing evidence that it is more than what leaders do that makes them successful. It is who leaders are. If leaders are people who tell stories that other people choose to follow, then why aren't company stories just as important?

For the past few years I have been developing the concept of a company story. In testing this idea with thousands of managers from all ranks of business, I found consistent themes. Most organizations fail not because they are badly managed. Evil people with bad-spirited intentions do not run most businesses. The opposite is true. Over the years I've found managers who want to do well but just can't seem to get the hang of this management job. My conclusion is that they fail because their stories are not consistent, congruent, or believable.

Basically, employees want to believe in their management. They want to come to work every day to excel. People need a cause to believe in and work toward. Leaders in history have known this need and have played it to both good and bad returns for humankind. Hitler understood the need for people to believe in something. As evil as it was he gave them a story. Churchill also had a story, which led his nation out of its darkest hour.

The best example of how a leader creates a company story is one I experienced in a movie. Critics had been very unkind to Kevin Costner's release of *The Postman*. During the first part of the movie I could understand their unkind critique. Then suddenly the movie took a serious turn. As the main character in the movie, Costner visits a community under the guise of being a postman. All he wants is a little food and a refuge. As his character develops, a story emerges. The scene where he swears in another postman, Ford Lincoln Mercury, makes a moving case that people need a story, need direction, and need hope. The remainder of the film is about the energy field developed from the story Costner tells, how it is picked up by his believers, and how it emerges as the second American Revolution. Although the movie is a fantasy tale, there are important messages that we can translate into your business planning.

THE THREE REASONS COMPANY STORIES FALL SHORT OF EXPECTATIONS

The company story is a composite of how you represent yourself to employees, customers, and the general public. It is tied closely to your reputation, reinforced by your integrity, and defined by your behavior. Your story is the essence of who you are, what you believe in, and how you act out your character in a business play. Think of your story as if it were presented in a theater. Your story can be a comedy, a tragedy, or a musical. There will be a cast of characters, some good, others not so good, each telling their own version of the story.

Most organizations are in trouble because their main characters in the play, the managers, tell stories that don't hang together. Three problems are associated with their composite company story. First, the story is badly told; second, it is not acted out in a coherent manner; and third, it doesn't ring true. The sales department is living one story while operations follows a different theme. Finance has its own world while marketing occupies still another cloud. Is it any wonder employees are confused? They seem to be working for different companies simultaneously.

When a Story Is Badly Told

A badly told story has its roots in an incomplete business plan. Most organizations have bits and pieces of the items making up the plan. Managers are usually proud they have a philosophy statement posted in the lobby. They point in triumph to the value statements listed in the company literature. Somewhere you will be shown a vision. Each of these elements is appropriate and necessary in both a well-constructed business plan and an authentic story. If a single element is missing from the plan, the story is incomplete. The danger of an incomplete story is evidenced when the flaws show up in execution of the plan. An incomplete business plan results in a fragile document presenting a story that doesn't ring true. An incomplete model implodes.

I saw this happen once with a national sales team from a chemical company. We were doing a team-building session to determine how the sales staff would support the company as a self-directed work team. During the examination of their goals I asked to see a copy of the vision statement. My thought was to cross-examine the goals as they supported the vision. There was no vision statement. We had a well-written plan with all the pieces but the vision portion. Coincidentally, the company president dropped by the session to support the team. During the first few minutes of his arrival he was asked about the vision. "Of course I have a vision," he replied. "Well, we can't find it anywhere," came back the chorus. From the several hours of discussion before the president departed came a clearer picture of what the team had to do to complete its mission. Moreover, the president went back to his executive team and revised the company's plan to include the vision. How something so obvious can be missing from a business plan is startling, but it happens.

When the Story Pieces Don't Add Up

Failure to virtually link the elements into a coherent plan also contributes to an incomplete story. Because the parts and pieces are not interconnected there is no coordinated, disciplined implementation. It is possible to actually have the elements working against each other. For example, values may contradict the philosophy. The vision and mission could be disconnected. Principles could be developed that cancel each other. These disconnected behaviors cause customers and employees to hold the company management suspect. They sense something is not right or it is just not working.

When the Story Isn't Believable

Another equally fatal flaw in telling a story is to be incongruent. For example, you claim to love customers then treat them badly. You claim to value employees yet they become targets of opportunity for reengineering or downsizing, even in good times. You profess to provide the best products in your industry yet they don't work as advertised. People are astute and getting smarter. They pick up on the fact you don't live your own company hype. Your story simply isn't believable. Consider public awareness of a company's environmental protection position. Let one incident occur then watch the media have a field day with the inconsistencies. Politicians suffer the same fate when they make public promises they cannot keep. They become inconsistent with their story, telling each special interest group what the group needs to hear.

The Antidote to a Badly Managed Story

There is an antidote for a badly managed story. The key is building a congruent story by eliminating the very issues that create incongruence. The first step is to get a business plan in place. To do it as defined in this text, you will be forced to deal with the key planning elements as discrete elements and then again as an integrated framework. This is the only known process to make the message authentic, congruent, and believable.

Being authentic requires truth and hard work. It requires an acknowledgment of who you really are in terms of what you believe in, how you behave, and what you expect. If yours is a lethargic organization, don't claim high performance. Being authentic means identifying all the problems in your system, communicating to employees that you know the problems, and finally telling them how you intend to fix those problems. Everyone must share this hard work across the range of business activities and down the management structure. Everyone must participate in careful organizational analysis and the required actions to fix the problems.

Being congruent requires constant vigilance on the part of the whole management team. This means you must do what you say—every single time. There are situations where you will slip. Honest mistakes are okay. Employees do not expect their management to be perfect. They do expect them to live up to their word and match word and deed.

Reaching a state where you and your management team are believed is a journey with history working against you. A mismanagement example made public doesn't help your case. Building trust to counter this history is not an overnight event. After your story is completed, communicated, and demonstrated you will experience hesitance and resistance from employees. They won't be quick to jump on your train. There will be a test period to see if you really meant what you said or if this was simply an annual pep talk from upper management. Remember two points: Employees have heard it all before, and actions speak louder than words.

HOW SLOGANS WORK AS WINDOWS INTO YOUR COMPANY

Stories work in multiple directions with multiple audiences, as shown in Figure 1-1. The internal story is directed toward the management of the organization and the total workforce. The internal story is developed and presented by the management teams for internal consistency of the organization's operating procedures and direction. Management teams often tell fragmented stories, so the slogan helps consolidate the story within the team. The slogan provides the rally point for those who are supposed to lead and manage the system. Consider the slogan as an easily remembered theme used every day by management to keep focused on the job at hand.

Figure 1-1. Your story works in two directions.

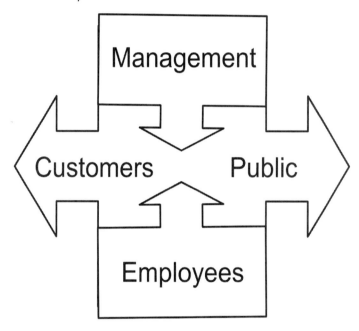

The second purpose of the internal focus is for communications with employees. Slogans provide an outward demonstration of the direction of the company. They give the employees a place to stand while getting work done each day. Slogans or themes have been used for centuries to rally people to perform. When a company is experiencing its darkest hour on Wall Street, a rally cry around a core theme may be necessary to pull morale back from the brink.

The outward direction of the slogan to the public is usually developed and presented by the marketing department as a staff responsibility. Marketing's targets are public image and customer appeal. Although both audiences are important, the second is the most critical. This appealing to customers is called branding and is essential to selling products, goods, and services. Companies spend billions of dollars each year to achieve worldwide brand recognition. The condensed message for this branding effort shows up as the slogan.

In this section I describe the outward manifestation of the story, but remember this is a planning book, not a marketing thesis. Keep the internal orientation as it relates to planning in mind as we discuss slogans.

Major dollars are paid to marketing personnel for their expertise in representing the company in assorted media events. Their product is usually an ad campaign or program to catch public attention. There is nothing wrong with that approach except that it is usually just that—an annual advertising campaign and not the actual story of the company. Smarter companies separate ad campaigns from the portrayal of their image. These companies are communicating a more permanent or long-term message. It screams out for you to know who they are, their values, and their place in the world business pecking order. They want you to buy them and not just their product. These companies send messages in cleverly worded bits and pieces called slogans.

For years, slogans were viewed as those cute sayings that appeared in advertisements or commercials. They were intended to be anchors in the consumer's mind. That thinking and usage needs revisiting because those slogans actually provide a window of understanding about the company. The slogan signals to us, the public and customers, what story the company wants to tell. I experienced this firsthand while flipping quickly through the pages of a magazine in the Calgary Delta Crown Room. What became very clear was the theme or hidden message communicated in the slogans. Here are a few examples of companies, their slogans, and my interpretation of what story the advertisement may have intended to communicate.

Company	Slogan	Message
Qwest Communications	Ride the light	Speed of communications
International Paper	We answer to the world	International social responsibility
Celestial Seasonings	What you do for you	We help you be good to yourself
Toyota	People drive us	People's choice
Subaru	The best of the all-wheel drive	Four-wheel drives can be classy
Chrysler	Engineered to be great cars	Leading technological advancements
Timex	The watch you wear out there	A real-world watch for everyday life
GMC	Do one thing. Do it well.	Standards of excellence, quality of product

It is interesting to compare companies in the same business or industry for similarities or differences in their stories. Look at the automobile examples in the previous list. Subaru chooses to tell a story around a unique feature—its state-of-the-art four-wheel drive, while Toyota puts the people, machine, and environment together. Chrysler and GMC tend to focus on the engineering appeal and the quality of product, respectively. The first appeals to those who are intrigued with mechanical perfection. The second appeals to buyers who feel comfortable driving a GMC because it is well built by a company that doesn't waste any time on poor manufacturing processes. The message from these examples is that your story can be unique within the same industry. It can be used to make a powerful connection between you and your consumer. And finally, the story can be communicated by using a device called the slogan.

A strongly pushed slogan or image can backfire when the same message is communicated internally. If your story is consistent, then you have no problem. If you are putting up a good public front or false front that is inconsistent with how the company is managed, you have a problem. There must be alignment between the outward and inward stories.

I have a unique opportunity to get behind some of the public stories while working for well-known companies. Often I find conflict with the image presented to the public. While no company is perfect and there will always be irritants, some company stories just don't hold together, no matter how active their marketing efforts. This book is your game plan to eliminate the problems of how you present yourself to employees, the public, and your customers. A theme of this model is consistency in what you say and do. If you follow the integrated model in all the elements, your consistency is ensured.

ORGANIZATIONAL ENERGY FIELDS: THE INVISIBLE FORCES THAT HOLD YOUR COMPANY TOGETHER

One of the objectives of a well-crafted, complete story is to create synergy. This combined effort or synergistic effect produces energy in many places within the company. These fields of energy become an invisible force that holds your company together (see Figure 1-2). While the concepts of field theory are still relatively new as they are applied to an organization, we must believe that people working together toward common goals display a different level of excitement than a loose collection of individuals with no defined purpose. That excitement is created by lots of leaders telling lots of good stories about the organization. It is about leaders creating myths, legends, and fables of the company that tend to attract people. It's the stories told around the coffee station. Leaders can create energy, synergy, and bonding to corporate stories by appealing to people's sense of belonging, challenge, purpose, and contribution.

Figure 1-2. Four fields of energy that generate passion.

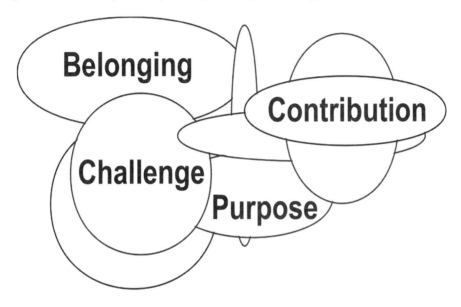

Fields of Belonging

People want to belong to something. That's why they join clubs, work in groups, and live in communities. They want to be part of a winning work organization. I've never met a single person who said, "I think I'll go to work for a losing company." Use this basic human need to create a field of energy around membership in your organization.

Fields of Challenge

People want to experience challenge in work and life. That's why they search for the cure for cancer or participate in extreme sports. Give people a challenge. Ask them to do the impossible. Stretch their knowledge and ability. Tap into their unused energy. Channel it toward your goals. You will be surprised at the results.

Fields of Purpose

People want to know that their work has meaning. That's why they need to know if what they do has relevance. Show everyone how he or she fits into your business plan and why it is important for every employee to be successful. It is amazing how easily your goals will then be accomplished.

Fields of Contribution

People want to know if their work has contributed to the activity. Have they made a difference? Show employees where their individual efforts help the team achieve its goal and you have a satisfied workforce. If I can make a difference I will work at a different level than if I believe that my work is just part of a giant struggle that leads to no conclusive end game.

THE NINE TOOLS FOR GENERATING EFFECTIVE BUSINESS ENERGY FIELDS

Effective leaders can use the elements of a business plan to create the necessary energy to make things happen. They know energy fields and business plans cannot operate independently. A business plan that has an inconsistent story will be flat, lackluster, and boring. There will be no passion or sense of purpose. Employees will not work with pride or display esprit de corps. There will be no sense of urgency to complete the plan. Lethargy toward the written plan will be evidenced.

On the other hand, well-crafted business plans generate all the human power you need for accomplishing ambitious goals. Turning people on turns on the business plan. Throughout this book I describe how to use each of the business plan elements as a tool for creating empowered people. Each element has a unique value to your business plan and the underlying company story. Margaret J. Wheatley describes our present understanding of energy fields. "We have moved deeper into a field view of reality by our present focus on culture, vision, and values as the means for managing organizations. We know that this works, even when we don't know how to do it well."[2]

Here are nine critical elements (see also Figure 1-3) I believe are core to any organization's ability to create energy fields:

- Vision Statement (creates passion)
- Mission Statement (creates purpose)
- Strategic Goals and Objectives (set direction)
- Strategies and Tactics (generate action)
- Philosophy Statement (creates ethical boundaries)
- Focus (creates efficiency)
- Value Statements (create a scale of importance)
- Principles (benchmark behavior)
- Strategic Intent (signals commitment)

Figure 1-3. The nine elements to create energy are all pieces of a puzzle that, when fitted together, create workforce momentum for the plan.

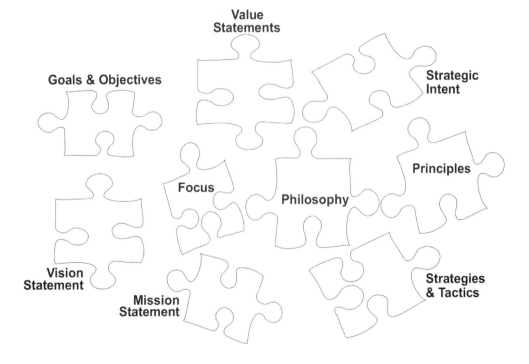

The vision statement is used to create passion. Sadly, I've been in a number of companies where there was no demonstrated vision. It is tragic to meet good people who want to be successful but are without direction. One thing I have noted repeatedly is that companies with visionary leaders seem to be the ones with people who are passionate about their work, their job, and their company.

The mission statement is the second stake in the ground, being the opposite end of the vision statement. The mission gives your story purpose. Without a purpose life has no meaning. Without a carefully constructed mission statement your company cannot effectively conduct its daily business. When your mission statement is unclear, employees fail to connect to why they work at what they do. The employee-mission disconnect is a major reason for inconsistency in a company story.

Strategic goals and objectives give direction to your story. People must have direction because it has an underlying sense of security. Direction gives structure to ambiguity. Without goals a company's story has no end point or place to go. Having a goal gives employees a way to measure the value of the story and to check accomplishment of the story along the way.

Strategies and tactics are part of the direction-setting that will help accomplish your vision, which needs two parts to be complete. First is the "what" as defined by the goals and objectives. Second is the "how" as defined by the strategies and tactics. They are the long-term and short-term methods to define how you plan to move toward the future.

Your story must have an operational core, which is set by the philosophy statement. This is a statement about how you intend to run your business. It is an integral part of the story because it benchmarks your position in codes of conduct and ethical situations. The philosophy statement also signals to people that what you believe is central to your success. "We will be okay if we follow this philosophy of doing business" is a thought that frequently visits the minds of managers. Having a well-defined philosophy gives an anchor point in turbulent times because it provides psychological stability.

You must have a single business focus to create congruence for your story. You cannot be all things to all people. Salespeople try to please the customer. Manufacturing wants to make products effectively. Research and development (R&D) tries to crank out new products. The company is split into a number of individual special interests. This causes your story to be fragmented, which is dangerous to your concentration of effort. A multiple focus pulls the company in multiple directions. Employees get confused when attempting to carry out their daily activities.

Your value statements create a scale of importance within your story. Value statements signal to employees what is acceptable and what is not acceptable. Values are critical to the completeness of your story.

Organizations must operate within a set of principled behaviors. A solid set of principles can be used to benchmark your story. Ask yourself a simple question: "If we do this, are we violating any sensible business principles?"

The final element is the strategic intent statement, which communicates your commitment to making the plan work. It is the bridge between the mission and the vision.

Your company is made up of a mass of energy fields created by the nine core elements just identified. In subsequent chapters I will define and describe how to develop each item, how to analyze each in operational terms, and finally how to add each to your basic business plan and story. Look for additional ways to create energy fields within your organization. When you find a source of energy, use it for as long as possible. There is nothing wrong with capturing the hidden energy of your company and bringing it into full use.

Growing Up to Be What You Don't Want to Be: The Three Stages of a Company's Life Cycle

Organizations grow from an entrepreneurial start to eventually become bureaucracies. There is a fixed pattern to this growth with a clear definition between stages that can be observed, described, and modified if necessary.[3]

Every organization has a life cycle. That is a truth you cannot avoid. However, you can eliminate some of the dysfunctional behaviors that are found at certain points in your company's climb to growth and success. The complete cycle of an organization can be described in many ways with many labels. For planning purposes and understanding your company story, you can do fine with a simple model that I call a growth line. In this model you must be able to fit yourself into a category and then understand what story you are telling, look for congruence in your story, and be willing to change your story if necessary.

Organizations can be generally characterized as falling into one of three categories or into a transition stage as illustrated in Figure 1-4. Those three stages are entrepreneurial, professionally managed, and bureaucratic, and each has a corresponding story. No matter how long you have been in operation, you will fall somewhere on this hypothetical growth line. A key to understanding the growth line and how it connects to the idea of telling a company story is knowing that each stage has a distinctly different story to tell. Your approach to planning is influenced by where you are on the growth line. Organizations risk death as they grow through three stages. Eventually all organizations attempt to return to their entrepreneurial roots.

Figure 1-4. Where is your organization on the growth line?

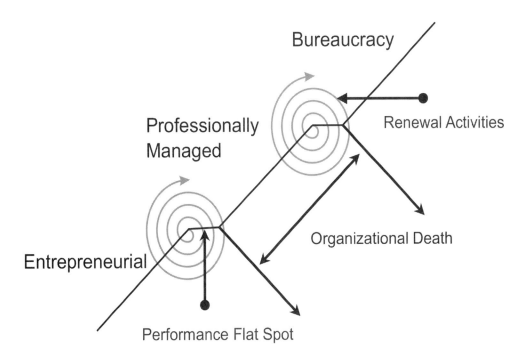

Stage 1: Matching the Stage and the Story

Your position on the growth line is reflected in your story. I can listen to your story and place you with great accuracy on the line. Two significant pieces of management knowledge can be found by knowing where you are on the growth line and how you tell the corresponding story. The first lesson is the story and stage match. Are you entrepreneurial but acting like a bureaucracy? If you are at the professionally managed stage but your story is entrepreneurial, inconsistency occurs. If the story doesn't match the stage of your company development, mixed messages are sent to employees. The results are a story that breeds distrust and disbelief.

Stage 2: Growing Your Story

The second lesson is that of a transition. As you move from one stage to the next, your story will change out of necessity. A professionally managed company has a different story from the other two stages of organizational development. A bureaucracy certainly operates on the opposite extreme from an entrepreneurial company. This leads us to the belief that you must change your story depending on where you are on the growth line.

There is one exception to the match situation. If you are a bureaucracy, you don't want to encourage a story of bureaucracy. Although you may accomplish the consistency of being in the bureaucracy stage and telling a bureaucracy story, unfortunately, it would be the wrong story. In this instance you want to change both your story and your operating behavior.

Failure to change your story is a serious foundation for failure and explains why so many rapid-growth companies get into trouble. Management doesn't adjust its story as the business grows from entrepreneurial to professionally managed. As a company reaches a stagnant state the story gets institutionalized to the point that it is dysfunctional to your business process. In these cases your story automatically becomes unauthentic, incongruent, and unbelievable.

Take the example of a food distribution company I encountered. The owner wanted to become professionally managed because he realized that the business requirements had outgrown his abilities. He hired an excellent general manager who was given full operational control of the company. The failing behavior of the owner was to continue to be an entrepreneurial spirit. He played at being the president of the distribution company and used it as his personal cash account to underwrite his side ventures. It became common for the owner to direct the chief accountant to transfer large sums of money for outside purchases. When confronted, the owner's position was, "It's my money. I own the company. I can do anything I want with it." The withdrawal of funds created havoc with the company planning and seriously damaged its ability to pay its suppliers and other recurring bills. The company went into bankruptcy in a very short period of time. Two lessons are found in this story: The transition from an entrepreneurial start-up to a professionally managed business is more difficult than you think. The second lesson is that a company is not a personal toy of the owner.

Let's see how your story develops and disintegrates by stages. Every company's life cycle began as an entrepreneurial activity. Some stay in that stage for years. Others grow into the second stage in a short span of time depending on many factors. The story told during the entrepreneurial years is very exciting. Those are the go-go years. Everything is fast-paced where survival is the name of the game. Serving the customer is the number-one priority. You don't have the luxury of making mistakes or time to waste on the inconsequential. Little thought is given to job descriptions and less time to policy manuals. The company future is often decided on Friday when the money is counted.

The story befitting an entrepreneurial company is usually one filled with hopes, dreams, and hard work. It is about sweat equity and the promise of big rewards in the future. A charismatic leader who holds people in sway tells the story with passion generated from the depth of his or her personal convictions. People are sucked into the vortex. The story and its passion generation are what attract people to a start-up company.

In the second stage the company has grown to a professionally managed system. Managers realize the need to put systems in place to get organized. People with special skills such as human resources, logistics, or computer technology are hired to professionally manage each of the special functions. This is an effective method to pull the business process together. It is important for the congruence of your story.

The story often found in a professionally managed company centers around performance. Words such as *high performance, teamwork,* and *best of breed* are commonly bantered about. The story is replete with examples of heroism in getting the job done under adverse conditions. It attracts people who seek challenge, want a well-run machine, and are professional in word and deed. This professionally managed stage also creates passion within employees. In this case the passion stems not from the vision, as in the entrepreneurial stage, but rather from the challenge to accomplish great deeds. To create passion, build your story around educated, skillful people doing the right thing for the customer. Portray a company that puts professional competence in the limelight. In the words of Tom Peters, "Hire for talent, train for whatever."[4]

Stage 3: Accepting Stagnation of Your Story

If you are in the third stage your story will be very different. It will be one of stagnation, featuring all the ills associated with a bureaucracy. In the bureaucratic stage a company has perfected the lethargic model. Its management uses the textbook ploys to delay decision making, resist change, and fight progress. Your story in this stage will be filled with despair, failure, and hopelessness. Employees live out the story with sad faces. They are long past caring. Their model of work is to just make it through the day.

The greatest stagnation example I found in my consulting career came inside a large bureaucratic company immediately following a successful engagement at one of their plants. Within eighteen months, a team of two managers and I found and recovered $5 million of waste in their manufacturing processes. We carefully documented the engagement with the idea of repeating the newly identified cost-saving measures in other plants. Since the company had about thirty plants operating at all levels of success, we thought our plan would be a done deal.

To this day I recall with great clarity the briefing room of polished paneling, the leather chairs, and the long conference table. Key players were assembled around the room, ready to tell a convincing story of how we helped a plant that made only $200,000 the previous year become a star in the system. At the end of the briefing I asked for a decision to continue at another plant. The new client, a plant manager, eagerly nodded in agreement. The executive vice president in charge of operations leaned back in his chair and said, "Well, that's real nice, but that's not how we do things in this company." I replied, "Excuse me, we just saved you $5 million that goes to your bottom line. I don't understand your comment." He answered, "You know, all that fancy behavioral science stuff." I closed my briefcase and stepped down from the platform. We never saved the company another dollar and the executive retired a year later with his story intact. What I didn't understand at the time was that our work was uncovering and making public the ugly side of his story.

SUMMARY

Your story is not something you must acquire. Fortunately or unfortunately for you it already exists. You may or may not like what you hear but you must listen carefully to the signals that tell your story. Not all is lost if your story is less than desirable. You can shape it into anything you wish. You may decide to be creative or allow it to be dull and boring. It may be developed around purpose and passion, or it may evolve from a core of despair. You can be a powerful culture with people who believe in your story. Remember the key to a successful story is that it must be authentic, congruent, and believable.

THE KEY QUESTIONS: CREATING YOUR COMPANY STORY

Use the following questions to begin the process of understanding and building your company story. Expand the list as necessary. These questions are not intended to be all-inclusive; rather, they represent keys to opening your thinking on the concept of story.

1. Could you tell your company story with any sort of credibility?
2. What parts of your story are inauthentic or inconsistent?
3. What parts of your story do you wish to change?
4. How difficult will it be to get your revised story communicated?

THE PRACTICAL APPLICATIONS: BRINGING YOUR COMPANY STORY TO LIFE

Examine the stories of people, organizations, and countries as you encounter them. Begin to develop a sense of the underlying energy of an organization by experiencing the force firsthand. Think about the feelings, impressions, or messages you pick up the next time you visit a child's classroom, a bank other than your own, a hotel lobby, a nursing home, a new town, a friend's neighborhood, and the World Wide Web. Then practice the following exercise:

1. Identify each of the nine organization elements your company currently has in place.

- Vision Statement
- Mission Statement
- Goals and Objectives
- Strategies and Tactics
- Philosophy Statement
- Focus
- Value Statement
- Principles
- Strategic Intent

2. Determine where your business is on the growth line. How does that influence your story as written?

For example:

- If you are an entrepreneurial company, what must you do to move to the professionally managed stage?
- If you are professionally managed, what action must you take to avoid bureaucracy?
- If you are a bureaucracy, what action must you take to break out of the lethargy?

3. Write your company story in fifty words or less.

4. Develop a slogan to serve as a short version of the story for communications purposes.

CHAPTER

2

The Practical Guidelines for Building a Business Plan in Five Pages

This chapter explains the five major elements that make up the business plan, defines the critical terms used in business planning, demonstrates how the components of a business plan fit as an integrated model, defines logical steps in writing a business plan, and describes the complete business planning cycle. You will learn the activities required to implement a correct planning cycle and the methods to develop a 5-Page Business Plan model.

This chapter sets the stage for the development of the actual business plan document. Five major elements of the business plan are defined in specific terms. While the five are discussed as separate elements, the information for each is developed during a single planning session. Do not hold separate sessions to build strategic plans then operational plans. The efforts would be redundant and overlapping. Over a long period of time I tested the methods described here with clients and found the single session to be the most cost-effective and efficient way to manage the process. As information is completed at the one session, it is grouped into the five subordinate plans.

DEFINING YOUR BUSINESS PLAN

A business plan is a consolidation document that defines the parameters of how a business operates. It communicates strategic direction as well as specific goals, methods of achieving the goals, and the management development activities needed to reach the vision. It is a master document that serves as an umbrella for all events taking place within the company.

A business plan is the one place you turn to for completeness in your story. Since it contains the key elements of both hard and soft processes, it must be inclusive. Hard processes are those normally thought of as goals and objectives. Soft processes are the intangible but critical elements such as values, philosophy, and principles. In years past, planners avoided so-called soft or esoteric processes such as values because they could not directly connect them to the bottom line. Now smart executives work with values, philosophies, and principles early in their planning activities. They know the importance of integrating both the soft and hard processes. These executives see the relationship between goal failure and gaps in the operational values of their companies.

An important function of a business plan is to set the direction of the company. Setting direction means more than setting goals. The business plan serves to tell a complete story of where you are going, how you are going to make the journey, and what business behavior you will practice on the way. The plan becomes a road map, blueprint, and template for employees to follow in accomplishing the goals:

- *The road map* provides a path with markers of incremental progress along the way. Because the plan is well defined, employees can measure their success.

- *The blueprint* feature of the business plan provides employees an overall design for the company's actions. It shows how the parts and pieces fit together, defines the relationships, and explains the master schema of the future.

- *The template* provides models for business units and teams to build their own local action plans. If the company has a plan, then a work team must have a plan.

Business plans should meet certain criteria. They need to be user-friendly; therefore I present a simplified, workable document for a complex topic. The document needs to encourage rather than discourage its use. It needs to reflect the same goals and objectives that people pursue each day in their work. A plan fails when its goals are different from the work requirement. Another use of a business plan is to provide guidance when you don't know what to do. This becomes the direction and benchmark for your actions.

HOW THE 5-PAGE BUSINESS PLAN WORKS

One of the main reasons resistance to business planning happens is because of the paperwork it produces. When we think of planning we automatically envision reams of papers, three-ring binders, and thick bound reports. These perceptions cause people to avoid planning. It doesn't have to be that way.

The methods I propose short-circuit some of the resistance to planning by simplifying the documents. Over the past fifteen years

I have helped several companies condense the bulk of their plans down to five pages. These core plans contain the essence of what you need to do. The often-told legend of President Lincoln writing the Gettysburg Address on the back of an envelope holds a hidden truth. His address was short, to the point, and told a story that captivated the audience. A second example of the brevity concept is found in Winston Churchill's apology to a friend about the length of his letter: "I could have made it shorter if I had more time." We can build business plans using the same concepts of brevity, succinctness, and focused text. You can tell your story using a business plan with only five components of a single page each.

The Strategic Plan—Forming the Heart of Your Story

The strategic plan is the first of the five types of plans (as shown in Figure 2-1). It is the starting point for the other four types of plans and the heart of your story. Get this wrong and the rest of your plan and your story is suspect. Get it right and the power of your people will be unleashed because they want to know where the company is headed. Employees want to believe that something exists in the future. The strategic plan is a single-page document that defines where and how you want to position your company. It examines a list of factors that might influence your future. A diagram of how you format the strategic plan into a single page is shown in Appendix B: The 1-Page Strategic Plan. Topics you must address in your strategic plan are:

- Assumptions
- Guidance
- Vision Statement
- Mission Statement
- Strategic Goals
- Objectives

Figure 2-1. The strategic plan sets the direction of your company.

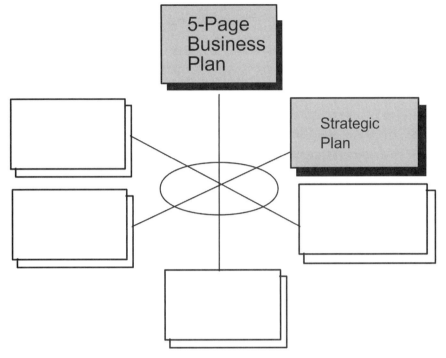

- Strategies
- Strategic Intent
- Philosophy
- Focus
- Values
- Principles

The Operational Plan—Bringing Your Plan to Life

The operational plan is the dynamic component that brings the strategic plan to life (see Figure 2-2). It is the first of ten years of the complete business plan and is developed simultaneously with the other four components. It defines how the company accomplishes its strategic intent on a daily or annual basis. It breaks down the strategic goals into objectives and tasks to make them more understandable and manageable. The operational plan also provides information to executives on how well the staff carries out its functional activities. Along with the execution of functional activities comes the requirement for staff coordination. Work cannot be effective unless it is closely coordinated across staffs or functions. The operational plan also helps management teams implement actions. Because it identifies the persons held accountable, the operational plan becomes a good benchmark for reporting processes of key programs and projects. This becomes the benchmark for performance measures of both the individual and the company. A format for this plan is found in Appendix C: The 1-Page Operational Plan.

Figure 2-2. The operational plan sets the strategic plan into motion on a practical level.

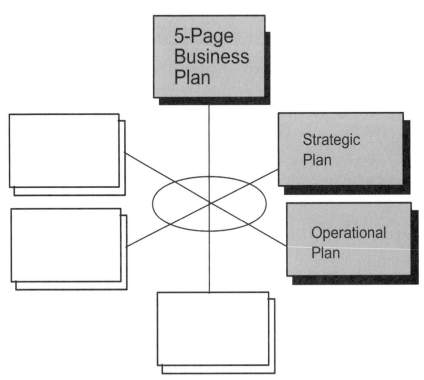

The Organizational Plan—Defining Your Corporate Structure

The organizational plan (seen in Figure 2-3) is the third of the five types of plans you must develop. It defines the structure you must have to put the complete business plan in place. Organizational planning begins with the concept that structure follows strategy. The strategies come from the strategic plan. The organizational plan is more than a wiring diagram or chart showing assignments; it must help you do certain things. First, it ensures your people are all properly assigned to specific work or functions. Like the operational plan, the organizational plan aids coordination among critical staff sections. Another important function is cost control. The organizational plan illustrates adjustments that need to be made to streamline activities within the workforces. Structure should always be tailored to the requirements. Finally, the organizational plan must illustrate three ingredients:

Figure 2-3. The organizational plan matches the structure to the goals of the plan.

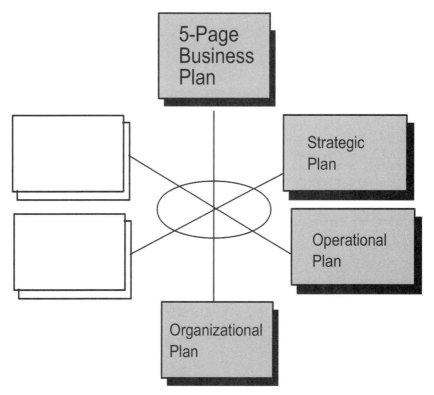

■ A chart showing reporting relationships

■ A clear definition of responsibilities

■ A clear definition of authorities

A template for the organizational plan is found in Appendix D: The 1-Page Organizational Plan.

The Resources Plan—Analyzing the Support You Need to Put Your Plan Into Action

The fourth of the five types of planning is the resources plan that can be seen in Figure 2-4. It defines the resources you must have to support the business plan found in Appendix E: The 1-Page Resources Plan. This plan begins with an analysis of the annual targets and the goals from the strategic plan. Normally you can develop the resources plan in conjunction with the operations plan since the two are so closely connected.

Figure 2-4. The resources plan matches requirements to the overall plan.

The resources plan provides a great deal of information to the reader because it examines specific support requirements. It contains, at minimum, information on ten categories:

1. *Staffing Levels.* What are your short-term and long-term staffing requirements? What kinds of skills will be needed at each level, now and in the future?

2. *Information Requirements.* What is the volume and quality of your information?

3. *Technology.* Do you have the most effective technology to do the job? Is technology just around the corner that will put your competition in the advantage? What is the cost of staying up-to-date with technology?

4. *Tools and Equipment.* What supporting systems do you and your staff need to get all the tasks completed?

5. *Intellectual Capital.* How smart are your people? How smart will they have to be in the future? What do they have to be smart about? How are you using the intellectual capital database that now exists?

6. *Time.* What critical milestones exist in your plan? Where are the important decision points in the plan? What can you do to use your time more wisely?

7. *Relationships.* What networks need to be developed? Can strategic alliances and strategic partnerships help your plan?

8. *Image.* What is your image in the public perception? What should it be? How will you develop this perception or change a negative one?

9. *Facilities.* Can you estimate the facilities requirements? Is the need for physical space increasing or decreasing? What effect has e-business had on your industry?

10. *Financial.* Have you considered the budget constraints for short-term requirements? What are the long-term capital investment requirements? Do the financial numbers make good business sense?

The Contingency Plan—Taking Evasive Action in a Crisis Situation

The contingency plan is the last of the five types of plan (see Figure 2-5). It is important but is often the most frequently ignored type of plan.

Figure 2-5. The contingency plan builds cases for alternatives.

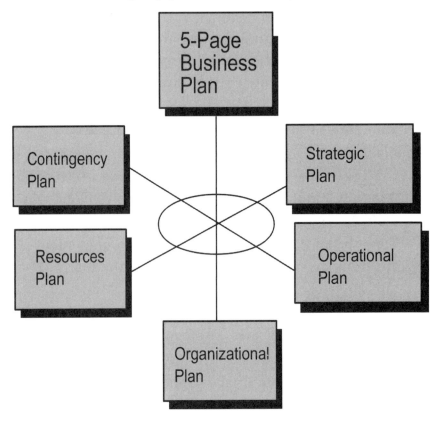

There are three types of contingency planning you must consider. The first is when your goals are not accomplished or are blocked somewhere in the execution. You must have alternatives developed to eliminate the blockage. It is a fallback position. Normally you develop several courses of action to get you to the goal. Multiple routes or alternatives permit you choices when the goal path becomes blocked. You don't change your goals, just the actions to get you to the goals.

Another type of contingency planning is a big picture issue. This is a disaster plan for a business-created crisis that could shut down your company—for example, a labor strike in a plant that was not expected or anticipated that catches management unprepared. A contingency plan should address such occurrences.

Natural disasters are a primary contingency that companies plan for. Like manmade situations, these occurrences can be predicted and planned for. What would happen to a business dependent on landline telephone communications if a flood wiped out the line? Remember the huge area of Quebec, Canada, that was paralyzed for months in the winter storm of 1998? How can you plan for those events? What is your recovery plan?

The third type of contingency plan is developed from an internal view that examines incidents that could happen to your business and that would cause significant concern. For example, what would happen if members of a key management team were all killed in a plane crash? Sad events such as this have happened before. A contingency would have to be in place to replace those critical people. This example is so real that at most companies it is standard operating procedure that teams not fly together as a precautionary measure.

Another serious situation could be in the area of workplace violence. How do you prevent a serious incident from happening inside your workplace environment? Acts of violence against supervisors and coworkers by disgruntled employees have grown at a disturbing rate in the American workplace.[1] Increasingly, embittered employees and ex-employees are seeking revenge through violence and murder for alleged mistreatment on the job. According to a Bureau of Justice, Statistics Crime Data Brief, homicide has become the second leading cause of death in the workplace. Additionally, statistics show that one in four workers will be harassed, threatened, or attacked on the job. The topic of violence has many variables, but given the high stakes involved, it is prudent for management to prepare to deal with workplace violence by implementing prevention procedures. In short, this is contingency planning. An example of the format used for contingency planning is found in Appendix F: The 1-Page Contingency Plan.

TIPS ON CAPTURING INFORMATION AND MINIMIZING PAPERWORK

A company-level business plan is usually written in a three- to five-day period with all members of the executive team participating. The end product is a business plan of five single pages as outlined in Appendices B–F. Over the past years I have helped a number of teams accomplish this seemingly difficult task within these time parameters. To do that successfully requires certain preconditions and specific actions at the planning session.

One problem at a planning conference is the capturing of information and the paperwork that follows. The only efficient way to record information and complete the final document is to have on-site computers and printers for the session. This allows you to pace the discussion by producing final written documents at the end of the session. Too much time is lost in translation if newsprint or handwritten notes are relied upon to capture the information. Computer support eliminates the lag time normally associated with the planning process. At the end of the session each participant is given a diskette with the plan and a printed copy of the plan if they desire. Another alternative is to e-mail the final copy to all participants.

Another important tip or technique I always use is to view the work-in-progress through an LCD projector. This provides a fast way to develop, edit, and finalize the volume of information that will be generated in the session. The management team can see their work on the screen and make immediate corrections. Just about any software such as Microsoft Word or Powerpoint can be used for this stage of the plan's development. All input and changes from multiple participants can be shown on the screen and manipulated as the decisions are made to finalize the content.

Using full-time computer support for planning is well within the means of any company today. It is not difficult to have the equipment and support personnel at the conference. Usually the president's administrative assistant or someone who can be trusted with the sensitive information that may be discussed provides the computer support.

Two additional tips can make your computing support dynamic and successful. Although I have provided formats for the final plan, don't worry about format at the planning session itself. Have the plan recorded in a simple word processing format that is fast and easy to work with. The second tip is to print the plan as you go. At several points in the conference print a copy for each participant. This gives them something in their hands, helps them review the items, and provides assurance that progress is being made toward the completed plan.

THE FOUR UNIQUE PHASES IN A BUSINESS PLANNING CYCLE

Sadly, the business planning cycle in most companies is not in step with the calendar, the execution of the work, or the need for planned thinking. Too often the plan for next year is developed in the middle of that year. It is a joke to your employees to issue a plan that is already half-expired. Stop that practice! It makes you look foolish and inept at planning.

So how do you get the cycle in the correct place? Two methods can be used. The first is to start earlier. That's not magic. Just do it earlier. More important, though, is to cut down the amount of wasted energy in developing the key points. Remember that you are going to capture the essence of your complete business plan in five pages. To do that seemingly impossible task means you need a tool to organize your activities.

The business planning cycle is the tool a successful organization uses to establish a business plan with all components in place for execution. It is more than a document. It is a completely integrated process consisting of four distinct phases (see Figure 2-6). They are preparing, planning, implementing, and sustaining. Each phase has a unique and powerful place in the planning cycle.

Figure 2-6. The business planning cycle has four phases.

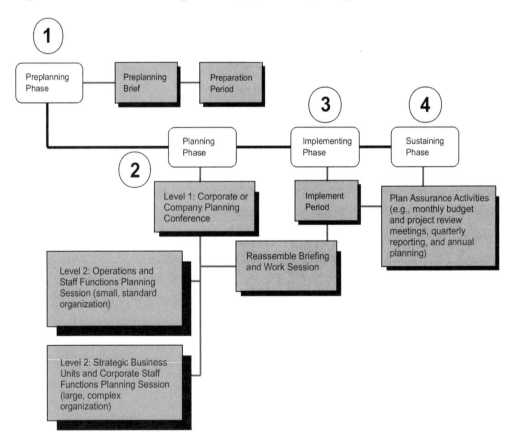

Phase 1: Preparing

The first step of the planning cycle is to complete a preplanning briefing (see Figure 2-7). If your existing plan is incomplete or this is your first time working as a planning team, a briefing is critical. Usually the team is assembled for an overview. The more people you have involved at this point the better because all managers and supervisors will be participating in the actual planning and execution at some point.

Several things happen at the preplanning briefing. One is to standardize the terms for the purpose of establishing a common language. Often terms are confused and people are working with different operational meanings. Standardization of language is a must. Use the preplanning session to address concerns and fears. Because planning has such a bad reputation, you can use this session to help smooth the way for further work. Clear definitions of what is to be accomplished should be communicated at the briefing. Make sure participants understand that your planning model is about to take a dramatic turn for the better. Business-as-usual cannot be allowed.

Figure 2-7. Getting ready to plan has two important steps.

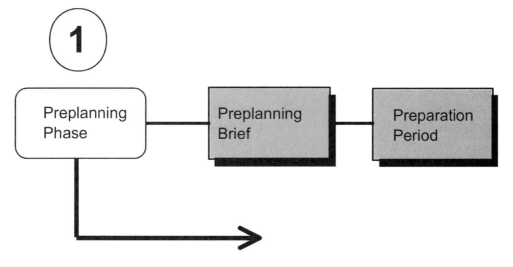

Another item addressed in the preplanning briefing is the homework assignment that must be completed in the preparation period. Generally two to four weeks are allowed between the pre-planning briefing and the actual business planning session. It is wise to use this time for preparation. Too many planning teams fail because they come unprepared or ill-equipped with data to make decisions. The business planning conference is not the time to be gathering data. At that point it is too late. Participants should not be allowed to show up empty-handed or to just "wing it," especially since the whole company must live with the results.

To help you get ready for the actual planning conference, I provide you with a set of questions as a preconference assignment that may be found in Appendix G.

Phase 2: Planning

The next step in the business planning cycle is to conduct the actual session (see Figure 2-8). All members of the executive or top team must attend this three- to five-day session chaired by the president. Key players should not be absent. If necessary, postpone the session until they can attend. At the conference the team jointly develops five one-page plans (which I call Level 1 plans). These company-level plans are the basis for each key staff or function to roll the process downward.

Figure 2-8. The planning conference builds five plans in a single session as phase 2 of the planning cycle.

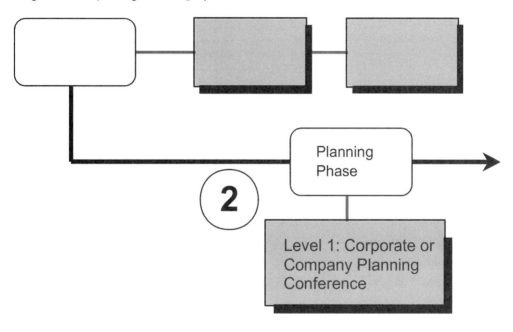

Each team member repeats the exact planning process for his or her team (see Figure 2-9). This is done at each successive level in a reduced scope and scale for the specific purpose of continuity. By repeating the company-planning model at the functional or business unit level you have achieved another level of understanding. This replication accomplishes steps to create buy-in and taps into the intellectual capital of your resources. Repeat the planning model throughout the company until all the managers and supervisors are involved in defining their parts of the plan. Appendix H: Plan Continuity provides formats to help either a staff function or a strategic business unit accomplish their part of the planning cycle.

Figure 2-9. The business planning must cycle through at least one more level—Level 2 for staff and business units. It may go to a third or fourth level depending on the size of the company.

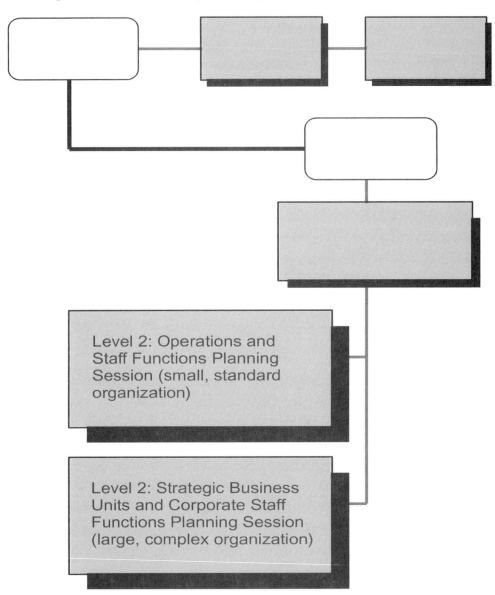

THE BUBBLE-UP THEORY: WHY PLANNING FROM THE BOTTOM UP DOESN'T WORK

The actual writing of a business plan can be as easy as it is simple in format, but first let's discuss who develops the plan. That's an easy question with a straightforward answer. The top management team writes a company business plan. The combined thought processes of your top managers and their agreement on what makes up the business plan is most important. The agreement of what is in the plan is more important than the mechanics of writing the plan. Said another way, the paper is not as important as the agreements to what goes on the paper.

Let's address the concept of upward planning popularly known as the "bubble-up theory." My views, which are supported by twenty-one years of consulting experience, are very clear. Planning from the bottom up doesn't work. Show me a company that has successfully started planning at the bottom and carried it through to completion in a reasonable time. Some organizations claim to have successfully used the bottom-up approach. In every case a short discussion reveals the reality of the situation. Bottom-up planning becomes a committee activity with lots of fanfare, noise, and expended energy. It fails because such an approach violates a number of logical and principled laws of businesses. Committees do not run businesses. Someone in authority needs to set the direction of a business.

What the bubble-up advocates are seeking is buy-in from employees, which is essential to the completion of the plan. The advocates are also asking for empowerment, decentralization, and use of intellectual capital. I have no argument with those conditions or requirements. The problem is that it sounds good but simply doesn't work. The same desired outcome can be achieved by approaching planning from the perspective I've outlined, which starts with Level 1 (company-level) plans and then further develops those plans at a level for staff and business units (Level 2).

Allow a reasonable amount of time between the company business planning conference and the session for the strategic business units. Usually a month is sufficient. Once the business unit plans are completed the executive team needs to bring the pieces back together to cross-check the feasibility of the original plan. Some adjustments may need to be made to the original numbers. Often requirements created at the top in the first company-level plan cannot be supported when broken down to operational-level requirements. This is why care must be taken in establishing requirements. It is possible to extend your plan beyond your capability.

Phase 3: Implementing

This phase (shown in Figure 2-10) is critical to the success of your plan, which cannot become just a one-year activity. Implementing the plan requires a minimum of two activities:

1. Quarterly checks
2. An annual update

Figure 2-10. The implementing phase puts the plan into motion. It is necessary to ensure the plan has a life span longer than the planning conference.

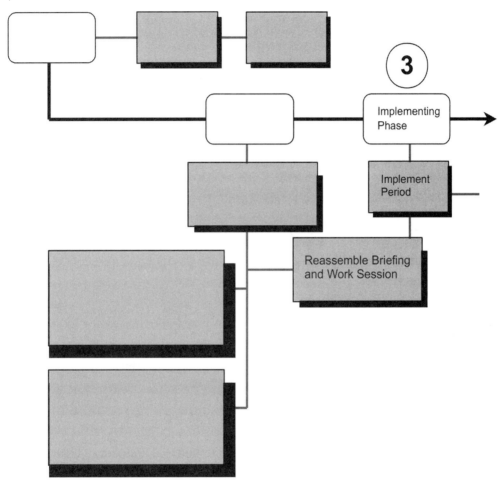

The plan needs to be checked on a quarterly basis (see Figure 2-11), which is consistent with the cycle of most businesses. During quarterly meetings you check to see how you are progressing against your projections. A danger exists in this phase. You may have a tendency to overcorrect on the plan. Take prudent actions but don't micromanage the plan.

The quarterly checks are a good time to see how your team is supporting the plan. Look for signs that the management team has involvement at all levels of the company. If you are getting the results you need then everything is probably working. If you are not meeting targets you need to start asking serious questions. Don't ask "why" questions, but rather precision questions. For example, you might ask:

- What caused you to miss your target?
- What are three things you plan to do to correct the situation?
- When do you plan to have the situation corrected?

The annual update is actually an extended version of the last quarterly meeting. Plan for a little extra time at this session because you will need to review the complete year. Once more the danger will be for you to overact on the numbers. I will give you a hint. In all my years of consulting it is rare to find a company that was too ambitious with the numbers for the first year of its plan. The single most common reason an organization doesn't reach its goals for the first year of the planning process is the lack of management attention. The management team wandered off-track, didn't honor their commitments, and didn't hold each other accountable. If you don't meet your annual target, look inward first.

Figure 2-11. The sustaining activities must include regular measurements of quarterly targets.

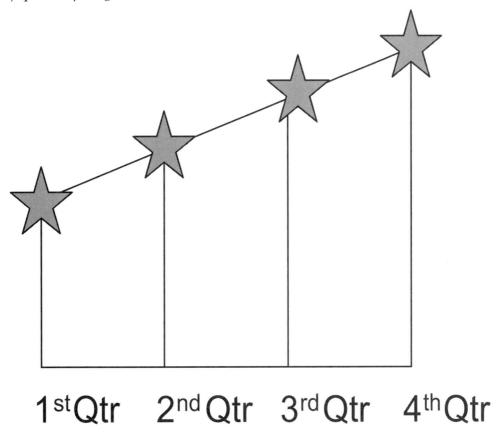

1ˢᵗQtr   2ⁿᵈQtr   3ʳᵈQtr   4ᵗʰQtr

Phase 4: Sustaining

Following the business planning session you must anchor the organization for continuing the planning cycle and implementing the plan (see Figure 2-12). I strongly suggest you do more than just develop a plan with the idea of communicating it downward. Little is accomplished if a great plan is produced but not supported by other organizational behavior. Make sure you have all the skills gaps identified before you begin any development. This includes preparing any other organizational assessments, employee surveys, or reports about your organization's performance. Combine this information into one focused development program.

Skills Development

Training and education activities needed to sustain and ensure your plan's success become self-evident as you build your business plan and identify performance shortfalls. The most effective core themes fall into logical groups, such as project reviews, leadership training, and budget meetings (Figure 2-12). These are usually safe bets as places to look for performance improvements:

- Coaching skills
- Communications skills
- Financial awareness
- Process efficiencies
- Leadership skills
- Managership skills

Traditionally business planners find problems in these areas. Building education and training activities around these themes produces a high degree of payoff.

Coaching and Communications Training

One of the best modules of training I've found is to review or refresh coaching skills. You will have a lot of tasks that must be completed in a short period of time. If the organization is to work at maximum performance then the coaching skills of your managers and supervisors may need reviewing. I suggest a custom package developed around situations found in your company. These hands-on training activities can be fun while teaching employees specific skills for how to better communicate expectations.

Sue Arnold at International Wallcoverings understands how coaching is a follow-up activity to effective planning. Her team understood the necessity to get the plan to all levels of the organization and to coach employees to do those things related to the plan.

As an interim step in the planning model, Sue and her team developed, reviewed, and sharpened their own coaching model.

Figure 2-12. During the sustaining phase you must pay attention to the leadership and managership activities required to keep the planning momentum.

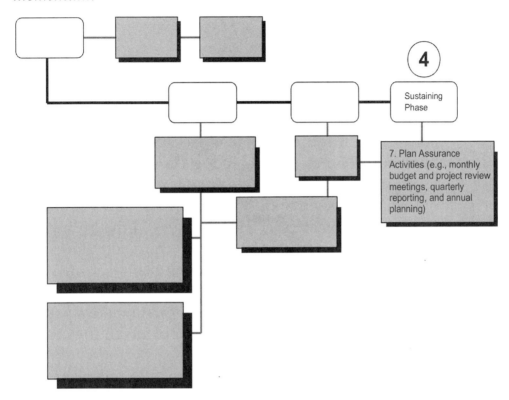

This included extensive training on precision communications techniques to keep focused on results. Now the team speaks with one voice on both what is to be done and how it is to be accomplished. This makes a highly effective management team.

Explaining How Money Works

I also recommend you teach your employees more that just what you intend to accomplish. You need to teach them the business acumen behind your goals. You need to teach employees to be businesspeople. This effort starts with teaching them the simple concepts of how money works. I'm not suggesting that you create a company of accountants, but rather that you teach employees the value of money. Amazingly, many people who should understand the financial concepts of business are remiss in their knowledge and applications. Even more scary are organizations I've encountered where managers and employees alike don't understand the concept of profit.

A remedy for this shortfall is to do what a small, East Coast manufacturing organization did to overcome this problem. As a follow-up to planning, a person from the accounting department took on the task of educating company employees about the ebb and flow of money within the system. She packaged a one-hour program that was initially presented to mid-level managers. Key to her success was explaining money in simple terms using examples from the factory floor. Her presentation focused on one item—profit. By showing how to manipulate everyday activities in the business to increase profit she was able to win over the shop floor. The increased profits were then tied to increased quality of life items such as pay raises, better healthcare, and other fringe benefits.

The outcome of these efforts was very rewarding. By popular demand she took the presentation to all four plants in the company. She demonstrated commitment to the topic by going to plants at early-morning hours, talking to every employee on every shift. Over a short period of time the company was able to see the results of various teams as they became more aware that every day you either make or lose money for the company.

Process Mapping

Another training event that supports the business planning cycle is business process mapping. Little is accomplished by selling more goods and services if your profits are draining out the bottom through organizational process inefficiencies—often called "heat loss." This session is the greatest single education and skills session that you can do to improve your bottom line by eliminating these wasted efforts. Basically the one-time training can be replicated forever within your company.

Mike Mulligan of EM Science, which is a part of EM Industries, uses business process mapping to identify improvements. He perfected the techniques as a result of this business planning model.

Mike's story is a good example to follow. He had his teams go through a brief training cycle to illustrate the power of looking at business processes. Jointly the teams compiled a list of what they thought needed reviewing. Management attention was given to five major processes. Each was assigned a functional champion who put together a working team, developed schedules for completing the project, and defined the expected deliverables. Now, whenever a project is finished, Mike and his team select another process to be examined. The management thinking is to keep the list short but focused. Mike carries the process mapping one step further. He connects each critical process with managerial performance. Each process owner is responsible for delivering what he or she promises. This fits the requirement for accountability and makes his story congruent. Mike rightfully expects and requires accountability.

I have worked with a number of other companies teaching and installing this simple process. A hospital was able to cut down the cost of patient notification from $350 to less than $2. A wallpaper manufacturing company discovered thousands of rollers used to print paper were not being recycled but instead were being stored in expensive warehouse space. At a chemical company the cost of returned chemicals was found to be staggering, so a plan was developed to reduce the returns. I could continue at length with examples of easy money returned to the bottom line.

The business planning cycle should include support for many types of education, training, and skills building to sustain the process. It does little good to know what to do but not how to do the tasks. A viable method to increase the skill levels of your managers and employees goes a long way to creating a success from the plan.

Building your education and training as an adjunct to the planning model prevents what I call random or event training. Huge amounts of training are conducted each year because someone thinks it is needed. These training modules are usually based on whims, novelty of some instrument, or a fad of the time. Seldom is training and education connected directly to the business plan. I believe you need to invest your training dollars wisely by making sure that every course is connected to the goals of your plan. If someone attends training you need to show where the course fulfilled a shortfall in skills to accomplish a part of the business plan.

Training must be connected to and integrated with your company's strategic plan activities. It must also be vertically and horizontally linked internally. That means the training begins at the top and works vertically down the system. Then, the objectives are linked horizontally so that every training event is tied to the next event in a continuous flow. Where this has high payoff to you is in building credibility within the ranks. Too often training begins and ends at the supervision level. Try teaching empowerment concepts to first-line supervisors in an abusive system. Within five minutes the supervisors will ask, "Has my management had this training? If not, see me after they have participated."

Leadership and Managership Training

What I found worked well at a Midwest business-to-business catalogue sales company was to separate the training into two major groupings. Over a three-year period Ralph Cannon, the VP for human resources, used the vertical and horizontal method to provide leadership and managership training and education to 100 percent of the company's managers and supervisors. The first year began with the basics and subsequent years built upon critical leadership and managership topics. By carefully controlling the learning events, Ralph was able to increase the skills to a high-performance level as measured against business goals. For this vertical and horizontal training integration to work, he made sure the information had continuity down the management chain to employees first. This meant that everyone got the same topics but tailored for their specific level and needs. The second successful element of horizontal integration was a building plan. Start with the fundamentals, train employees to perfection, and then add more knowledge and skills to the package each year. After three years of concentrated activities and follow-up, this company had a well-schooled management team.

For your own training to support your business plan, I suggest you build a custom package tailored to a number of identified shortfalls from the gaps found in the planning processes.

SUMMARY

You can condense your core company business plan to five pages. Your top management team then cascades the plan down through the system. Extensive preparation and homework must be completed to define the necessary information from which to plan support for the five pages. With careful preconference preparation you can carry out a detailed business plan. Once the plan is defined you determine what education and training must be conducted to reinforce the plan. These steps are all part of a business planning cycle that has been tested with real businesses making significant improvements in their performance.

THE KEY QUESTIONS: BUILDING YOUR 5-PAGE BUSINESS PLAN

Use the following questions to set the stage for building your 5-Page Business Plan. Don't restrict yourself to the confines of the eight questions. Push to explore all additional topics as they relate to the five-page model.

1. What is your understanding of the purpose of a business plan?
2. Does your written business plan match what you say and do—that is, does it match your story?
3. Does your written business plan contain all the elements suggested in this chapter?
4. Do you have the five major components—the strategic plan, operational plan, organizational plan, resources plan, and contingency plan—defined similarly to those in this chapter?
5. Can your complete business plan be written on five sheets of paper?
6. Are you prepared to lead your management team in preparing a complete business plan?
7. Are you willing to set at least four days aside to develop a company-level business plan?
8. Are you prepared to complete the business planning cycle by providing the education and training necessary to support the finished goals?

THE PRACTICAL APPLICATIONS: BEGINNING A SUCCESSFUL PLANNING CYCLE

By following the sequence of events outlined here, you will have the mechanics in place to begin the planning cycle:

1. Draft the templates for your five single-page plans.
2. Notify your team of your intentions to complete the business plan.
3. Schedule the preplanning session.
4. Schedule the planning session.
5. Assign homework and collect data.
6. Arrange the logistical and computer support for the planning session.

A note of caution: If you start the process, be prepared to carry through to the sustaining phase.

3

Strategic Planning: The Five Critical Considerations That Can Help Your Plan Succeed

This chapter presents five critical issues to consider when building your business plan and constructing the accompanying story. Stories fail when these issues become traps or pitfalls. This chapter presents the issues and offers concrete examples of how to avoid the pitfalls. These issues have to do with:

1. How management theories shape your business behavior
2. Your attitude toward planning
3. The effects of time on your story
4. Guidance from which you build a business plan
5. Assumptions you make to construct a successful plan

You must meet and deal with all five considerations for a successful story. The absence of any one piece creates a hole in the planning model and makes your story incongruent.

The first issue is your understanding of the roots of our business models. As managers and leaders, we have centuries of business thinking embedded into our psyches. That thinking is based on a model now considered obsolete or at least under suspicion. A completely new way of viewing the world has opened our thinking about the leadership of people and the management of companies. In a nutshell, every business model we know is up for review. Concepts once held dear, like the span of control of five to seven people, are now being questioned. The traditional chain of command is being replaced with other ways of thinking. Rigid organizational structures, once thought to be permanent, are being replaced with evolving structures of a fluid nature. It is a confusing time for those managers who mastered the principles of one type of management only to find it being replaced at the height of their careers by another school of thought.

The second piece is your overall attitude toward planning. A timid company approaches the planning process differently from an arrogant company. A conservative company produces a plan far different from an aggressive company that doesn't believe in planning in the first place. Timidity and arrogance are the two ends of the continuum for failure, each with a different story that ultimately fails.

Third is the time consideration of your business plan. A story stretching out over ten years is significantly different from one that reaches out only twelve months. Your story will be enhanced if it covers a longer period of time. This makes it more believable. The resulting plan will appear more logical if your time frames are real-istically matched to the grand scheme of your vision. This match creates congruence in your story.

Fourth is the guidance you receive from higher headquarters, corporate headquarters, or those in a position to approve or reject your plan. It does little good to build a plan if it falls outside the box of your board of directors' guidance. Better to know the expec-tations of those who control your destiny before putting efforts into an extensive planning process. Better to know that your story fits the profile of their story before you strengthen a culture and then have to change it. Your business plan has high potential for failure if you neglect to consider the issue of guidance.

Fifth are the basic assumptions you make for your planning. What guesses are you making about the future? Assumptions are those things you believe to be true that affect your plan if changed over time. The more accurate your assumptions, the more definitive your plans become. Your plan fails if your assumptions are grossly off the mark. The validity of your story is also questionable if your assumptions don't make sense. This creates a problem of congru-ence, authenticity, and believability.

HOW TO EMBRACE THE FAST-CHANGING LAWS OF THE BUSINESS UNIVERSE INTO YOUR COMPANY STORY

How the business world must serve its environment is changing in front of our very eyes. We must not only recognize but also embrace the change. The context of your business training called for man-agement behavior that was straightforward. You were required to write your managerial story in rational, cause-and-effect terms. Logical thinking was critical to developing your story. Your business produced things, so your management style was deterministic. You solved problems based on simplistic laws that boiled decisions down to predictability of what worked and didn't work.

Management and leadership were based on one-way communication, centralized authority, and command and control. Businesses were treated as a giant machine with interchangeable parts. Unfortunately, people were considered part of that machine and treated accordingly[1] The structure was traditional, with clear lines of reporting and command and control (see Figure 3-1).

Figure 3-1. The old model of management was rational, logical, and linear while the new model requires interactive relationships as the foundation.

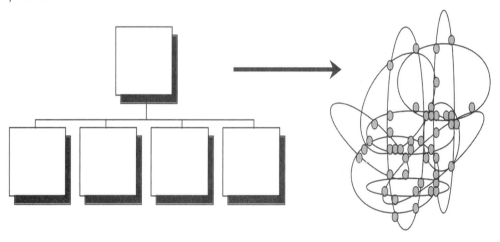

   In management circles there is a name for the aforementioned management theory—Scientific Management. This theory was derived from the Newtonian concept of how the universe is ordered. For a long time this construct of order was helpful in organizing our management knowledge when applied to business situations. However, not all parts of the theory fit today because we are experiencing modern times calling for modern management. In fact, every model we are using is subject to being questioned in light of applicability. Therefore, we may make the following observations:

- Traditional models are not bad—they just don't work as well anymore.

- Every business model we learned is shifting.

- Every model is therefore suspect.

Lurking in the background has been a competing theory of how businesses should be led and managed. Events, circumstances, and the nature of the evolving fundamental processes of society have brought the competing theories into vogue. Now you are being asked to look at your business from a shifted point of view. Concepts such as self-directed work teams, empowerment, and shared decision making are terms frequently found in your business meetings. Instead of just making things you are now being asked to put your customers' needs in the center of the ring and respond accordingly.

Consumers take quality as a given, want the product yesterday, and expect to pay less and less. The Henry Ford quote, "Any color you want, so long as it's black," worked well for his time but wouldn't survive till the sun goes down in view of this shift in management thinking.[2]

No area of business is protected from the effects of the shifting business models. Areas once considered safe are the focus of attention. Consider services being outsourced as a prime example of the shift from owning everything to paying for services as needed. That's what the whole outsourcing movement is about. Think of typical company staff functions such as human resources, information technology, and administrative services. Many companies are turning to experts in the functional fields and paying them a fee to perform the services. Give serious consideration to how the shifts in thinking are affecting the roles of each part of your business. (A case study at the end of this chapter provides an exercise designed to help you understand the new roles of each of your functions and departments as they move from a highly structured approach to one of a fast-breaking, fluid business situation.) We must become more flexible in applying the lessons from a virtual model. Terms such as *strategic partnerships, alliances,* and *outsourcing* are the watchwords of the new business language.

Jim Dean has thirty-plus years of involvement with the human resources business. When he and I discussed the changing role of human resources in the new millennium, he observed that the role of the human resources manager is shifting from the traditional model to that of the champion of change as it relates to a virtual model of business. Jim goes further to suggest that human resources managers should be the champions of the company's business planning process. He sees that role as necessary to connect the strategic with the tactical functions of a business. His reasoning is logical. Who else touches the major resources and all parts of the business in the same fashion as the human resources business unit?

To avoid the trap of outdated management models consider the following four planning techniques:

1. *Challenge every belief you have about leading and managing your business.* One of the first places to look is at your theory of people. Do you see people as part of a big machine or as a valuable resource? For example, do employees need to be involved in planning, or can the management team just tell them what to do?

2. *Challenge every concept you have about customers.* Are customers and their inherent complaints a necessary part of doing business, or are they the key to your existence? For example, when do you consider the customer's needs and wants in your product development? Traditionally we asked the customer's opinion last when developing a new product. In the new models of the business future, customers will be at the center of the equation.

3. *Challenge your internal time orientation.* Customers are demanding goods and services in real time. Are you prepared to operate on a next-day-delivery concept? Is your model of the world still "Please allow four to six weeks for delivery"? FedEx and the other overnight-delivery services

have rethought, redesigned, and reoriented the time issues.

4. *Challenge the roles and functions of your organization.* How can you redefine roles to make them more challenging? For example, examine your organization's structure. Can you get more done through strategic partnerships and outsourcing?

BAD ATTITUDES: HOW ORGANIZATIONS GET INTO TROUBLE WITH POOR PLANNING

Another area of concern deals with an organization's ability to react or not react. Let's look at two cases: the timid company that sits in the hot water until it boils to death and the arrogant company that believes its own press clippings until it appears in the obituary column of the business section.

In the first case the parable of the boiled frog is appropriate. Like the frog that dies as the water is brought to a boil, a timid company dies while making slow, incremental adjustments to its situation even as business conditions heat up around it.[3] It makes minor changes to its behavior, fine-tunes its existing story, and polishes old behaviors. The arrogant company, on the other hand, refuses to believe the water is heating up. After all, it's in control of the thermostat. Let's examine in more detail how both types of companies refuse to examine their internal thinking.

Timid Companies: Thinking Small and Failing to Take Risks

The story of timid companies is marked by a failure to live up to their fullest potential. They build stories behind an elaborate set of excuses designed to keep the company in the middle of the road, never venturing too far to either side. Managers of timid companies are not bad people. They don't set out to be average; they are just not the risk takers of the business world.

Most organizations are successful to some degree in spite of their management, not because of its behavior. Managers in timid companies get in the way of their own success because they tend to think small, stay in a low-performance comfort zone, and avoid risks. This mediocre behavior is generally acceptable in the average American corporation where the "industry average" is the performance benchmark. If an industry average growth is 10 percent, a timid company is satisfied with getting close to that mark. Their story at year's end is a glowing admission of limited thinking. Praises and self-congratulations are made for setting and meeting average performance goals. Such self-limiting behavior creates mediocre management.

Thinking small is an extremely limiting managerial behavior. With few exceptions, most managers today are trained with a numbers mentality that leads to thinking inside a box. Words such as *practical, reasonable,* and *attainable* are replete in our business language. Managers brag about making money the old-fashioned way; they earn it one dollar at a time. Executives take pride that their companies are conservative, as if working at less than full potential is a badge of distinction. Reaching for the stars is something relegated to a handful of entrepreneurs.

The most interesting story I can tell you about thinking small and allowing timidity to run rampant involves a banking corporation. A business partner and I had developed a relationship with a large state association. Keep in mind this was only one state out of fifty, so the potential to expand our services was staggering in magnitude. This association wanted us to help them develop a credit card for their membership. We gathered the facts, did an analysis, and developed a business case. The information was pretty exciting, so we approached the banking corporation with the plan. After several successful meetings between the bank and the association we ran into an unexpected barrier. When the bank's project manager briefed executives they rejected the plan. Their stated reason was interesting, to say the least. It was, "We're not sure this credit card business isn't just a fad. We don't have a card, and we're not sure that cards are a good line of business."

This bank's rejection of the business case was not based on research into the card business and a subsequent management business decision to stay out of the competition. The bank's management had never investigated the concept at all.

Ironically, the month before we presented our business case, I counted nine unsolicited credit card offers that came across my desk. If the credit card business was a poor venture I wondered why so many people were in the game. While writing this chapter, I decided to check out my suspicions on credit cards. I wanted to see if the fad had passed. For a one-month period we kept a few unsolicited cards that came into our office. Here is what we received (and this list doesn't even include the many phone calls we had for the same service):

- Orvis Conservation Platinum Visa Card
- NRA MasterCard
- FCC National Bank Gold MasterCard
- FCC National Bank First Card Platinum Visa
- American Express Small Business Services Corporate Option Platinum
- City Bank & US Airways Platinum Visa

I guess these are businesses that think the card business might be a worthy venture after all.

Thinking small also encourages another destructive behavior. Being conservative is safe, comfortable, and attracts little attention to poor individual performance. Using team-generated, conservative numbers makes it easy for an average performer to hide in the management crowd. With the current emphasis on using teams, it becomes easy for group dynamics to become a screen for limited individual thinking. Bold thinkers stand out in a crowd where the group norm is a safe, conservative approach to business goals. Average thinkers also hide in that same crowd. But the blame for misusing a group doesn't just rest on the individual. Much of it can be linked to the training and skills of those responsible for creating and leading those management teams.

Seldom do senior managers have the necessary sophisticated group skills to create a total team of bold thinkers. The fine art of group dynamics is not taught as a part of our formal education. The average manager in corporate America cannot even run an effective meeting, the simplest demonstration of group dynamics skill. Why should we expect managers to be able to orchestrate, with virtuoso ability, the complex and intricate processes of humans interacting in business groups? Without group skills, team mentality at many organizations actually becomes a vehicle to encourage lackluster performance.

The antidote for timidity in planning is to think big and outside of the box. Consider the following planning techniques:

- *Eliminate the use of "industry averages."* You should know what they are but not allow them to become the basis for performance or goal setting. To use them as benchmarks for higher performance is fine. Just don't let them become de facto ceilings.

- *Plan as a team.* With effective team management you can create the synergy necessary to overcome the pitfalls of committees and other dysfunctional groups. By using team planning, you can tap into a wealth of intellectual capital that may be otherwise missed.

Arrogant Companies: Three Deadly Excuses for Not Writing a Business Plan

Arrogant companies are the other side of timidity.[4] They tell quite a different story. Often it is hard to get them to define their story because they are moving fast and making lots of money.

Profit hides many management evils. When you are making money it is hard to be convinced of the need to develop a business plan. That's arrogance pure and simple. Sadly, the reasons for arrogant companies to avoid planning won't withstand close scrutiny.

A company that doesn't plan can operate for a period of time, existing day to day or year to year, but sooner or later the story plays out.

Arrogant leaders of arrogant companies often use three common themes or reasons to skip writing a business plan. These deadly avoidance behaviors are made even more potent when found in combinations:

1. *When life is good customers line up and profits roll in with no end in sight.* "Why should we do strategic planning?" a successful management team asks. The more profitable a company, the more arrogant it becomes. Managers begin to believe their own press clippings, which leads to a belief of infallibility. Arrogant companies are so busy making money they get lulled into a false sense of security. They don't believe they need to do strategic planning. Ironically, the best time to plan is when you are making lots of money and having a string of successes. Then you can afford the luxury of planning. When you are failing is the worst time to plan. That's when you can least afford it. Either way, the need for planning doesn't disappear.

2. *We're good.* Arrogant companies have a distorted view of themselves as successful management teams. They falsely believe their successes are because of their astute performance. They would be devastated to learn that their successes may be a matter of circumstance, not brilliant management. If a company is successful, doesn't that mean management is doing the right things? Maybe that's true but maybe not. Does it indicate a well-trained, disciplined management team with the skills needed for sustained growth? Maybe it does and maybe it doesn't.

3. *Planning is a waste of time when we could be making money.* Arrogant companies see planning as missed opportunities for generating more dollars by doing more of the same as they are doing now. This track soon runs out. Planning is

not a waste of time. It is about using your time to prepare for new opportunities. Doesn't it make more sense to be in control of your company's future than to leave it to fate? Wouldn't it be wise to think through what you want to accomplish long term rather than live from day to day?

Arrogant companies are easy to spot from my vantage point as a consultant. Most frequently these are family-held businesses, entrepreneurial ventures, or old-line staid corporations. Don't try to tell such companies that they need to do planning. You have to wait until they start to hurt. They must hit the flat spot on the growth line before you can get their attention.

One such case comes to mind. I was asked to work as a sub-contractor for a large consulting company that had a growing strategic consulting business unit. The weeks of telephone discussions went well. The actual meeting went in the other direction. The reception I received at their corporate headquarters was the most insulting of my consulting career. The interviewing team was the most arrogant, self-centered group of professional consultants I had ever encountered. Their smugness was evident in every theme of our conversation. The final comment that sealed the meeting's fate was this: "You don't understand. You are just a little player. If you expect to work for us you'll have to give up some of your autonomy."

That attitude was indicative of a group that failed and was disbanded within six months. They had no business plan. I suspect there was a connection.

The following techniques for dealing with an arrogant attitude are simple but radical:

- *Wait until they fail to get attention.* Unfortunately, this is not a healthy course of action, but sometimes it is the only way.

- *Focus on the idea of creating greater success than the present.* This often hooks high-performing organizations that think they are creating the optimum results. Ask two questions of the management of this type company:

1. How much more money could you have made if you had been better organized?

2. How much money did you leave on the table by the way you now operate?

These are killer questions that usually lead an arrogant company to planning.

How to Choose the Best Time Frame for Developing and Executing Your Story

There is a direct connection and suspected high correlation between timid and arrogant companies and their time perspectives. Timid companies do not reach out to the future. Arrogant companies think the future is the next quarter. Both of those orientations eventually fail.

The proper length of time covered by a business plan is one of the hot topics among planners and business executives. Heated arguments are made for both long and short time frames. The proper time span in your business plan is critical to its subsequent development and execution. A proper story cannot be constructed if your plan is too short. It is not believable.

Proactive Long-Term backPlanning

Your business plan should cover a period of time sufficient to see the trends for your industry and your own business performance. This is called backPlanning because you put a stake in the ground and work backward (see Figure 3-2). Most businesses tend to plan for three to five years. While that is better than one to three years, the time should be more in the ten- to fifteen-year zones for strategic planning. A solid recommended time frame is ten years. Longer backPlanning time frames are better for several reasons:

■ *A ten-year period gives you more start points to put critical actions in place.* There may be many things you would like to do but cannot start them all next year. A wide time span lets you spread the start points over a number of years and make reasonable commitments.

■ *A ten-year span gives you time to ramp up if necessary.* You may need to continue business as usual for several years until you build momentum.

■ *A ten-year time frame makes your story more believable.* Employees can see a series of progressive actions to accomplish heroic deeds more easily than attempting to create overnight successes. The latter is not believable.

■ *A ten-year time frame allows you to build early successes.* Trying to compress a huge success into a three- to five-year span often leads to failure. You must guarantee a series of incremental successes starting small and growing.

Figure 3-2. backPlanning is a concept of starting at some future point in time to establish a vision and goals, then working backward to confirm the mission. Execution is then a forward activity from the base of the mission. Consider the phrase "back planning and forward execution."

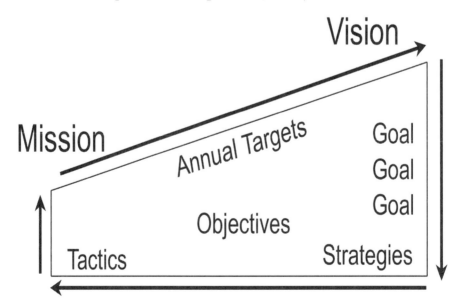

Robin Jolley understood the need for long-term planning in his role as resources manager for a lumber company. While his plan far exceeded our recommended ten-year span, it was necessary for the wood products industry. His mission was to keep the division supplied in trees for lumber. Since the company bought from itself first, he had to know how many board feet were available at any given year. This helped him to project the shortfalls and advise the company to buy more land, plant more trees, or be prepared to buy from the market. A shortfall might mean buying from a competitor at an unattractive price. How long does Robin's strategic plan reach forward? Try fifty years. Why? Think how long it takes to grow a tree to any size.

While Robin's plan is an extreme, it illustrates the concept of long-term versus short-term planning and the industry-specific nature of a time frame. Of the thirty companies that have implemented the model described in this book within the past five years, 95 percent have opted for the ten-year zone. After careful consideration of their industry rhythm they saw the value of reaching out to the future.

Planning requires more than just forward thinking in time. It also requires a look backward (see Figure 3-3). I suggest you extend your timeline back for a minimum of ten years. If you can plot data further back in time, that would be even better. The rule of thumb is to put as much information on the board as possible. You need extensive historical data to ascertain where you have been in performance and how the projections are forming. This is done using trend analysis of your time schedule.

Figure 3-3. Extend your time analysis backward to give as much depth to your business plan as possible.

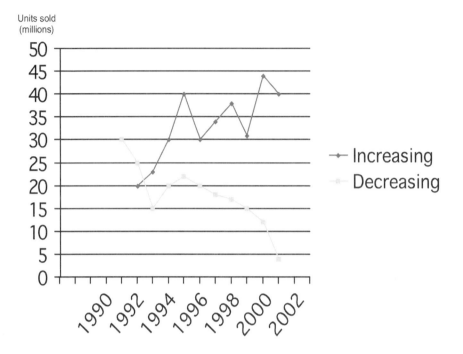

Since all businesses have a sine curve of good times and bad times, you need to know how those are developing. You must know where you are in the cycle. Is your industry up or down? How long has it been that way? Is it on the upswing or downswing? How much longer will it go in either direction? These are the critical questions that must be answered from your timelines.

The normal resistance will be to shorten the timeline and not push out but instead proceed in a "planning creep," or an incremental growth fashion (see Figure 3-4). The justification for not pushing is to give you time to react to the changing market or environment. There is some sort of crazy belief that if you focus only on the short term (say, six months or a year), you can better respond to situations. That belief is actually counterintuitive, meaning it is exactly backwards. With long-term planning you can be in a position to deal with the new situations. Conversely, if your story is always short term you will always be in the reactive mode. Your model of the world will always be to play catch-up. You will never be the market leader or even close because all your energy will be spent trying to stay even. There is no way for you to break out. If you are a reactive-type business with a short-term orientation, I suggest you reconsider your basic assumptions and how they affect your time frame of planning.

Figure 3-4. Planning creep is a common business trap limiting a company's potential.

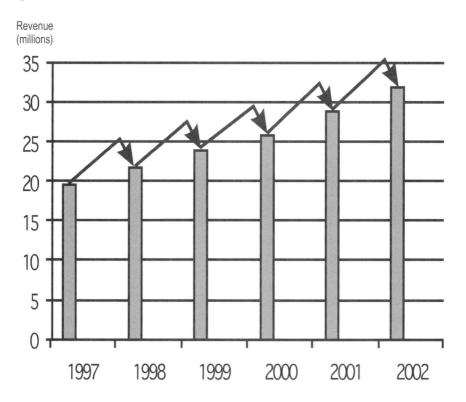

To successfully carry out long-range planning you must alter the creeping methodology. You stand in danger of planning and thinking too small, not thinking in bold terms. Planning creep is moving toward the future by "adding 10 percent" to last year's budget and goals. When these outcomes are added over time they do not give the same results as well-developed goals. Planning creep is moving cautiously toward the future in a nonrisk mode. It is safe, will get your plans approved, and will get you rewarded for accomplishment.

In the normal planning process, planners build on past success. An example is in sales volume. If $10 million in sales was good, let's try for $11 million. Over a period of years a company continues to plan and implement in this fashion but finishes dissatisfied. It finds itself somewhere it didn't want or expect to be. The result of planning creep is mediocre or average performance.

Planning creep is the desired format for some shareholders because it is predictable and safe. It is called "blue chip" investments. This is dangerous for four reasons:

1. It fails to meet expectations.
2. It doesn't live up to organizational potential.
3. It fails to use full intellectual capital.
4. It leads to stagnation of mind and action.

Predicting the Future Versus Designing the Future

Another common excuse to avoid long-term planning is the belief that "we cannot predict the future." This is a frequent quote from business students in management classes. They are playing "gotcha" with the teacher. Often these participants are in a high-tech field with rapidly changing technology—for example, computers or networks and related fields. A simple challenge is appropriate to this foot dragging: "Do you really think Bill Gates and Microsoft refuse to plan because they can't predict the future? My guess is that they design the future."

Asking managers to think long term isn't the same as asking them to make predictions. What you are being asked to do is to describe where your organization will be at some point in the future. Anyone can do that. With a little thought and imagination any manager can describe some future setting.

Setting Time Frames

To properly set time frames in your planning session consider the following questions:

- What is the trend data of the past?
- Where are we now on the cycle of our industry?
- How have the variations of ups and downs changed over the past few years?
- What industry data do we have projecting trends for the future?
- Will looking at a ten-year window give a more complete understanding of future requirements?

HOW TO TELL YOUR STORY EFFECTIVELY WITH (OR WITHOUT) GUIDANCE FROM TOP MANAGEMENT

Another reason a story fails or gets into trouble early is because it doesn't fit into the expectations of upper management. If the plan is outside the guidance of the board of directors it will not be approved. If it is designed and implemented without approval, it will certainly raise questions about the management team's behavior.

Business planning begins with guidance that defines the boundaries within which you must plan. It determines the box within which you must play. The boundary conditions found in your guidance may be explicitly stated or annoyingly vague. If guidance is specific it may contain things you don't want to hear or require performance you don't expect. If the guidance is vague it can be either a frustrating or a freeing experience. How you react to vague guidance is a message about you as a manager.

Often senior managers whine and complain about the lack of guidance. Interestingly, these same managers don't seem to have the courage to ask for guidance. When it is suggested they might ask, it seems a novel idea to them. Some managers are happy with no guidance because it becomes an excuse for no action on their part. Blaming upward becomes easy.

When managers complain that they have no guidance, my response is usually unexpected. I answer, "Isn't that great? Now you can do anything you want to do." Normally those personality types don't see the humor or get the message.

In reality, having no guidance is a freeing experience. Bold, risk-taking managers believe having no guidance is a license for them to act. Likewise, smart planners do one or two things: They move without guidance and force the issue, or they determine their boundaries before doing detailed planning. Responses to asking for guidance vary. Sometimes there is no guidance and you will have to go it alone. Other times the guidance will not be what you expected. Worst is the vague guidance "go out and do good." If you have no guidance, you still must carry out your planning process. In fact, you have an opportunity to force management into making decisions and assuming responsibility. Forcing the issue makes boards of directors get very clear when they often wish to remain vague. Since the board must approve a business plan it becomes a de facto method of forcing them to do their job.

Guidance becomes the critical success factor required by the tasking authority or persons asking you to do business planning. Examples of tasking authorities may be the board of directors, corporate headquarters, or the company ownership.

Guidance may cover a number of areas. Some examples are:

■ *Budget Constraints.* What are you allowed to do with financial resources? For instance, you may be directed to place a hiring freeze on the workforce for the next year with a possible extension for three years. Knowing this piece of information would certainly be helpful in planning your resources.

■ *Product or Service Range.* This refers to what you can and cannot sell. For example, you may be told to increase your product line by generating 20 percent of your long-range profits with new business lines.

■ *Political Restrictions.* In certain geographical areas or industries, rules, regulations, and laws often make significant differences to your bottom line. For example, you may be directed to avoid locating a new service facility in a certain state because the state government is basically antibusiness with punitive tax rules.

■ *Critical Success Factors.* This is a common piece of guidance because it defines what you will be measured on at intermediate and long-term points of the plan. For example, the board of directors may define exactly how much money is returned per share of stock, per quarter.

■ *Expected Performance.* You may be given a revenue goal and told to reach that goal. This may be both short term (i.e., next year) and long term (i.e., for the life of the plan). For instance, you may be directed to grow the business from $100 million today to $1 billion in revenue by the end of ten years.

■ *Time Requirements.* Often the guidance giver has a time frame in mind to see specific targets accomplished. For example, you may get guidance to enter five new countries, one every other year for the life of the plan.

MAKING ASSUMPTIONS: BENCHMARKS FOR CROSS-CHECKING YOUR SUCCESS IN THE FUTURE

Your business plan must be built on a solid foundation that can be later checked. Assumptions are guesses you have to make about future conditions holding true for your business. They become benchmarks for your thinking later as you review and update your plan. An example of an assumption might be "that access to the healthcare marketplace would be maintained."

Assumptions fall into three types:

1. *Past Predictive Assumption.* This assumption is built on the chance that an occurrence in the past will happen again. For example, a record flood will hit the Mississippi Delta region again within the next one hundred years.

2. *Present or Steady-State Assumption.* This assumption is built on the belief that something that is presently happening will continue. A case in point: The frequency of violence in the workplace will continue to be a significant management problem in the next decade.

3. *Future Predictive Assumption.* This assumption is built on the belief that something that has not happened will happen in the future. For instance, you may make an assumption that electrical technology will develop to the level of applicability that it replaces petroleum-powered vehicles.

A perfect business plan has zero assumptions. A poor business plan has many assumptions. A great business plan probably has four or five assumptions. Excessive assumptions mean you have not sufficiently defined the problem. If you think you have too many assumptions, keep defining the situation with facts until you arrive at a few remaining issues that must be assumed.

Correctly including your assumptions in your story and business plan is also a protection to you should the situation change. In subsequent years you can check your thinking. Another protection is when someone changes the plan on you. If upper management changes its requirements, then you have every right to revisit the goals of the plan. Remember that you will resource your plan based on a set of assumptions. If those basic assumptions change, your resources will be out of alignment with your plan.

To correctly integrate assumptions into your plan consider the following:

- *Assumptions are the basis for plan change.* If the assumption fails, the plan must be changed. Act accordingly if this happens.

- *Assumptions must be limited to things that you cannot validate.* That is why they are still assumptions.

While writing assumptions is an art and requires careful team discussion, some outstanding examples can be found in real company business plans. Here are seven examples of assumptions that were valid for each of their owner companies:

1. Our proposed credit line will be approved.
2. No natural disaster occurs that affects the price of lumber within the next two years.
3. We have no loss of clients from our existing customer base over the next year.
4. Access to the healthcare marketplace will be maintained.
5. We can find and hire a qualified information technology person within our salary offering by third quarter of next year.
6. We have no unexpected turnover of key team members within the next twelve months.
7. The Canadian–U.S. dollar exchange rate will stay stable for the next year.

CASE STUDY:
COMPARING HUMAN RESOURCES FUNCTIONS

In future organizations, the functions of staffs as they currently exist will be severely challenged. The function will no longer be a centralized, controlling body governing the life and death of the activity. Instead, the structure will be decentralized with the control going to the actual working level of the organization. Here are two scenarios for a selected staff function.

THE NEWTONIAN METHOD OF SCIENTIFIC MANAGEMENT: BUILDING A LARGE POWER BASE

In the Scientific Management model, staff function was built into a large power base. It was to the vice president's advantage to control as many activities and people as possible. Take the area of human resources. You can actually get a degree in human resources management. The disciples of HR have their own language, hold annual conferences, and confer upon themselves near mystical powers over the organization. The model is centralized control where HR specialists take over the functions of managers. In the Scientific Management model the human resources staff function:

* Manages the recruiting process

* Manages the hiring process

* Manages the firing process

* Develops the compensation packages

* Establishes promotion criteria

* Develops and maintains the company's
  training program

QUANTUM MECHANICS: EMPHASIZING RELATIONSHIP MANAGEMENT

While certain functions will remain, the major differences will be the shift of emphasis on responsibility. The simple illustration is the traditional turn to HR for questions and actions involving company motivation. HR is not responsible for company morale. Motivation is an ingrained function of all management and all employees. In the future, HR will be placed in a monitoring role and in less of a police role as the center of control shifts to empowerment and self-responsibility. The operation or role of the HR function in the hiring process may be revised as follows:

1. Instead of waiting for HR to fill a position, the work team tells HR what type of individual with what skills it (HR) needs to recruit.

2. The work team hires its own members and simply reports to HR for record keeping. There is a transfer of traditional HR functions to the work team.

3. The work team can fire its peer members who are not producing their fair share of performance. The work team reports such personnel action to HR for record-keeping purposes.

4. The work team enters all personnel data into a computer database and eliminates the staff record-keeping function of HR.

5. Work teams determine their own compensation and rewards systems based on internal budgets and guidelines.

6. Promotions may not follow a traditional career path but may require workers being assigned to or accepted on a variety of more highly evolving or specialized teams.

7. Individuals are able to select education, knowledge, and training from a menu of options that HR prepares for the organization.

SUMMARY

To build your business story you need to understand the changing world around you. This means you must explore every business model and construct you presently use for viability. Is it still working? Examine your attitude. Is it timid and, if so, what must you do to break out of the ultraconservative mode? If yours is an arrogant company, are you willing to risk your future over this dysfunctional behavior? Are you willing to admit that there may be business over the hill that you have not considered? Have you asked for or received guidance? If not, you may be outside the boundaries and have your plan rejected. Are you willing to risk the time, effort, and embarrassment of a disapproved plan? And finally, what assumptions have you made to build your story? Are they valid assumptions or just quick passes at the requirement? Can those assumptions be used for benchmarks in the future to cross-check your management team's thinking? If you can successfully answer these questions, you are ready to move to the next part of developing your story.

THE KEY QUESTIONS: UNDERSTANDING HOW CRITICAL ISSUES INFLUENCE YOUR COMPANY'S STORY

Use these questions to determine your level of understanding how the two competing models of management influence an organization:

1. How would you describe your beliefs about an organiza-tion? Choose a or b:
   a. My company should operate like a well-oiled machine.
   b. My company is a giant network of existing relationships.
2. Would you consider your approach to planning timid or arrogant?
3. If you are a timid company, what is blocking you from breaking out of timidity?
4. If you are an arrogant company, what attitude and behaviors must you change to become fully functional?
5. What is the time frame for your business plan?
6. What is preventing you from stretching out to a longer time frame?
7. Where do you fall on the sine curve of good times and bad times in your industry?
8. Do you know the boundaries of your guidance?
9. What assumptions have you made about your business situation?

THE PRACTICAL APPLICATIONS: FRAMING THE CONTEXT OF YOUR PLAN

You are now ready to create three items for your business plan:

1. *Develop your timeline.* Be bold and look for a longer time frame for your plan.
2. *Write your guidance.* If you do not have clear guidance, ask. Add this information to your strategic plan.
3. *Write your assumptions.* Add this information to your strategic plan.

4

Vision and Mission: The Two Key Anchors That Add Passion and Purpose to Your Story

This chapter defines the heart of your story. To build an effective plan you begin by putting two stakes in the ground. The first of these is the vision statement and the second one is the mission statement (see Figure 4-1). This chapter deals in detail with both elements. Here I tackle controversial issues such as top-down versus bottom-up visioning. Because they are often confused and considered the same thing, I clearly separate the definitions and purposes of vision and mission by describing the roles and functions that each has in developing your plan. I go further by explaining how to look at your mission in a new light. This new concept is called mission analysis and gives you a detailed review of what is required by the mission statement.

Figure 4-1. The mission and vision serve as the two end points for the path of your plan.

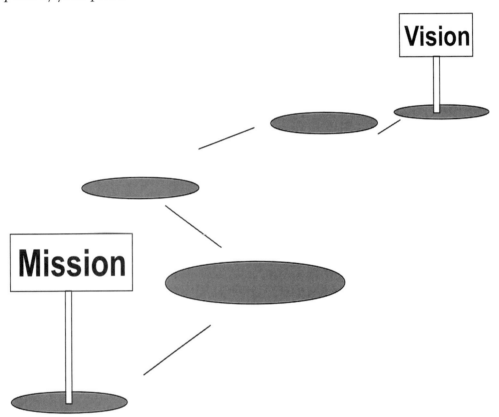

Putting stakes in the ground gives you anchor points for your plan and creates stability by defining start points and end points of your planning. One stake defines where you are now and the other defines where you want to be in the future. Neither can be absent from your story since they are the originators of your plan's purpose and passion. By knowing the two end points of your plan, you can add pieces and parts of the planning process. From these anchor points you build an integrated model of many critical items, which combine to form your story.

THE TWO CRUCIAL PARTS OF THE VISIONING PROCESS

Let's put the first stake in place. The vision stake contains two parts (see Figure 4-2):

1. The vision itself
2. The vision statement

These two parts are different but so closely integrated and interdependent that they cannot be separated. Both must be present in your thinking and should be developed at one time in the process.

Figure 4-2. The vision and the vision statement together provide the direction of the plan.

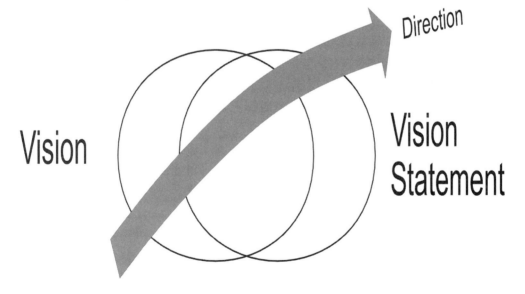

One part, the vision statement, is short and to the point, whereas the vision itself can be lengthy and somewhat vague. As you build your plan, these two parts must be discussed. The vision statement becomes part of your written documentation in the business plan itself. The longer vision may be captured in narrative as part of the company's recorded history.

TECHNIQUES THAT CAN HELP YOU CREATE A POWERFUL COMPANY VISION

The vision is the guiding focus of the company's direction. Without a direction the company is lost, wandering around the landscape of the business environment. Employees are disillusioned with the situation because they cannot see an end game. I believe that people come to work each day expecting to move toward some goal. That means they need direction to their existence. Companies without this fundamental element are doomed to exist from day to day, act only in a reactive mode, and be forever chained to the present.

Scenario Writing: Where Are You Heading?

Direction provided by the vision can be written many ways. A useful tool for developing the vision is called scenario writing. You may choose to describe multiple versions of your vision. Two examples or versions will give you different perceptions of how you want to proceed. One version may be an extension of the present situation but improved over time. This means you are satisfied with your present business but would like it to grow or be more profitable. Visualize making your existing business much bigger. A second vision scenario may ask you to change your current business into something different but better. This could mean growing from your present product or service line into something quite different. For example, you may be presently in the insurance business. Looking into the future you expect a certain part of your business to grow to the point where it becomes the dominant income producer. Your main income might then be from brokering stocks and bonds. Ten years down the road your company name may still be the same but your products may be completely different as you slowly gain more definition and clarity of what your vision really meant.

Keep Your Focus Future-Oriented

Other factors distinguish the vision as a concept that is different from the mission or other parts of your story. The vision must obviously be future-oriented. This means you must think outside the box of today and describe the world of the future. Since the vision can be anything you want it to be, it may be recorded as fragments or it may be a complete document. The vision can include a number of diverse points or it can be very focused. Because the vision is a description, it should be stimulating in phrases and wording. The vision must paint a picture that attracts employees through the use of visual imagery. This is what hooks people into passionate buy-in, subsequent followership, and cheerful implementation of the plan.

The idea that a vision has to be a completely thought-out, stand-alone piece of work is not necessarily true. Often just the concept of where you want to go as a leader can fire the imagination of the company. Consider Steven Jobs's idea that every person should have access to a computer. Consider what kind of story was built around that simple but elegant vision. Maybe entrepreneurs cannot fully explain their vision on the first pass, but they can anchor the idea. That is often enough to build successful companies. In the movie *Field of Dreams*, Kevin Costner was visited by a voice that told him, "Build it and they will come." His character then began a quest to find out what that voice meant. In the beginning he had no clue, just a belief that the message was important. During the journey he found another believer and then a third, who reinforced his vision. Later Costner's character "bet the farm," putting his entire future at stake to fulfill the dream and make it a reality.

Add Keywords to Fire the Imagination of Your Employees

The stimulating factor of a vision cannot be underestimated. By using keywords in telling a story the leader stirs the imagination, bonds employees with common purpose, and creates hope for the future. Howard Gardner's simple but elegant description seems to fit: "And still others have investigated the primary purpose of stories—binding together of a community, the tackling of basic philosophical or spiritual questions, the conferral of meaning on an otherwise chaotic existence." In his book Leading Minds, he builds example after example of the power of stories and linking people through a common imagery.[1]

The vision must include concepts that capture people's attention and create the passion necessary for successful planning. Inherent to the visioning process are words that convey the following information:

- *Size.* What size company could you become in ten years? Just how big do you want to grow the company? How hard are you willing to work?

- *Geography.* Where do you want to be located in ten years? Are you willing to do what is necessary to expand, often into other countries with different rules, regulations, and business climates?

- *Markets.* Are you willing to shift markets from your existing one to an emerging market, one that could be risky?

- *Products, Goods, and Services.* Are you willing to give up old-line products and sacred cows for new ventures that may be different from your company's history? How different would it be to move from a producer of goods to a deliverer of services in ten years?

These are just examples of items you must consider when developing your overall vision. Combine these key concepts when painting the picture of the future. Substitute the words *planner* or *president* in Gardner's quote and you build a case for using imagination in the planning process.

There is one more idea I'd like to introduce. I find it cold and distracting when writers downplay the power of emotion in an organization's plan or story. The component of emotion is critical in developing the psychological tie-in of employees to the business plan. But don't confuse the value of employees' emotional connection with the concrete aspect of the vision. Too often the analytical writers try to equate vision and the visioning process as some blinding flash of the future without substance. They are simply mixing the strategic goals of a business plan with definition of the vision. This shows a lack of understanding of planning as an integrated model. Of course you must convert your vision into measurable, doable actions. To believe the vision carries itself on its own strength is fantasy. (Further explanation of the conversion of the vision into strategic goals is offered in Chapter 5.)

THE VISION STATEMENT: HOW TO DESCRIBE YOUR COMPANY OF THE FUTURE

The second part of the visioning process is the vision statement. This is a statement that captures the essence or spirit of how you describe the organization of the future. Here are some guidelines for getting started:

- *Make your description short and to the point.* Sometimes the description is vague to the outside reader. That's not bad. Because the complete vision is a long paragraph or numerous pages, the shorter vision statement is ideal for inclusion in the business plan.

- *Don't be concerned with the vagueness or brevity of the vision statement.* Vagueness in sentence structure gives you an opportunity to have a quality communications event with employees. In fact, you want them to ask about the definition of the vision statement because it gives you a chance to explain details of your thinking. This was not meant to be a license to create a deliberately vague vision statement. There will be enough of those.

■ *Don't try to write a vision statement that is so clear it will be understood by 100 percent of your employees on the first pass. That is just not realistic. If you want clarity in your vision statement, ask yourself this: Can you fully explain it to anyone who asks?*

Here are several examples of vision statements taken from business plans of assorted organizations. While they differ in length, all are short, powerful, and achieve positive responses from employees:

Examples of Vision Statements

■ To be the respected leader and credible information source for all issues related to the forestry community.

■ The people of HRD Canada, New Brunswick Region, make a difference in the lives of New Brunswickers and Canadians. By contributing to the improvement of social and economic conditions in our province, we are working toward the achievement of people's full potential and the elimination of poverty in our communities.

■ Our vision is to dominate the world market with our products.

■ Beat big blue!

■ To build the smallest, most user-friendly computer in the world.

■ The Creative Kitchen Company will become well known for solving complex kitchen renovation problems.

■ The company customers will turn to for help in resolving their difficult business situations.

■ To be rated among the top 100 companies to work for in North America.

- To build houses, each leaving only a wheelbarrow full of scrap.

- To set new standards of on-time delivery and accuracy at the international level.

- Our products will achieve public recognition for quality, durability, and safety.

- To touch every household in North America with at least one of our product lines.

- Our bed and breakfast chain will become the symbol for your "home away from home."

- To become the most highly sought-after tree service in the state of Virginia.

- To make our seafood line the most recognized within North America.

- To provide our customers with exotic flowers from around the world today.

- To have my gowns featured in *Vogue* magazine.

Martin Luther King Jr. touched spirits and enflamed souls with his famous "I have a dream" speech. If you don't believe in "this vision thing," consider how that one speech changed a nation and forever shaped history. Consider how a new president at Savage Arms saved the company when he appealed to the employees with words to this effect: "This company is a piece of American history. We are too valuable to let it die. We are going to salvage this company."

Getting a vision down to a single phrase or sentence is not an easy task. The best way to extract the vision statement from the discussion or scenario-writing exercise during a planning session is to let it evolve. Capturing a powerful vision statement is not something that can be done on cue or at a scheduled time in the planning process. You often find a team discussing the vision at length and not being able to immediately define the vision statement. That's okay. Don't force the issue. Sooner or later the team will circle back around to the issue of vision statement and write an acceptable version.

A critical by-product of the vision statement is the creation of passion, which is the outward expression of emotion. The dynamic of passion surrounding the vision and the vision statement creates an energy field or field of vision. Admittedly, this is an intangible but nonetheless real organizational dynamic. When visiting an organization that has a well-communicated vision, an energy field is very much in evidence. It manifests itself in the way people carry out their duties, the way they deal with customers, and the way they approach one another. A company with a field of vision is an exciting place to work. People know their work is important, is meaningful, and has purpose. This energy is translated into higher motivation levels and better performance.

A significantly higher level of performance can be found in organizations with a vision than those without a vision. Often you find good people, people who want to perform but have no emotional outlet. There is no vision to create passion for their work. I am saddened to find good companies with good people and good products managed by presidents with no vision. While there are many leaders with outstanding operational skills, these same individuals often have little or no visionary skills. Because visioning is a core competency of a leader it goes without saying the leader is responsible for setting the vision and facilitating the executive team in developing the vision statement—and ultimately, for being the cheerleader for the field of vision. The president of the company is the number-one advocate of the vision. Without a public display of emotion of the vision, the business plan will have a stillbirth.

The president or leader of the business unit creates the initial vision. This is done in draft and communicated to the executive team in the first planning activity. It is one of the first pieces of information discussed in the preplanning meeting.

The suggestion of the president being responsible for the vision is very different from the current popular trend of bottom-up visioning. In my consulting experience I have never found a single instance where the bottom-up approach to building a company vision has been successful. Occasionally management teams try to claim this distinction, but on close examination their claims are easily refuted.

Now let's tackle the controversy of a leader's single vision versus that of the masses. A single leader vision pushed down stands a high chance of failure. A leader can have a compelling vision but not get it institutionalized. That can happen when the management team doesn't buy the vision or they don't communicate it downward with the same degree of passion.

DON'T CONFUSE THE MESSAGE WITH THE MESSENGER

The question of who writes the vision gets further muddled when we examine the center or core of the message. Is it something the leader wants to do, or is it a summation of unspoken needs by a multitude of people? Let's not confuse the message with the messenger in this case. Often the president is simply someone who centers the vision for the company by putting it into words or symbolic meaning. This means he or she simply articulates what is felt consciously or unconsciously in the hearts and minds of the employees. The vision, therefore, is not one person's dream. It is the expression of many dreams, hopes, and desires. But someone must take the lead to articulate, champion, and energize those dreams[2] Someone must create a rally point in time of uncertainty or chaos. That someone is not a committee, a group, or a mass of employees. It is the ethical responsibility of the top management team to assume the mantle of leadership and have the courage to put the stake in the ground.[3]

Sharing the Vision: How to Encourage Employee Involvement

What is confused in this controversial issue of top-down versus bottom-up vision development is the need to have employees involved. Having input and buy-in is more than important. It is critical to have a shared vision for a simple fact: People support what they develop more quickly than something handed to them. This translates to ownership and vested interest (see Figure 4-3). Building a case for shared ownership is not a new topic. Peter Senge develops a strong case for shared vision when he writes, "Likewise, when a group of people come to share a vision for an organization, each person sees his own picture of the organization at its best. Each shares responsibility for the whole, not just for his piece. . . . Each represents the whole image from a different point of view."[4]

Figure 4-3. A company's vision is inclusive of the direction for all subunits such as staff functions and strategic business units.

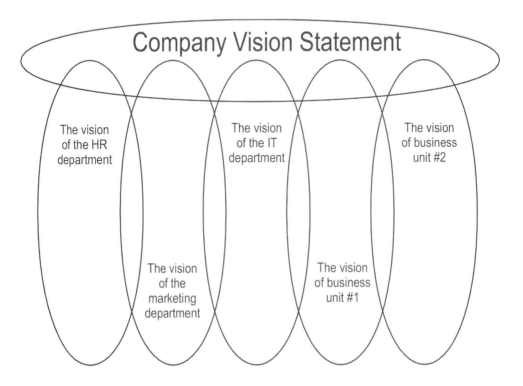

This common bonding of different perceptions allows the employee individual participation. This supports the belief that people willingly follow a vision. This moves employees from pure compliance behavior to a collaborative model where it is in everyone's mutual interest to achieve the vision.

When to Use Multiple Visions in Your Plans

How many visions can a company have in its plan? (See Figure 4-4.) Admittedly, there is a gray area where common sense and a rule of thumb must apply. Usually a company has a single vision, which eliminates confusion, provides direction, and promotes stability. The case for a single vision can be successfully argued, but there are exceptions. Corporations or companies with large divisions may have multiple visions as long as they nestle together as supporting

Figure 4-4. Corporations with diverse businesses may have multiple visions as long as they converge at the higher level.

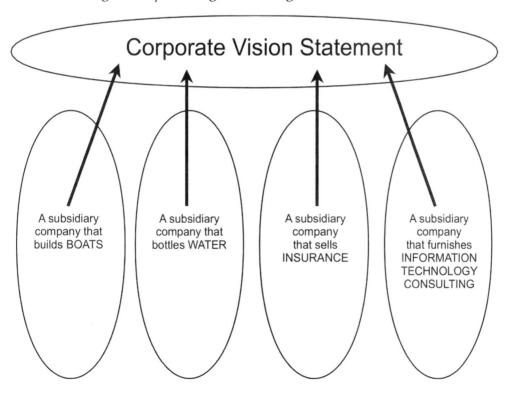

visions. Saturn probably has a different vision statement from General Motors. Chrysler's automotive division may have a different vision from the division that builds tanks for the U.S. military. A strategic business unit or company within a corporation cannot have a vision that carries it in a direction different from the core vision. If your situation necessitates multiple visions make sure they are in alignment or agreement.

In summary, the vision must start at the top and be strategically placed. It must be communicated in the form of a vision statement to every last person in the system. Management teams at every level must be held accountable for putting the vision into operational terms at their level. Finally, the vision is too important for you to fool around with by establishing committees and focus groups to develop, discuss, and argue. Demonstrate leadership and act like a fully functional manager. Take responsibility for establishing and communicating your vision statement. After all, it really is your job.

RALLYING THE EMPLOYEES: HOW TO CREATE PURPOSE WITH YOUR MISSION STATEMENT

Your mission statement becomes the second stake in the ground for building your story, writing your business plan, and achieving any behavior changes necessary to reach the strategic goals. A mission statement defines the business you are in today by stating your purpose. Ask yourself this question, "If we went out of business today, what hole would be left in the business world?"

The mission can also become a rally point for employees. To know I make a difference changes my attitude toward work. Having a rally point is especially important during times of high stress common in today's business world. Leaders throughout history have recognized and used rally points to bring people together. Finding a common enemy is a tactic often used to rally everyone. Translated to business, it means beating the competition, overcoming obstacles, and meeting challenges—all of which can galvanize a company into unprecedented action.

The mission is quite different from the vision in other ways, however, and the two must not be confused. The vision statement is future tense while the mission statement is present tense. The vision may be a collection of ideas or a conceptual description of where you want to be in the future, whereas the mission is a single defining sentence of what you are today.

There are similarities. Both are written as if they are permanent but may be changed given the right conditions. Neither is whimsically changed. Both vision and mission can be upgraded and revised after careful consideration of changing events. Changing either item is a serious management activity that should be taken only after you've given careful, deep thought as to how to complete the transition. Changing the vision or mission involves cultural changes that must be dealt with over a period of time. Resistance frequently occurs to these changes because people normally resist newness. Change your mission when you have substantial information that what you do as a business has significantly shifted.

The Three Critical Functions of a Mission Statement: Communicate, Appeal, and Define

The use of a mission statement has become distorted over time. It is grossly misused. Examples of misuse would be comical if not so serious to the health of the offending companies. The common misuse is to think of the mission statement as a slogan that goes on your letterhead. Frequently it is used as a public ploy or marketing device. While these uses are admirable they are not essential. In fact, they are secondary and optional. Can you put your mission on your business card? Of course, but the function of communicating what you do for your customer is secondary to the mission's value of describing the parameters of work to employees.

The most important function of the mission statement is to communicate purpose. It helps employees understand what the company does and how their roles are incorporated into that purpose. The mission gives meaning to daily jobs. It provides understanding of roles and responsibilities. Parallel to the vision, which provides the ingredient of passion, the mission provides the foundation for establishing purpose. Your mission statement must contain some sense of higher-order purpose (see Figure 4-5). Take the following mission statement example: "Our mission is to build starter homes." While this mission meets the suggested definition of short and simple, it fails to promote some concept of "higher order." Would this mission statement create energy in employees? Probably not. Consider this revision: "Our mission is to help first-time buyers become home owners." What difference would the second mission statement create in your employees? The second version adds richness; the business isn't just throwing up houses on

Figure 4-5. The mission must have a higher-order purpose, and it must help employees understand why they come to work each day.

speculation. There is an emotional component that comes from employees knowing they make a difference in their work. Does building houses for sale on the open market have a different appeal from watching a young family go through the process of buying and moving into their first real home? You bet it does! The higher-order mission puts you into partnership with the home buyer.

Now let's introduce another dimension into the mission statement, that of product identification and specificity. Does your mission statement give the customer a clue to your business? If your company name of ABC Homebuilders were separated from the mission statement would it be self-explanatory? Does your mission statement box you into a specific product, or does it leave room for interpretation? Either way is okay, the decision is yours. On one hand you can be very specific: "We build single-family, stand-alone, starter homes." This makes it easier for you to communicate your product description to your sales forces. It means first-time starter-home buyers can find you more easily in the yellow pages. But there is a downside. As your business grows, your mission may also need to grow. At some point you may need to move up to the midrange or custom-home market. This movement requires a mission change that must occur when evidence suggests your old mission statement is no longer your prime function.

Your mission may leave room for interpretation. This gives you the space to grow without changing your mission. The danger is that the more general the mission statement the more chance for confusion. Consider the mission statement:

We help first-time buyers become home owners.

There is room for both employees and customers to misinterpret this statement. For example, a new employee may think you are a mortgage or loan company within a niche market.

So how do we get out of the box? Let's balance the critical items. The mission must communicate purpose, appeal to a higher order, and define product. The mission statement then must present two levels of sophistication: first to employees for the emotional hook and second to the customer for the products, goods, or services they seek. Perhaps our test mission statements could be revised one more time as follows:

> *We build affordable starter houses to help first-time buyers become home owners.*

This mission hits both levels of sophistication. The customers connect with both the product and the partnership between them and the builder. The employees understand the product and connect to the meaning of their job. The latter is most important because employees need to feel that they are contributing members of the company team.

Here are examples of simple but powerful mission statements from several industries and organizational levels. These were taken from real business plans that are producing results.

Mission Statement	Line of Business
We identify, develop, and support implementation of human resources.	A human resources branch
We generate income for the company.	Sales department
We help companies build effective business stories.	Consulting company
Our mission is to be your home away from home.	Motel chain
We open the northland.	Transportation and communications company
We provide affordable accounting services to the private citizen.	Accounting firm
Our mission is to help small businesses compete through affordable management services.	Consulting firm
We provide a safe, secure harbor facility for your overnight boating events.	A marina
We offer a variety of good food at a reasonable price.	A diner
We deliver your local business correspondence with a 100 percent guarantee.	Courier service
Our limousine drivers get you to your destination safely, every time—on time.	Transportation service firm
We make older houses elegant homes.	Renovation company
My mission is to put a shine on your shoes and a spring in your step.	Airport shoeshine stand
My mission is to help you enjoy the lunch hour—outdoors.	Sidewalk vendor

I used simple but real examples of a single-sentence mission statement. Now, let me explain why I chose that format. How the functions of a mission statement are communicated is often distorted by the very sentence structure of the mission statement. Complex mission statements lead to misunderstanding and confusion. From a business viewpoint it seems practical to keep the mission simple, clean, and focused. Given this rationale the solution would seem to be a single sentence. Unfortunately, that is not the case.

Two schools of thought exist in management guru circles. Consultants have confused the buying public once again. The previous examples were cases for a simple single sentence. Another line of reasoning has businesses developing a long, convoluted document that includes many items such as product, geography, customer targets, quality, and services levels. And this list is not complete. All this effort sounds logical, but it is in fact unrealistic, confusing, and unproductive. There is a place to address quality, but it is not in the mission statement. There is a requirement to deal with the issue of global versus national distribution but not in the mission statement. Discussing your values is important and deserves attention but not in the mission statement. The 5-Page Business Plan (introduced in Chapter 2) is an integrated model, so the mission statement does not have to include these confusing items.

Here is how our clean mission statement for the housing industry might have looked if written according to the second school of management theory. "Our mission is to provide quality, service, and value through affordable housing. We build value-conscious housing for budget-minded families desiring locations within the city of Jacksonville. Our workforce is dedicated to quality construction by using the latest building techniques and material. Our sales force is committed to your satisfaction by matching your desires with our extensive portfolio of models. We seek your endorsement through responsive customer service. Our company values our employees, Total Quality Management, impeccable customer service, an environmental friendly building process, and good community citizenship."

Quite a mouthful of platitudes, isn't it? Mission statements such as this example are abundant in businesses across the world. Even worse are mission statements that are so vague and universal they say nothing. This one was copied off the wall of a well-known hotel chain: "Our mission is to ensure your satisfaction. We work hard to provide friendly service and fast responses to your needs."

I would feel more reassured if I knew they understood their mission as having a clean, comfortable, reasonably priced room ready for my arrival each and every time I make a reservation. As a customer, I cannot do anything with the first version of their mission statement. As an employee I would be even more confused.

Remember your audience—the employees who must execute the mission. I recall a case many years ago when this need for clarity became very evident. It was a miserable, cold, snowy Saturday in January. A team from a government ministry and I were working on their planning documents. We had written and rewritten the mission statement a number of times, but none of the versions seemed to capture the message. The different versions had been put through readability checks for education levels and ease of comprehension. The minister even asked the opinion of some employees who just happened to be in the building. Much to his dismay, they rejected the draft statements. We refined the mission down to a simple statement, written at the eighth-grade level, and took it back downstairs. The employees universally said, "Yeah, that's what we do." This anchored my belief: Keep the mission statement simple so people can understand what you do!

WHY PROFIT HAS ITS PLACE—BUT NOT IN YOUR MISSION STATEMENT

A dangerous item often found in a mission statement is a reference to profit. Does profit belong in the mission statement even if it is thinly disguised as shareholder value? The answer is a big resounding no! If you think otherwise, consider this acid test—an actual case. Pretend you are a regulated utilities company asking for a rate increase. The public is already unhappy with the costs of your services. How appropriate is it to have this mission statement on their next bill: "Our mission is to make as much money as possible for the family shareholder groups." This was the mission statement of a multibillion-dollar utilities company. Can you believe it? There is a place for profit, but not in the mission statement.

I was invited to participate in planning with that company. To get ready for the conference I asked for advance copies of the existing plan. The mission statement was missing, so I called my contact person, asking for a copy. There was a long pause before he answered, "Yes, we have one of those. We developed it about two years ago. We've been lucky and kept it restricted to the top five officers in the company."

After much discussion, the mission statement was faxed to me. That's when I discovered the profit mission statement. Now you know why it had been closely held by only a few company officers. I would keep it a secret, too!

If you believe that your mission is to make money, we must have a straightforward talk right now. If making money is your company's mission, then ask this probing question: "Why are we in the business we are in?" In some cases your profits may be so small you would be better selling your company and investing in some good long-term stocks. Why go to the bother to make as little profit as you do in your business if you could invest it with more safety and less effort?

I once suggested a similar solution to an arrogant banking client in Baton Rouge who was in deep trouble. After trying to deal with him for several hours with my team getting nowhere, I asked a pretty straight question. "What is your business?" I asked. "I don't understand your question," he replied. I rephrased the question and asked what his mission was. "It's to make money," he said with this incredulous look on his face. I suggested he should try drugs and crime. They were quick ways to make money, he could make more money, and he didn't have to pay taxes. He thought I was kidding. I wasn't. I think I made my point.

MISSION ANALYSIS: HOW TO KEEP IT SIMPLE BY DEFINING YOUR CORE TASKS

Let's revisit the challenge—to keep the mission statement simple. Make it a single definitive statement that describes the essence of what you do. A single-sentence mission statement is easier to communicate and execute than a complex set of tasks thrown together in an emotional fashion. All my clients use the single-sentence format. They see the value of clearly defining what business they are in and being able to explain it in simple terms to their employees.

A single-sentence mission statement allows you to scrutinize what you do. This is called a mission analysis. As a young military officer I was taught early the value of understanding what my mission included and, more important, what it did not include. This understanding allowed me to gather my resources, shape my actions, and deploy my Infantry unit in a mission-focused manner. The greatest sin of a combat officer is to be "off mission." This creates unit failure and leads to organizational failure.

How do you as a business leader do a mission analysis? The same way I did as a combat commander. You do a mission analysis by defining two significant elements found in your mission statement. The first is your specified task. The second element is the implied tasks.

The Specified Task: The Heart of Your Mission

The specified task is the single thing that your mission requires you to do. It becomes the heart of your mission. If this is not done, then your mission is a failure. Notice the singular. A mission can contain only a single specified task. This is compatible with the concept that you cannot serve multiple masters. When you have multiple missions, history suggests you don't do any very well. The multiple efforts become average.

When I lived in Denham Springs, Louisiana, I marveled at a sign on the lawn of a resident: WE FILE INCOME TAXES AND SHARPEN SAWS. To give them credit, they were certainly diversified or at least multiskilled. I wonder which one was the core competency. No problem stopping in around April 15 to get your taxes calculated while dropping off the chain saw. How would you write the mission statement for that enterprise?

The Implied Tasks: Unstated but Essential for Achieving Goals

The second part of your mission statement is the implied tasks. These are things unstated but necessary for mission accomplishment. Breakdowns in getting a job completed can usually be traced to the failure to understand the number, complexity, and variety of implied tasks. Only by breaking the mission down to discrete tasks can these variations be understood.

The reason you must include implied tasks in your mission analysis is to understand the correlation between work and functions. Every staff function has work to be completed, but does each function understand how it relates to the others? The tendency is for work functions to consolidate into "stovepipes," with each work function concentrating only on its purpose. By defining all implied tasks, people are better able to understand how they must work together to accomplish the desired targets.

How does the concept of mission analysis apply to a business mission statement? The mission analysis of a combat unit or a commercial business is done in exactly the same way. There is no difference in the mechanics. To illustrate, let's revisit our home builder's mission statement for the purpose of mission analysis.

Mission Statement
- We help first-time buyers become home owners.

Specified Task
- Construct houses.

Implied Tasks
1. Secure house sites.
2. Create marketable designs.
3. Generate sales.
4. Hire appropriate trades.
5. Maintain a trained business team.

Applying the Mission Analysis

Business planners must know how to use the mission analysis to full advantage. Planners work on two assumptions that must be well understood by all other managers within the company. The first is that a manager automatically does an analysis of her mission as part of the planning process. The second assumption is that those managers are well trained, so it is not necessary to remind them to pay attention to the implied tasks. Their job is to be intimately familiar with the functions necessary to carry out or execute the coordination found in the implied tasks. Senior managers use these assumptions to empower leaders and speed the organizational communications process. Everyone in the system plays by the same set of rules and understandings.

There is significant lack of understanding in business about the value of a mission statement and even less understanding of the critical components of the mission. In seventeen years of private practice I have found hundreds of examples of poor understanding and implementation of mission statements by business leaders. What is even more startling is that I never found one case where a company had conducted a detailed analysis of its mission and the mission's implications. I'm puzzled at how a management team could communicate its daily requirements if there is no understanding of the core purpose of mission.

HOW TO CONVERT YOUR MISSION STATEMENT INTO DAILY ACTIVITIES

Once a mission is analyzed in terms of specified task and implied tasks, there is still work necessary to connect mission to the business plan. So far I've defined what's to be done. Now we must add two pieces to the formula. They are functional task requirements and coordinating requirements. What actions are necessary to complete the mission? These should align with the tasks and task combinations that are defined in your goals and objectives. That means every unit in an organization must have a purpose (i.e., a mission) and things to do defined in terms of functional tasks. Furthermore, these tasks must be coordinated across functions and functional lines to ensure integrated accomplishment. Because the tendency is to operate in isolation, the president may have to be so bold as to issue instructions to staff units forcing them to coordinate.

The lack of mission statements below the company or corporate level is astounding. In my twenty years in the Infantry I never served in a unit that wasn't crystal clear about its mission down to the individual level. This is a way of doing business that is ingrained in all levels of a military unit. It is drilled into your thought processes until your own mission becomes second nature. A rule of thumb is that a leader must know his or her mission, the mission of the higher headquarters, and the mission of adjacent business units.

By contrast, in businesses I seldom find mission statements written for staff functions, strategic business units, and functional teams. In less than 1 percent of my consulting engagements did I ever find a company that understood that every organizational unit down to the individual level required a mission statement.

Let's review the function of a mission statement. It is to define the purpose of a unit, whether it is a company, a sales department, or a project team. A simple test determines if a unit needs a mission statement. If I walked into your facility and asked the information technology (IT) department its mission, could the IT staff tell me? If the answer is no, then how can they perform these jobs? If they cannot explain what purpose they serve, why should the president of the company continue to pay the IT department? Obviously they cannot state the purpose or reason for their existence. If they have no purpose, then they need to be immediately eliminated to save unnecessary expenses. Think this is a silly example? I think not. In fact, I've used it dozens of times to stimulate thinking at various levels within a company. I challenge you to try it sometime. You will be amazed at what you find.

Summary

You must have two stakes in the ground to build a story and a subsequent business plan: vision and mission. One creates passion and the other provides purpose.

The vision has two parts:

1. The vision itself
2. The vision statement

The mission has two levels of tasks:

1. The specified task
2. The implied tasks

The mission must connect employees and customers to a product and a higher-order emotional appeal. Complete both of these components with details for your story. Be able to explain both to employees. And finally, include them in your written plan.

THE KEY QUESTIONS: PREPARING VISION AND MISSION STATEMENTS

Ask yourself these questions when you create your vision and mission statements:

1. Do you have a written vision statement?
2. Are you confident that all employees share it? How do you know?
3. Can you produce on demand a document that outlines your complete vision elements?
4. Would I find your employees passionate about their place of work?
5. Do you have a well-written mission statement?
6. Is your mission statement a single sentence?
7. Do all your functions and units have their own mission statements?
8. Have you conducted a mission analysis for your company?

THE PRACTICAL APPLICATIONS: WRITING YOUR PRESENT AND FUTURE STATEMENTS

Keep these steps in mind when writing your statements:

1. Develop a vision by writing several scenarios.
2. Write your vision statement.
3. Add your vision statement to your strategic plan.
4. Write your mission statement in a single sentence.
5. Add your mission statement to your strategic plan.
6. Conduct a mission analysis.
7. Ensure coordination among those responsible for the implied tasks.
8. Develop a list of all the immediate tasks required from your mission statement.
9. Add the task list to your business plan documents.

CHAPTER

5

Strategic Goals, Objectives, and Tasks: How to Set Them and Then Make Them Happen

In this chapter I encourage you to stretch. You will move to another level of sophistication by breaking out of planning creep or incremental planning. What I propose is not risky to your business. It is risky, however, to your psyche. This is the break point in the storytelling. Here is where you find out if you actually mean to run your business in a different manner than the ho-hum way of yesterday. Get ready to take the next step.

113

HOW TO CREATE STRATEGIC GOALS THAT DELIVER WHAT YOU PROMISE

Vision should not be a stand-alone item. It works in conjunction with the other parts of the business plan. The next step is to form a goal-vision connection to introduce goals into the planning model. It is common to treat vision and goals as separate units without a relationship. This goal-vision disconnect is frequently found in planning. A team develops a vision and somewhere later in the agenda the team develops a set of goals. Seldom if ever does the planning team ask, "If this is our vision, how can we define it in terms of strategic goals?"

Translate your vision into something of substance by developing four or five strategic goals that collectively accomplish your vision. Continue to build a logical story by adding these goal pieces until a clearer picture of the future begins to emerge. Keep adding parts and pieces that make sense until you have the whole plan.

This approach reminds me of a children's story. It goes something like this: A man was wandering across the country and needed to eat, but he had no money. He stopped in a village, but no one would feed him, so he resorted to trickery. Producing a smooth, round stone from his pocket he proclaimed it to be a magic soup stone. Soon he convinced the villagers to boil a huge kettle of water into which he dropped the stone. After letting it boil, he tasted the water and declared it almost ready, but thought carrots were needed to complete the taste. The villagers hurriedly found carrots to add to the pot. Tasting the soup again the man declared it really nice but just short of perfect. Perhaps potatoes were what it was missing. By repeating this wily scheme over and over the man was able to trick the villagers into putting enough ingredients into the pot to make a rich soup from plain water. Planning is much like making the soup. Start with a basic ingredient, but to make a really good company story add bold goals to give it character.

Goals are the measurable manifestations of the vision. When you add your strategic goals together they should equal your vision (see Figure 5-1). By adding the goals you give measurement potential to the vision.

Figure 5-1. Goals make up the body of the vision. They are the incremental units of measure to accomplish the vision.

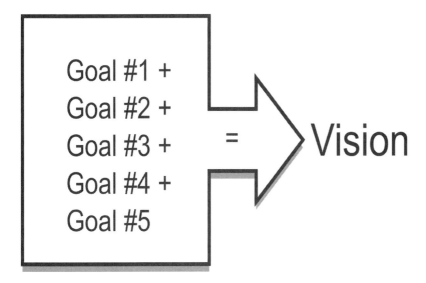

A powerful vision without concrete definition and measurement abilities is a dream, fantasy, or delusion. It might even grow into a nightmare. Too often it translates into unfulfilled expectations for employees, bitter disappointment for those who failed to accomplish their plans, and distrust by the board of directors of those managers who promised so much. The bottom line is that everyone is tired of promises. Employees have been promised great returns if they just work harder. Managers work to make the numbers and are then disillusioned when executive decisions thwart the plan. Failure is created by influences outside the managers' control. Boards of directors were promised certain levels of performance from the president. In turn, they promised shareholders to share the riches. Boards do not like to go back to shareholders with an "oops." Expectations are not properly managed in situations where planning has failed.

Diagramming Your Vision: Tips on Structuring Your Goals

Because the vision is sometimes vague or fragmented, we use goals to bind it together to give it a level of cohesiveness. Because it is made up of hidden but concrete components, a reverse engineering process can be used to understand the vision and formulate the goals. Remember diagramming sentences in English class? Breaking a sentence into components? Diagramming a vision works the same way to determine what is measurable and concrete.

Let's take Henry Ford's vision as our practical case exercise because we have a frame of reference for the company's successes and failures. Obviously we could reconstruct the company, but let's not do that. Instead, we can apply what we have learned so far from this book, our common business sense, and our intellectual capacity. Imagine Henry Ford as he might have mused over coffee: "Let's see, I've got my vision and my mission. What goals will make my dream come true? How can I hold off that guy Sloan over at General Motors?"

Ford's Vision Statement (Actual)

"I will build a motor car for the great multitude. It shall be large enough for the family, but small enough for the unskilled individual to easily operate and care for—and it shall be light in weight that it may be economical in maintenance. It will be built of honest materials—by the best workmen that money can hire—after the simplest designs that modern engineering can devise. But it shall be so low in price that the man of moderate means may own one—and enjoy with his family the blessings of happy hours spent in God's great open spaces."[1]

Ford's Mission Statement (Hypothetical)

The mission of Ford Motor Company is to put Americans on wheels.

"If those are my anchor points, my mission, and my vision, I need concrete, measurable goals," he might have said.

Ford's Strategic Goals (Hypothetical)

Henry Ford might have then come up with these three strategic goals:

1. Become the number-one selling automobile maker in America.

2. Become the standard motor car for the American public.

3. Build a low-cost, high-quality line of cars that attracts a significant portion of the potential American buying public.

Those three goals inherently include key elements to make his vision a reality. They say a lot and address major elements such as:

- Market position (number-one selling automobile)
- General market (American buying public—great multitudes)
- Targeted market (family)
- Sales territory (America)
- Industry position (the standard motor car)
- Product differentiation (low cost, high quality)

Just to dream would not make the future happen. There had to be more. Consider how Henry Ford may have used the goals to connect his vision with reality. Ford knew that the key to his success lay in the ability to mass-produce cars. He knew what he wanted in terms of the final product. By taking a hard-hitting approach he could make his vision happen. Nor was he distracted in developing his product. There was such a demand for the basic product that Ford knew the manufacturer that got the cheapest mass-produced car to the market would be the winner. This is probably what prompted him to state, "Any color you want, so long as it's black."[2] He was too busy filling orders to be worried about something as insignificant as a customer's preference of color. In those market conditions at that time, it was an effective decision.

HOW TO TRANSLATE YOUR VISION INTO REALITY

A vision with corresponding goals is still not enough to get from the theoretical to the practical. Astute business leaders know that every business has a core function or a "locus of control." Henry Ford clearly understood this concept with his manufacturing line techniques. Sam Walton certainly understood that a more effective distribution system was needed to change the retail model.[3] The late Ray Kroc of McDonald's grasped the concept when he developed the formula for his franchise system. Michael Dell of Dell Computer Corp. had insights to change the marketing and sales of computers long before the rest of the industry caught up.

Ford was building more than motor cars. He placed his product into a context of a higher order or meaning. He was completing a dream by reaching out to the common man. Buying a Ford automobile placed the average person in the same league with the aristocrats. Both could move from the old-fashioned horse and buggy into the modern era together. Henry Ford was a true visionary who painted the future in bold strokes and forever changed an industry and a nation. Likewise Sam Walton, Ray Kroc, and Michael Dell each gave us a world today that could have been significantly different without their abilities to envision the future and set bold goals.

Painting Your Story With Bold Strokes

Your story must be painted both in the spoken and printed word with a breathtaking boldness. You started that boldness in the vision and must continue in a fashion that moves the painted picture from one of potential to probable. Translating a vision into reality is achieved by developing strategic goals that are more than an extension of your current behavior. Strategic goals must be a stretch, otherwise they defy the definition of strategic. They must take you into an area that cannot be supported with the complacent management behavior found in most organizations. These goals must add a challenge that management teams and employees find stimulating. The magnitude of the goals must be challenging but not absurd. While the ability to reach the goals must be a stretch, it should not be an impossible feat. The freshness of your goals must break management out of complacency but not kill the team spirit in the process.

THREE STEPS FOR SETTING BIG, BOLD GOALS

Routine goals meet the requirement, but not the spirit, necessary to generate the passion found in the field of vision. Most of you will set routine goals by natural reaction. To fire up a story and get employees' energy flowing, the goals must be far more than routine. They must be blatantly bold.[4] This boldness is sometimes difficult for timid management to grasp. A team from a $150 million company may find it difficult to set a goal of growing to $1 billion in revenues in ten years. A complacent team may find a stretch goal of reducing quality issues tenfold in three years just a touch demanding. Life in most organizations is tough enough without adding more work. Comfort is the leveling factor. To suggest bigger goals, which immediately suggests more effort, is a little discomforting to the people who must implement. When challenged to change existing behavior, the natural reaction is to resist. Great courage is required to break the bonds of normal behavior and reach for seemingly impossible performance.

Courage to set bold goals comes from pure, old-fashioned leadership. A manager can calculate the numbers and figure the odds. A manager can perform a risk analysis and make the appropriate decisions. Those are necessary but not enough to carry the day.

Leadership is necessary to energize the spirit and galvanize the bold goal setting. I'll not go into the parameters of leadership except to say it is a responsibility of leaders to step to the forefront by creating stretch goals.

Step 1: Fire Up the Management Team

Big, bold goals don't just happen. The norm is business as usual, so you need a way to set bolder levels of sustained performance. Two methods can be used to establish big, bold goals. One way is to fire up your management team. This takes energy, leadership skills, and time commitment. Being a cheerleader for the kind of group dynamics capable of producing a big, bold goal is tough on the leadership capability of any manager. A law of physics provides a useful illustration: Bodies at rest tend to stay at rest. This law of inertia implies that teams that set unimaginative goals will continue to set unimaginative goals. Tremendous management energy is required to break the inertia. Leaders trained in group dynamics can be successful in using the potential synergy of group membership.

Step 2: Get Leadership to Step Up to the Plate

A second way to generate a big, bold goal is to have the executive leadership initially set the requirement. This forces your management team to step up to the plate and take a swing at the ball. The team cannot be sitting in the bleachers watching the president pitch while the employees play the outfield. The management team must assume the responsibility for carefully analyzing the organization's potential and determining exactly what level of goal achievement is possible.

Here the quality of your management team comes into play. You need team members with experience, wisdom, and judgment. There is a correlation between high-performing team members and good planning. Expect and demand all your planners to come prepared to make decisions on their professional opinions as well as data from their respective specialties.

Step 3: Validate Your Strategic Goals

In setting such high expectations leaders have psychologically committed to making the goals happen. To counter the problem of employees not trusting the goals, management must make an open sign that the goals are real. The best visible sign that a goal is to be taken seriously is the allocation of resources to that goal. You can talk and talk and talk, but the fact is that you are going to have to commit to the goals. There must be genuine dedication of resources to make big, bold goals a possibility.

Another technique is the designation of responsibility and accountability for the success of the goals. Goals are looked at with a more critical eye if people realize early in planning that they will be held accountable.

In working through the details of the strategic plan there must be validation of the strategic goals through the use of data. Market trend analysis, customer surveys, professional reports, and other reports are sources of critical information. You base goals on the synthesis of these pieces of information. Adding a dash of good old-fashioned intuition is also acceptable after you have done your homework. Don't ever go into a planning session with a blank sheet of paper, throw up some numbers, and expect to be successful. Wild, unsubstantiated numbers turn people off. You counter panic by calmly demonstrating mastery of the facts. One reason that big, bold numbers are not used is that managers are too lazy to do the analysis to determine the potential. It is too convenient to fall back on the industry average. Those numbers are easy to determine and the supporting numbers are equally easy to fabricate. It is hard work to do risk assessment, potential assessment, and probability analysis.

A distinct difference is found between an organization that throws around big numbers without a chance of achieving them and one that sets huge goals with determination to succeed. Unrealistic numbers paralleled by management systems unable to achieve the goals is an impossible situation. Often a management team sets unrealistic numbers believing they are following the concept of bold goals. There is no real examination of the future. Scenarios are not examined, markets are not analyzed, and revenue-generating income streams are unrealistically calculated. As these bogus numbers are communicated to the workforce, apathy quickly becomes the norm. Unexplained, unrealistic numbers are the death knell to morale and your plan.

SEVEN CRITICAL QUESTIONS TO ASK WHEN SETTING GOALS

Here are critical questions you can ask when you have finished your analysis and are trying to set the goals. Begin with this fundamental question—Why do we want to accomplish this goal?—then ask the other seven questions:

1. *Attainability.* Can the desired end product really be accomplished or achieved now that I have looked at all the facts and figures?

2. *Management Ability.* Will it be possible for the company to build a series of actions and decisions over the lifespan of the plan to complete the goal?

3. *Products, Goods, and Services.* Do we have enough of each to reach the goals?

4. *Core Competencies.* Are we skilled enough to reach the goals? What skills will we need in the future that we don't have now?

5. *Intellectual Capital.* Do we have the native intelligence to reach our goals? Are we using all the "smarts" of our people? What will we have to change to increase our usage of intellectual capital?

6. *Work Ethic.* Are we willing to work hard, make the extra effort, and commit 110 percent to reaching our goals? Isn't it just easier to stay in the comfortable middle than to put all this energy into big, bold goals?

7. *Market Potential.* Is the existing market big enough to allow us to reach our dollar requirements? How do we get more market share?

If the answers to these central questions are yes, then your plan is on track. If the answers are no, then you have another series of problems. If you answered no, you must go back through the planning process to resolve the problems. A number of possible solutions exist:

■ *Reexamine your assumptions.* Have you mixed facts with assumptions? By changing your assumptions you may change your goals.

■ *Revisit your mission statement.* Look carefully at your specified task and the implied tasks. Is your mission still valid or did you miss the basic question—What business am I in?

■ *Reexamine your data.* Are you looking at real data or emotional positions?

HOW TO CONSTRUCT REALISTIC GOALS

While goal setting has certain logical steps, it really begins in a more loose fashion. Having facilitated hundreds of goal-setting sessions over the years, I see a pattern emerge that generally looks like this:

■ *Get a group discussion started.* Begin the discussion with a simple question: What will it take for us to reach our vision? In profit organizations, the first element to surface is growth. This is usually stated in terms of gross sales. After some discussion the goal expands to multiple goals (such as gross sales and profit) when the group comes to understand that the first goal is not well thought-out.

■ *Get something on the board.* Put the first goal (usually gross sales) on the board and discuss the scope and scale of the goal. Here is the time-consuming part of your planning session. Getting agreement on the goal is sometimes difficult if the group is not aligned. There is a belief among consultants that reaching agreement on a ten-year goal is more important to the success of the plan than the actual number itself. Remember, the number may change, but you need immediate commitment from the team toward the goal no matter what the specificity.

■ *Get another goal on the board.* Once a solid goal has been established it becomes easier to fill in goals two through five (arbitrary numbers for illustration purposes). Move the group discussion to the next most important goal from a list of potential topics such as market share, product release, and customer satisfaction improvement. These are topics drawn from the vision.

■ *Finish the goal list.* Work through the vision topics until the group is satisfied that the list is comprehensive. Remember the rule of thumb that four or five strategic goals are enough to make the vision complete. The team should ask the question, "Do these goals make our vision happen?" When the answer is yes, stop the goal-setting process and move on.

Realism is achieved in your bold goals by looking at the cold, hard facts of your industry and your organization's situation. Consider the diagram in Figure 5-2. Before we go too far with this example, let's explain the parameters. I use a financial goal of gross sales because it is the easiest one for most businesspeople to comprehend. I could have easily substituted another goal. The steps of describing this financial goal can and must be replicated with other competing goals.

Figure 5-2. Bold goal setting avoids planning creep (A–B), establishes high expectations, and requires stretch from the workforce (A–C).

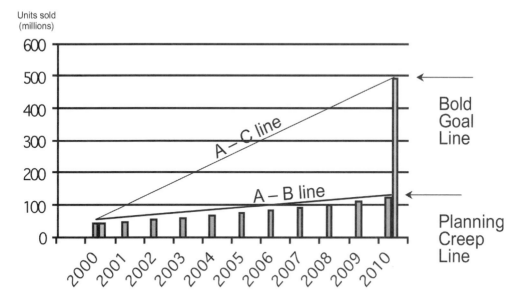

In Figure 5-2, let's assume you are at point A at year-end 2000, with $50 million in gross sales. Assume you are in a stable market and have a 15 percent market share. Since you use planning creep as a model and industry growth is 10 percent, you intend to stay even. If you do what you have always done you will only stay even. This puts you at point B in ten years, which roughly calculates to $130 million in sales. You creep toward the future by extending the existing model outward and are pleased with the numbers.

Now let us assume you used the backPlanning model (see Chapter 3) and realize that $130 million in ten years will not permit you to achieve your vision or realize your dreams. You reconfigure the model to within a target of $500 million in ten years. To move from $50 million to $500 million is a big move. The problem is the saying, "You can't get there from here." We often know where we want to go but can't seem to make it happen without changing some of the fundamental ways we do business. How tantalizing it must be to see success just out of reach.

However, you can break out by asking and answering hard questions. For example, if you are a $130 million company in a $10 billion industry you have just stayed even. If your strategic goal is to become a $500 million company in that industry, you have some growth to accomplish. We could get into a huge presentation about market shares and the accompanying good or evil examples, but we won't. This is not a marketing strategy book.

You may decide to move to $500 million by capturing market share. It is your call. Just remember: To gain market share, someone has to give it up. If the market is valuable, your competitors won't give it up easily. If the market is declining, your competition may readily give you all the market share you want. Be careful basing great successes on grabbing market share. Your story can become significantly flawed if you base it on size of market share.

FOUR DOWNSIDES TO USING MERGERS AND ACQUISITIONS AS A GROWTH TOOL

When the financial goal falls short of the desired number, mergers or acquisitions should not be used to fill the difference and round out the plan. The tendency to use an acquisition to make the numbers is a dangerous flaw in thinking. Repeatedly we see the use of an acquisition as a planning convenience. This gets the team off the hook of explaining how they plan to make up the long-term goal. This is either an avoidance behavior by management to avoid the planning pain or just capricious business behavior.

Given what is known about mergers and acquisitions failures, this avenue of revenue must be given careful thought. A wealth of intellectual capital exists on the problems of bringing two organizations together. The information is very clear. Billions of dollars are spent annually on acquisitions with very little return. In fact, the lost ground is a hidden cost that needs to clearly be studied, published, and taken to heart. Yet we read the papers daily and find fanfare and much-heralded stories of mergers and acquisitions.

Companies are going crazy with the combinations. Give those managers a year and revisit the story. Ask IBM how much was spent on the Rolm acquisition, the Wilkerson Group acquisition, or the Chem Systems acquisition. Check the status of the three today. In a few years you can probably add Chrysler and Daimler to the list of unsuccessful mergers and acquisitions.

Before you include an acquisition to make up numbers for your plan, consider four problems usually found in conjunction with the deal.

Problem 1: Culture Clash

On the surface there often appears to be good business reasons for a merger or acquisition. Those legitimate business reasons and projected numbers are offset by the potential losses that occur from the hidden costs of the transaction. On October 14, 1998, *USA Today* carried such an example, headlined "AHP-Monsanto Merger Dies From Culture Clash." The accompanying article described failure to bring a $35 billion "merger of equals" to closure.[5] There is no such dynamic as equals. One company will always dominate the other. This dominance is not necessarily in physical size. It may be strength of character, quality of management, and force of leadership.

Problem 2: The Clash of Management Egos

A second problem is the ego of the two merging management teams, specifically the presidents. The merger of American Home Products (AHP) and Monsanto Company was in trouble, according to the *USA Today* report, because "[t]he power-sharing agreement between strong-willed bosses John Stafford of AHP and Robert Shapiro of Monsanto quickly turned into a two-headed monster." A clash of egos is normal. Why is anyone surprised? If the egos don't get in the way, then the operating styles of the two leaders eventually clash.

A perfect example of the style problem was the Cendant story reported by Peter Elkind in the November 9, 1998, issue of *Fortune*.[6] The article supported the idea that clashing styles destroy the merger. "One man ran his company like boot camp, the other like summer camp," Elkind wrote. Consequently, even before the Cendant scandal broke, it was already "a merger made in hell" and "the decade's dumbest deal." One of the key figures was reported to be a control freak and the other a dreamy visionary. How do you think the mergers of these two styles would play out even in the best of conditions? How would you, a vice president, carry out your duties when faced with the style conflict that eventually rolls down to the operational level? What effect does the open warfare have on the organization as support for both sides forms among the employees? What does all this cost and how much is deducted from the bottom line?

Egos of the individual leaders also must be considered as a strong influence. People who want to do big deals are generally caught up in a personal issue. They want to be the rainmakers or the dealmakers. The issue is to see how big of a deal they can put together so their place in history is confirmed. Very little of this has to do with the actual benefit to the organizations or the ensuing heartache and damage to people's lives. The Cendant acquisition fits this situation. "One thing [Cendant president and CEO Henry] Silverman did not spend much time worrying about was the human factor—the 'small stuff,' he calls it," wrote Elkind. Tragically, this is the very thing one should spend the most time on in the merger process.

Problem 3: The Human Factor

A third problem with mergers and acquisitions is the failure to consider the human resistance to change. Integrating the people of both companies is the most dangerous and difficult part of the process. Resistance to change is a major drag factor in getting two organizations aligned. Regardless how similar the two companies may appear, the operational differences will be significant.

Employees will always find their way of doing work the best and resist converting to another process.

I sat at a planning table with two oil companies that had just merged. On paper and on surface examination the two companies appeared to be the same with only a name difference on their respective letterheads. In operational reality they were quite different. The planning session almost came to a stop because the two internal camps couldn't even agree on some of the most fundamental management activities.

Problem 4: The Process Itself

The fourth flaw in mergers and acquisitions is the very process itself. No due diligence is done on the cultures and the hidden costs to create operational alignment. Plenty of work takes place on the "what you are buying" but none on the "who you are buying." The syllabus of an unnamed but well-known multibillion-dollar international company reflects this approach. Their three-day program on mergers and acquisitions is all about what they are buying. They train their acquisition project managers on how to do the deals with the idea of improving their closure rates and making better decisions. Of the thousands of pages of instructional materials only two pages referenced the human factors. The three-day training I attended included neither plans for assessing the culture and defining the resistance points nor any plan for post-merger integration of the cultures. This syllabus is normal for mergers and acquisitions training. The parent company acquires an average of twelve companies a year, and even with extensive training the results are considered dismal. The company is running about 100 percent in its failure to successfully merge the acquired companies' cultures into the parent's.

Talking to mergers and acquisition teams about the dangers of post-culture integration is like talking to a Martian. We are speaking two dissimilar languages in two separate contexts. Merger teams are typically number crunchers who have little understanding of people issues. If you plan to buy a company or merge with another business, the very least you can do to prevent pain is to develop a post-merger cultural integration plan.

The Bottom, Bottom Line to Mergers and Acquisitions as Growth Vehicles

Do not use these approaches to fill gaps in your planning because finding, acquiring, and integrating another organization is not easy. The time you lose chasing an acquisition can be put to good use achieving real-time internal growth. Don't expect a huge financial lift the first year following an acquisition. Expect and plan for five years before you see a profit from the acquisition. That's considering everything going as planned. This lag time must be calculated into your goals. Lastly, don't underestimate how much resistance to change you'll encounter from the two merging cultures. Instead of going forward you may in fact lose ground.

Mergers and acquisitions are not ruled out for establishing big financial goals. They are discouraged unless you know exactly what you are doing and understand the true financial implication.

IT MAY NOT WORK TOMORROW: WHY YOU NEED TO RETHINK YOUR BUSINESS APPROACH

If your business does plan to grow in size, you need to come to an immediate recognition that whatever you are doing now may not be the answer for tomorrow. You may have to fundamentally change the way you approach your business. This may mean changing your:

- *Market Segments.* Are the people you sell to today the same as who you will sell to in the future?

- *Market Approaches.* Will the same marketing strategies that worked in this decade be viable with progress in e-commerce or e-business? How must you change to enter the same markets?

■ *Products, Goods, and Service Lines.* Are your offerings becoming obsolete? Will you have to shift from making things to servicing things?

■ *Management Styles.* With the mobility of the workforce and employees' abilities to find other opportunities, how will you adapt in terms of leadership and managership? If your management culture cannot attract a viable workforce, how will you get the most fundamental mission-essential task completed?

The message should be clear. You may have to do something radically different to achieve lofty goals. Usually management teams create more of the same, though they may think they are breaking out of the box. In management classes I use a gimmick to get participants' attention when their answers are unimaginative. I hand them a small polished rock with the comment, "You're polishing old rocks. It is the same idea, just made more smooth."

THE STRATEGIC GOALS CHECKLIST

If you plan to set big, bold goals you must do staff work validating the possibility that the goal crosses all aspects of the business. Are the goals comprehensive and complete? Where will your achievements come from? Here's a checklist with some possible strategic goals to help you get started:

Financial
1. To maintain a 25 percent return on investment (ROI) over a five-year period
2. To achieve 30 percent of sales from new products by year 2005
3. To become a $3 billion company by year 2008

Growth
1. To enter three new market segments within the next five years
2. To triple in size within ten years

Market Share
1. To hold 14 percent market share by 2005
2. To be the dominant supplier to the world with our product

Global Locations
1. To enter five new countries within the next five years
2. To establish an international presence

Market Segment
1. To establish dominance in the high-end youth clothing market
2. To become the product of choice of the upper one-third income bracket

Mergers and Acquisitions
1. To complete one successful merger annually over the next ten years
2. To buy our biggest competitor within ten years

Product Leadership
1. To be the recognized product leader in plastic injection molding
2. To be number one or two in the areas in which we choose to compete

Research and Development
1. To introduce one significant technological breakthrough within the next three years
2. To support field applications with more robust research design

Image
1. To rank in the top ten most admired companies within eight years
2. To be a recognized logo in the majority of countries around the world

HOW TO SET CRITICAL OBJECTIVES

Planning is a process of defining an end state in some level of detail, then subsequently breaking each detail into more specificity. We started with a global concept—a vision that was broken into more concrete terms or goals. These are still too large to work with on a daily basis. They must be further broken down into units of work. A simple and functional method is to divide each strategic goal into a number of objectives as shown in Figure 5-3. Four or five objectives per goal seem to be the rule of thumb.

Figure 5-3. Multiple objectives are the intermediate steps toward the strategic goal and ultimately the vision.

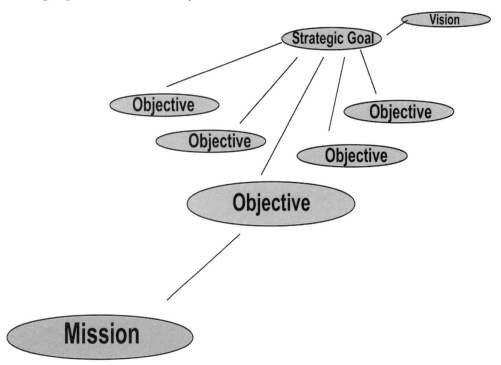

Let's examine a goal and apply the concept of decomposition—breaking it down into further measurable objectives. These objectives must have some elements of realistic application. They must be:

- *Specific.* Does the objective have a well-defined outcome or end state?

- *Quantifiable.* Can the objective be measured in some practical way?

- *Achievable.* Can you accomplish the objective with some sense of reasonable effort?

- *Timely.* Can the objective be accomplished within a reasonable time frame consistent with the plan and its internal requirements?

■ *Responsible, Authoritative, and Accountable.* Who has the primary charge for completing this objective? How much authority will that party be given to act out the tasks necessary to get results? How do you plan to hold the person accountable for the success or failure of the objective?

The financial goal is used as an example because all organizations must make a profit or work within a financial constraint such as a budget. If the strategic goal is to become a $3 billion company by year 2008, what intermediate points can be established that span the time frame? Accomplishing the four or five intermediate objectives ensures the completeness of the goal itself. Consider the following objectives for a chemical company:

■ *Objective 1.* Make every single strategic business unit profitable by year-end 2003. In this case the chemical company had a number of business units that were low to marginal performers. The planning team decided that a target was to have all business units at an acceptable level, none dragging the others down.

■ *Objective 2.* Achieve the maximum profit potential on every strategic business unit by 2004. The team further decided that just being profitable in objective 1 wasn't enough. Each unit had to be producing the maximum amount of return. The team decided to set a profit target for each unit in subsequent plans, increase the sales, and decrease the operating costs.

■ *Objective 3.* Eliminate nonperforming strategic business units from the company's portfolio by year-end 2001. The team saw the need to get rid of politically correct but costly units. They understood that although history was against them in this move, it was vital to their plan.

Time Factors in Setting Objectives

Usually a planning team gets caught in the excitement of what has to be done. Subsequently all the objectives seem to stack up in the first quarter or the first year for completion. A recommendation is in order. Space your objectives over a period of time by laying them on a Gantt chart to see the stacking effect. This gives the planning team some sense of when the objectives must be completed and their approximate relationship with each other. Rearrange the spacing by considering the following:

- *Establish an organizational priority for the objectives.* Some objectives have higher organizational impact than others. Often an objective gets a priority because of some higher management attention or need. Sometimes they are just fun things to do and have the favor of the management team. This is not necessarily bad.

- *Examine the sequence of the objectives.* What must be done first, then second, and so forth? Can any of the objectives be done in tandem? Some may be able to run at the same time as others. Is one objective necessarily done first because other objectives hinge on the completion of its activities? Line the objectives up in order of critical achievements.

- *Consider the resources required to achieve the objective.* What and who will you need to do the job? Are the resources committed for too many other objectives? Are the resources available? The objective may depend on your hiring someone for a key position.

- *Consider the workload.* The tendency is to overload a management team. Consider the volume of work, the ability and energy level of the team, and a realistic view of time. Can you keep the pace with too much loaded into the organization calendar?

TASKS: HOW TO FOCUS ON WHAT REALLY NEEDS TO BE DONE

We still need to achieve a third level of definition of what has to be done. The goals are the first level while the objectives are the second level. The third level is tasks, which are important to bring the vision down to the operational level (see Figure 5-4). The tasks are those things that must be done in the next year to get the company on the path toward goal accomplishment. The task list will be extensive because it includes all the routine, mundane things to make the business operate.

Figure 5-4. Tasks are the many mission-essential things you must do each day. They are the intermediate steps to the objectives.

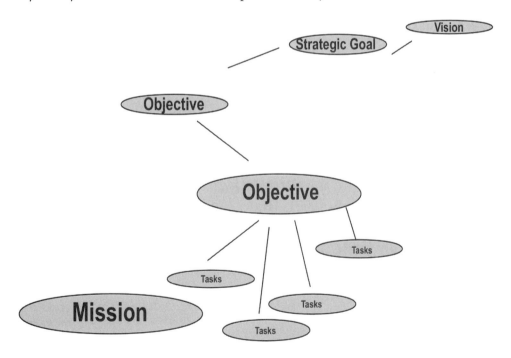

The best way for your planning team to develop the task list for the operational plan is to step away from the information and ask a question: What are all the things we need to do next year to get this plan in place? This question leads to a series of items, which are your tasks. Take care when assigning responsibilities and times to the tasks. Like the objectives, tasks seem to all stack up for completion in the first quarter of the planned year. The planning team could become overwhelmed unless common sense is used to assign time priorities. Everything cannot be completed first.

The reason we develop the level of definition called tasks is to define work to be done. The problem is that three sets of tasks appear in the planning model. One set is derived from the goals, objectives, and tasks just developed. Another set of tasks is the implied tasks from the mission analysis. There is a third set of tasks that creates noise in the model (as shown in Figure 5-5). Human resources complicates the picture with its own set of tasks called job descriptions, position descriptions, or performance measures. No wonder the employee is confused. The metaphor is one catcher and three pitchers. Three sources of tasks are throwing multiple balls at the employee. Why don't we make it simple for the person who must conduct the daily activities of our business? Why don't you scrap those reams of papers called job descriptions, position descriptions, and performance evaluation reports and get to the bottom line? Combine the three task groups into one list of four or five key tasks the employee is to do each day. Grade the person on that short list. This is a good way to reduce the paperwork of the HR department, eliminate the frustration of the employee, and get your organization back on track doing the things it needs to be doing to be successful.

Figure 5-5. Employees are confused when tasked from at least three sources.

Which of three tasks is the employee really supposed to do?

HOW TO PUT YOUR GOALS AND OBJECTIVES INTO MOTION

Vision and mission create passion and purpose. Goals, objectives, and tasks establish direction. The action part of the formula, which I call strategies and tactics, is missing at this point. This part of the chapter defines how you put the goals and objectives into motion. Goals and objectives make up what you are to do, and the strategies and tactics describe how you plan to do it.

Strategies: Big Picture Tools for Accomplishing Your Plan

Strategies are the big picture techniques for how you will accomplish your plan. They are global and sweeping in scope and scale (see Figure 5-6). By contrast, tactics serve the same functions as strategies but on a smaller scale. Strategies are therefore strategic in nature and tactics are operational in nature (see Figure 5-7).

Figure 5-6. Strategies are the big picture "how" you plan to reach your goal.

Sullivan and Harper nailed the definition:

> *Strategy is not about Attila the Hun or Sun-tzu;*
> *it is not about the management disciplines; nor is*
> *it about econometrics, numbers, or programmatic*
> *objectives. At its essence, strategy is an*
> *intellectual construct linking where you are today*
> *with where you want to be tomorrow in a*
> *substantive, concrete manner.*[7]

Therefore, strategies are critical to defining how you intend to bridge to the future from the present. Your plan must include viable strategies to get you there.

Figure 5-7. Tactics are the short-term "how" you plan to reach your goal.

Examples of strategies are easy to find in business literature. Here are a few, some of which you'll readily recognize:

- ◼ Nike signs celebrity athletes well in advance of their hitting their peak exposures.

- ◼ Pepsi's use of rock stars to endorse its products was a strategy that caught the competition asleep with respect to the younger market.

- ◼ Apple Computer's decision to use a closed architecture in its early days (as opposed to the PC's open approach) influenced the future of the company.

- BMW's strategy of independence from the automobile groups required the purchase of British Motor Cars to fill out its product line.

- Ford Motor Company's aim to show profit, not volume of sales, defined industry leadership.

- Another Ford strategy developed premium marques among specialty lines. Consider that the company owns Jaguar, Volvo, Lincoln, and Aston Martin now as well as Land Rover.

- Motorola used six-sigma methods far ahead of the majority of American industries.

- EZCertify.com's strategy is to place the government certification process back in the hands of the user by offering simplified software.

- Antique Works fills a niche demand by providing features for estate sales that are normally ignored by other auction houses.

- InternetTrain.com's $10-a-module Internet training is a trend-setting move to rewrite the books on how training is priced and delivered.

- Grimes Logistics stays close to its customers' wants, needs, and expectations. In operations the customer is the center of the universe.

If you are having trouble identifying strategies, look at the business section of any newspaper for examples of how companies are attempting to solve a particular problem, gain customers, or introduce a new product. You will find excellent examples in articles describing how the company plans to move forward.

To set strategies is not a complicated management maneuver. Once the strategic goals are completed, review them and ask a simple question: How can we accomplish these goals? Get a number of ideas on the table for discussion. Think big and bold for the strategy. You may find that one strategy covers a number of goals or that each goal requires a strategy.

A word of caution is necessary when setting strategy because it defines how you implement your story and your plan. A wrong choice leads to disastrous consequences. Consider Apple's strategy to keep a closed architecture in the early days of the Macintosh computer. This strategy severely limited the ability of programmers to write software for the system. What would have happened had the Apple management team chosen a strategy to open the information to developers? Where could Apple have been today? One cannot predict the future, but it is a good bet that Apple's point-and-click system would have been the standard of performance today.

Another example is the failure of BMW's strategy. In March 2000 BMW announced it was selling Land Rover to Ford, admitting the strategy of going counter to industry consolidation was not working. This miscalculation of strategy cost BMW 3.15 billion euros and three executives their careers. The write-off was not equally offset by the sale of Land Rover to Ford.

Using Tactics to Reinforce Your Strategies

If using premium brands (like Ford) is your strategy for the long term, there must be an operational twin called a tactic for the short term. As objectives nestle into goals, then tactics nestle in support of strategies. An example of a tactic to support the plan can be illustrated by expanding a strategy.

A venture capital group, Alchemy Partners, bid to buy the remainder of Rover cars from BMW. Its strategy was to acquire a product line in trouble that needed an infusion of new management. Its tactics for the potential Rover acquisition were to:

- Streamline the business.
- Turn it into a niche maker of MG sports cars.
- Sell the business.

GET STARTED WRITING STRATEGIES AND TACTICS

In developing your strategies and tactics, you may have to write and refine the drafts several times before you are satisfied. What is global in scale to one team member may be perceived as operational to another. What seems to be a "how to do it" for you may be a "what to do" for another team member. Keep asking yourselves the question, "Is this a what or a how?" If it is a "what" item, make it a goal by revising your goal list. If it is a "how" item, then make it a strategy or a tactic.

Here is a suggestion on how to initially write your strategies and tactics. Write your statement and decide where it fits using the criteria checklist provided here:

Criteria	Strategy	Tactic
Focus	Global	Targeted
Scope	Wide	Narrow
Scale	Large	Smaller
Time	Long term	Immediate
Support	Vision and goals	Objectives and tasks

Strategies have parts that are distinctly different from tactics. They include global focus, a wide scope, a large scale, and a long timeline. Strategies also support the vision. Tactics, on the other hand, are more targeted in focus, narrow in scope, smaller in scale, immediate in time, and support objectives. To determine whether you have written an item as a strategy or a tactic, examine how many characteristics it displays. If the bulk are in the strategic column it is a strategy. If it falls mainly in the tactic column then it is a tactic. For example, is the focus of the potential item global in nature with wide-reaching implications and a long implementation period? If so, it would fall into the strategy column. If the item were less than global and rather limited in focus, it would become a tactic.

A master action plan worksheet is provided in Appendix I to assist you with managing the volume of information generated for your plan. I recommend you have a central document for recording the (what) goals, their subordinate objectives, and all the tasks that have to be completed. A convenience is to have the (how) strategies and tactics recorded along with the action items. This gives you a good picture of the total requirements necessary to implement and execute the plan. To be complete, the action plan needs to include the targets you have chosen for measurement and accountability.

SUMMARY

This chapter has defined how you develop a bold story from your goals and objectives. Set stretch goals over a longer period of time. Carefully examine the capability and potential of the future to validate these goals. The end products of the goals and objectives are the tasks, which eventually lead to the development of a short-term action plan. The three components of goals, objectives, and tasks are reviewed in terms of how you plan to accomplish the future. Strategies and tactics are the long- and short-term "how to" get your goals accomplished. They form the bridge between the mission and the vision.

THE KEY QUESTIONS: BREAKING OUT OF COMPLACENCY

Ask yourself the following questions to break out of a complacent mode:

1. Is our organization caught in planning creep? If yes, what mind-sets must we overcome to break out of complacency?
2. Does my team understand the differences between goals with large numbers and big, bold goals?
3. If we set big, bold goals, does my team have the skills, courage, and tenacity to make them happen?
4. What education and training is required to help my team accomplish the goals?
5. What resources am I prepared to provide the team for long-term implementation?
6. What resources am I willing to commit to achieve the annual targets? Money is usually the biggest issue around this commitment.

THE PRACTICAL APPLICATIONS: WORKING ON YOUR STRATEGIC PLAN

The following six steps will help you with your stategic plan:

1. Analyze your current methodology for setting goals to determine if you are using the planning creep model.
2. Write four or five big, bold goals that collectively accomplish your vision.
3. Write four or five objectives that further define each goal.
4. Develop a master list of all the tasks that must be done next year to start implementing your objectives.
5. Define your strategies by looking at your total goal/objective package. Ask, "How can I make these things happen?" The answers are your strategies.
6. Define your tactics by looking at what must be done in the short term. Again ask, "How will I make these things happen given the short-term time frame?" The answers are your tactics.

6

The Six Driving Forces That Affect Your Business Plan— And How to Focus on the Best One for Your Company's Needs

This chapter describes one of the most important elements of your business plan. It is the element that provides alignment between and among the functions of your business. Without this element you cannot move toward coordinated goal accomplishment.

Typically planning teams spend time discussing the current state of their business situation. Equal time is spent discussing the future. Almost no time is spent discussing how to get from one state—as is—to the other state—to be. Goals will not do the job. To get to the future requires more than letting the organization run unchecked toward goals. The management team must drive the organization. I'm not using the term *drive* as in driving a reluctant mule toward the barn. It means instead taking an active rather than passive approach. It includes steering a course with all employees speaking the same business language, aiming toward the same goals, and moving with the same level of enthusiasm.

Employees reach a level of alignment throughout the organization when you clarify this element. Goal alignment of individuals with the organization's needs has long been a target of management theorists. Usually the wants and needs of the individual are compared to the wants and needs of the organization. That takes you nowhere. Too often the wants and needs of the organization and the employee are not compatible. What I'm suggesting is to align the business behaviors of all the people within the system. Alignment is achieved by using a single operational focus.

To move from mission to vision you have a number of business drivers that provide energy, power, and force to your story and create this operational alignment. Over the years I identified and refined six specific fields of energy that drive your goal accomplishment. I've also come to the conclusion that you cannot be all things to all people. This dissipates your efforts and weakens the results. You must have a single focus. The body of evidence found by Treacy and Wiersema concludes that companies that hold market dominance have a single focus. The authors describe with convincing arguments the three points of focus from which the single focus is selected. The three are operational excellence, product, and customer intimacy.[1]

The original work on the concept of business focus must be attributed to Robert Keidel, who compares businesses to sports teams. He explains how different organizations resemble baseball teams, basketball teams, or football teams. This comparison provides some fascinating answers to some tough questions about how and why organizations behave in certain ways.[2] What is attractive about the concept is not the sports metaphors, but the idea that different organizations have different points of focus.

Keidel approached organizational effectiveness from a teamwork perspective. He states, "In a nutshell, baseball requires situational teamwork; football, scripted teamwork; and basketball, spontaneous teamwork." That's not what caught my attention. He went on to describe how an organization rewards various types of behaviors based on the way they are designed. Keidel's work fired my curiosity. I was always puzzled why his metaphors and models didn't catch the business world's attention. His examples clearly had a message to me, so I took the challenge to push the key concepts further. I became intrigued by what specifically drives a business, what transparent forces seem to be at work within any system. Keidel found three while Treacy and Wiersema also name three. I found others. My work leads me to believe that six, not three, drivers actually exist. These seem to be found in all my client systems. Over a ten-year period I tested and retested the concept with a number of participants in management seminars and with clients in my consulting practice. My conclusion is that your story or plan will have a serious defect if you don't understand the business drivers. Furthermore, I believe that you must pick one from the list to create a single focus for organizational alignment. I labeled the six drivers as:

1. Players
2. Plans
3. Processes
4. Products
5. Properties
6. Payoffs

THE PLAYER-DRIVEN ORGANIZATION: PUTTING EMPLOYEE OR CUSTOMER FIRST

A player-driven organization requires the complete identification of all the people involved within and connected to the organization in any fashion. It includes all who touch the processes of the business. Often these people are labeled as stakeholders, which is at best a vague term. I have not heard the term used where someone in the audience didn't ask for clarification.

I keep the definition of player simpler. Listening to everyone who has a vested interest in the success of your company is important but not critical to this exercise. It is not relevant to the major parts of my model.

The two common groups of players I identified are the employees and the customers. Both are significant as dominant forces in your organization. You may choose one or the other but not both as your focus.

Hal Rosenbluth chose to focus on the employees as the central driver of his business. His rationale was that the customer comes second.[3] His belief was that a company that takes care of its employees doesn't have problems with customers. Putting employees first means taking care of your people, eliminating the common gripes and complaints that stand in the way of them doing a first-class job for the customer. This model must have worked because Rosenbluth Travel became a huge success.

Taking care of the employee first certainly has merit. We have all experienced walking up to a counter to be served or pay for our selections, only to be ignored. Doesn't it drive you just a little bit crazy when two salespeople, who are busy chatting about some internal store problem, ignore you? I want to shout, "Hey, look at me. Yes, me the guy with money in my hand. Me, the customer who wants to be served. Remember me, I'm the guy who contributes to your paycheck every Friday. I even put a little bonus money in your pocket each year. I've probably contributed enough to your 401(k) for you to retire. You may as well retire, since you are not serving me." I may make that speech someday.

A second player-driven type organization is one that focuses on customers. This organization does more than focus; it becomes very customer-centric. In Treacy and Wiersema's language they are called a customer-intimate organization. This organization's energy is spent solving the customer's problem. This core process of help-ing the customer with everything from finding the right size shoes to checking on the faucet installation is what creates the long-term relationships between the business and the customer. Customer-intimate organizations are clever. They know their market is the high-income category or people with money who want to be pam-pered. They don't cater to the handout crowd or people looking for a bargain. Don't go to Nordstrom looking for a blue-light special. You will never hear "Attention Nordstrom shoppers. Our blue-light special on aisle twelve for the next twenty minutes is mink coats, with matching accessories on aisle eleven." Sustaining a high cus-tomer–sales staff ratio to provide intimate service costs a great deal of money. Somebody has to pick up the tab. Guess who?

A customer-intimate organization understands that solving a customer's problems must be in real time. The answers or solutions must be immediate. In a customer-intimate organization the employee must be able to make decisions on the spot to solve a cus-tomer's special requirements. The required organizational structure is decentralized with a high degree of empowerment. Employees in a customer-intimate organization are rewarded for finding specific solutions to customers' problems.

Contrast that with my experience, and maybe yours also, while buying a car. At some point the salesperson has to check with the sales manager. Your offer is so low the company is giving the car away or the salesperson will be fired for making such a poor deal. Actually the salesperson is on break in the employee lounge drink-ing coffee while you anxiously await the news confirming your cunning ability to negotiate a deal. I caught that game early. Now the first question I ask a salesperson is, "Can you sell me a car?" The answer is always a startled affirmative. I then go on to say, "No, what I mean is can you sell me a car without having to go to the sales manager? If you can't, then I don't want to waste your time, so let me work directly with the sales manager. Otherwise I'm out of here." A Toyota salesperson in Baton Rouge must have thought I was kidding. When he returned he discovered I wasn't.

Customer-intimate organizations give employees a lot of room to make deals, work with the customer, and demonstrate value in the relationship. In my car dealership story, the salesperson had been told the rules up-front, yet he wasted my time and tried to play games with my mind. Don't do that to your customers, especially when they are sending signals that such amateurish behavior will not be tolerated.

A number of outstanding companies choose to use the customer-intimate model. Nordstrom, Cott Corporation, and Airborne Express are three examples I reference because they are in businesses with radically different goods and services. Don't be caught off base thinking that customer-intimate means assigning a personal shopper to your customer. Customer-intimate means solving the customer's problems, no matter what type business problem is presented. Each of these companies believes that time spent up-front with the customer in a one-on-one relationship pays great dividends in the long term. People and businesses pay premium prices to have their needs legitimized, their concerns heard, and their unique business problems solved.

Doug Christie, a sales representative for Bayer's agriculture division in Crossfield, Alberta, understands the concept of being close to the customer and customer intimacy. He is always on the job with no order too small or situation too minor for his attention. His clients know when they unexpectedly run short of vaccines or they need technical information, Doug is instantly available. His office has a twenty-four–hour phone contact number. Doug works the phone constantly, staying in touch with his clients. I jokingly said to him, "You must have that phone permanently attached to your ear." He just grinned, reached back, pulled out his wallet, and said, "No, not to my ear, to this." Not only is he a caring salesperson who loves his business, he also knows his "center of gravity"—taking care of those clients. It must work. Doug was recently named sales representative of the year.

THE PLANS-DRIVEN ORGANIZATION: ACHIEVING GOALS IS THE NAME OF THE GAME

A plans-driven organization is based on compliance of its membership. It believes in using a disciplined approach to moving forward. This organization requires rigid adherence to the plan. Rewards are based on absolute compliance with the pre-agreed plan. Such rigor requires an equally rigorous management system to sustain itself. Authoritarian management is the common approach. With a fixed structure there is little latitude for individual decision making or unilateral actions. In a plans-driven organization the name of the game is to accomplish the goals. Employees are rewarded for high compliance. Sticking to the plan is important. Because of this fixation with goal achievement, the customer tends to be placed in the back row of priorities.

A utilities company is probably a good example of a plans-driven organization. An electrical company must operate from a tightly managed plan to generate and deliver a certain level of power to its users. It must do usage calculations to determine the flow of its outputs and plan accordingly. To adequately serve the public, it must be thinking far ahead in terms of population growth, support requirements, and total management of the consumption requirements.

Plans are central to any organization that by necessity has a high compliance component. For example, a rigid plan would be followed by a team during an annual outage changeover procedure. Servicing nuclear rods is not the time to be creative. They would not be rewarded for skipping standard operating procedures, taking shortcuts, or making it up as they go along.

Another example of a plans-driven organization is the military unit preparing for war. The precursor to battle is thorough planning, but even this has limits. Every good commander knows that plans are obsolete the moment the first shot is fired. War is truly the role model for chaos. That's why the U.S. military, contrary to popular stereotypes, trains its soldiers to take responsibility, take charge, and take command. When the carefully planned attack becomes the typically chaotic scenario, nothing goes as planned. Stability is achieved in the chaotic situation by discipline, training, and dedication to the agreed plan.

A corporation represents a case for the concept of business drivers and a single focus. If the corporation is consistent with a uniform focus across all operating divisions, no problem exists. When a corporation is made up of diverse strategic business units, the problem of single focus is compounded. What is the correct driver for the corporation? If the planning team selects the wrong driver, serious operational difficulties will follow. Assume the corporation has a customer-intimate focus. What happens between the corporate staff and the operational staff of the business unit that is products-focused? What functional or dysfunctional behaviors are demonstrated in exchanges between the corporate staff and the business unit that is an operationally excellent unit? Imagine the communications conflict between the corporate staff and the business unit that happens to be properties-driven. In each of these cases you have a serious operational conflict. The management teams are behaving from uniquely different views of the same mission. There is no internal organizational alignment, as portrayed by the arrows in Figure 6-1.

Figure 6-1. When business units have different focus from the corporate focus, loss of direction, cohesiveness, and teamwork happens.

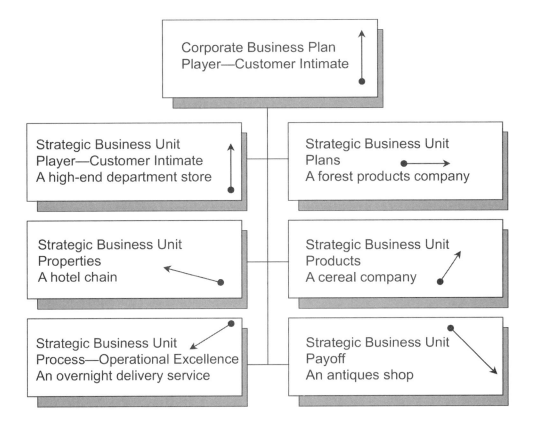

To resolve the conflict created by misalignment, as seen in Figure 6-1, you may choose to have all your business units come into alignment by shifting from one focus or orientation to a consistent focus across all units. There are two solutions: You may have them all become operationally excellent. You may choose to make them all product-focused.

Alignment can be done by that method. Before you jump to that solution too quickly, consider the cultural shift requirements and implications. You may not be able to get people to move from a product focus to an operational-excellence focus. I've watched organizations try to make the shift. Resistance to the change takes many shapes and forms. Employees will passionately charge that the organization no longer cares about the quality of its products. They see the company as a money-hungry organization trying to drive costs down. They equate steps like reengineering and down-sizing with cost cutting only for the sake of being more profitable.

A corporation with diverse business units must have a plan focus. The explanation is quite simple. What is the function of a corporate headquarters? It is a control function. What should head-quarters control? How about the plan? If I am the chief executive officer with five diverse business units, I want them to follow our plan. I don't care how they do it. They may have five different approaches (see Figure 6-2) and still be able to fill my corporate requirements. What I want from each of my unit presidents is their contribution to the bottom line of my corporate plan.

Figure 6-2. A corporation with diverse business units must be plans-driven. It is the only combination that allows diversity. The only thing that matters in this case is whether the business unit met its plan requirements. That's the bottom line.

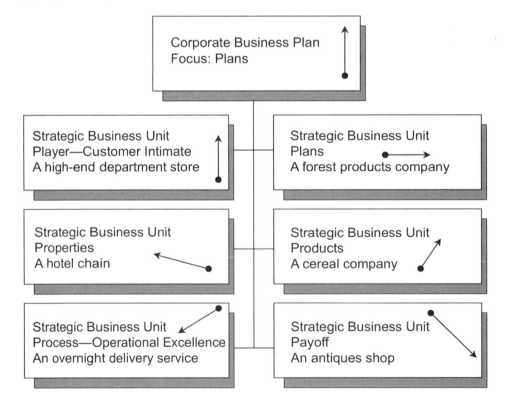

THE PROCESS-DRIVEN ORGANIZATION: CONTINUALLY SEEKING IMPROVEMENT

A process-driven organization looks for operational excellence in all that it does. These companies do extensive examinations of the flow of primary and secondary processes found within their businesses. They seek constantly to drive out inefficiencies. They are on a perpetual continuous improvement path. No process is too small to be ignored when looking for delays, blocks, and leverages to improve. This means they become very good at doing the same tasks over and over. Tight processes are the watchword when you look at an operationally excellent company's structure. There is no fat.

Operationally excellent companies focus on how they do business and reward efficient and effective behaviors in employees. Their people are taught not to waste any resources in getting the job done.

To achieve operational excellence, a company must advocate and practice teamwork as a principle of its culture. In today's business environment there is no place for the lone player. The processes required to stay ahead of production schedules, customer demands, and short cycle times are too complex to be mastered by one person or a handful of selected employees. An operationally excellent company is the right testing ground for using teamwork as a tool to promote the culture.

The Pony Express is a good historical example of operational excellence. The design of this mail delivery system was based on maximum efficiency for people and equipment for its day. The images of riders staying in the saddle for hours with no break, frequent horse changes, and frequent hand-offs to fresh riders at a full gallop have become part of the lore. As with many good business ideas the Pony Express's days were short-lived because of the costs and other factors. The process was so grueling and dangerous that the company encouraged only young, single, male applicants.

Wal-Mart wrote the book on distribution operational excellence.[4] It was the first of a number of companies to examine its processes, reduce the cost of those processes, and pass the savings to the consumer. Wal-Mart did not see the necessity to pay anyone in the middle to handle the product. The store's strategy was to reduce shipment time from factory to store floor and use the savings as a weapon against the competition. Wal-Mart went ever further with its remaining handlers. In simple terms, products enter a warehouse floor by two in the afternoon, go directly to a lane designated for a specific store, and are shipped out in the afternoon. The product enters the store and is immediately on the shelf. The production-to-consumer sequence is short, controlled, and efficient.

Another example of an operationally excellent company is FedEx Corporation. Its ability to manage process is legendary and has been copied by hosts of companies trying to emulate its efficiencies. FedEx manages its processes tightly, carefully designing routes, loading trucks, and managing the route time. The company's delivery people are like human machines—they represent the model of efficiency during their workday. The next time you have a FedEx delivery, invite the representative to take a coffee break and chat. It will not happen. They are cordial but focused.

Any company attempting to achieve the awards for excellence will have to examine the way it does business with the same intensity as Wal-Mart or FedEx. There is a move in management circles to clean up operating systems. Reengineering, Business Process Mapping, and six-sigma are techniques currently in vogue. Each technology has its various consultants, disciples, and true believers. All work well to some degree when properly applied.

THE PRODUCTS-DRIVEN ORGANIZATION: PRODUCING THE BEST AND STAYING ON TOP

A products-driven organization replaces the customer as king with the product as king. These organizations know their "center of gravity" is the product. A products-driven organization puts its energies into producing either the best product on the market or a series of products that stay ahead of the market requirements.

In a products-driven organization, two factors influence success. The first factor is the product itself. No effort is missed in making the product the centerpiece of the organization. When a company hits a winner, such as Sony with the Walkman, Volkswagen with the new Beetle, or DaimlerChrysler with the Chrysler PT Cruiser, it pushes the product to the fullest with continuous improvements. Companies with an early product lead often lose the advantage when they stop the product improvement. A competing company then buys the market with an improved model just far enough off the original design that patent or copyright infringements are not a problem. A products-driven organization can ride a single product for years if it has the foresight to pour the effort into maintaining the product's visibility in the marketplace.

An issue faced by every products-focused company is obsolescence. Continuous improvements help, but not for the pet rock or hula hoop. Some products are fads with a limited shelf life or life span, no matter the marketing efforts. Management teams have to make tough decisions about their approach to products since significant capital investment is required to generate a stream of products or refurbish the existing lines.

This was exactly the situation for Rose Marie Bravo as the new CEO of Burberry.[5] She faced a tough situation of reviving a proud old British brand. As a tough manager she was reported to be cutting the gray-goods market in Asia, focusing the product lines, and refreshing the image. Her situation was delicate since she did not want to alienate the old Burberry crowd of trench coat wearers while appealing to the fashionable new follower. This situation is familiar to any president of any products-driven company.

A second way for a products-driven company to succeed is to try to always top its own product through creativity. This is done through a business structure that is loose enough to allow for creativity. Out-of-the-box thinking is necessary in a products-driven organization because demand for innovations on the existing products is relentless. When combined with the requirements for a stream of new and better products, the culture, by definition, must promote innovation by individuals and teams. The reward system in a products-driven company is based on the creativity required to develop and sustain a steady stream of products.

Another example of a products-driven company might be General Mills or Post Cereal in the cereal business. Every day they fight for shelf space in the stores. Their packaging has to be eye-catching; their products taste-sensitive and cost-competitive. The pressure is on the development teams to improve the existing products or develop new ones. The next time you are in a grocery store take a close look at the products on any given shelf. How many will be marked in some way as "new" or "improved"?

I love being a consultant. It gives me an opportunity to contradict myself without missing a beat. I just told you about the need for freshness and creativity in your product line. Now I'm going to say you may not have to do anything with your product but keep on keeping on.

A product that hasn't changed since it was first introduced is the Randall knife. Based in Orlando, Florida, Randall Knives has patterns of knives that have been unchanged for several decades. The Number One fighting knife I carried in the jungles of Vietnam in 1969 is exactly the same pattern as the model featured in the company's 2000 catalog. The late Bo Randall and later his son Gary remained true to their purist designs as custom knife-making caught on in the late 1960s. Prior to that only a handful of custom knife makers could be found in the United States, and Randall was considered the dean. That was because of quality and style. When the Vietnam War and movies made big, obscene knives popular, many knife makers got into the act, creating absurd designs more for fantasy than reality. During this time Randall never wavered. Year after year the company filled orders for those who treasured a Randall knife for what it really is, a functional piece of art.

One Thursday afternoon I let my students off an hour early so I could make my semiannual trip to the orange grove where Randall Knives is housed in a cottage. The shop was empty and I took a few minutes to browse through the museum, looking at pictures of the famous users of Randall knives. Mr. Randall happened to stop by his office and I had a chance to thank him for the knife he sent me in Vietnam. We chatted briefly before I had to leave. To this day I remember the quiet, soft-spoken, silver-haired gentleman who had the courage to stand his ground and not succumb to the lure of the gaudy or the gauche. I could collect many fine knives, but my collection is restricted. Like the Rolls-Royce, there is only one Randall.

Training development companies such as the American Management Association (AMA) or its Canadian counterpart, the excellent Canadian Management Centre (CMC), are also products-driven. They develop a product or course offering, send out brochures advertising the course, and present the course. The gamble is that people like what they read and attend the course. Obviously, there is a little more sophistication to the process of delivering a product—but not much. At the end of the day, filling classes is still a guessing game no matter how sophisticated the marketing ploys and complete the customer research data. The constant problem with any products-driven organization is guessing what the public will buy.

THE PROPERTIES-DRIVEN ORGANIZATION: MAKING THE MOST WITH WHAT YOU HAVE

A properties-driven organization is one that recognizes it has certain properties of which it must take daily advantage. Those properties can be intangible or tangible. An intangible property of a company is its good name or its reputation. At sale time a company with an outstanding professional reputation brings more on the auction block than a company with a disreputable past. You are worth more as an honorable company with a good reputation than one noted for sleazy management practices and a terrible reputation in the marketplace. A markup of 10 percent to 15 percent is often added to the sale price of a great company because of this intangible property.

This whole concept of intangible property eventually leads to a discussion of reputation. Charles J. Fombrun wrote the definitive text on the subject of how important your intangible property is to your fiscal health.[6] It is a fascinating description of companies you and I recognize. Rather than have me describe it, read his book *Reputation: Realizing Value From the Corporate Image*. It should be required reading of all executives who don't appreciate the intrinsic value of their company's good name.

A second type of properties-driven organization pays attention to its tangible assets. Any organization that must lease, rent, or barter out its physical assets or intellectual capital on a revolving basis is properties-driven. Consider Avis or Hertz in the automobile rental business. How about the Holiday Inn or Motel 6? Don't forget Blockbuster Video or that string of rental companies just down the street that can rent you everything from art for your offices to mattresses for your beds at home. If these properties are not in rental use every day the revenue is forever lost. That's why car rental companies go to great efforts to make it easy for you to do business with them. They don't want any distractions that will divert you to their competition. Properties-driven organizations must never forget that ease of doing business is the separator between them and their competition. Their television ads gleefully point out how the competition inconveniences you. Recall the Hertz commercial portraying a group of business travelers having a hard time getting to their car in the rain. The junior member of the team was repeatedly questioned if this obscure rental agency did such and such like Hertz. The repeated response was, "Not exactly."

Some hotel chains haven't gotten the message. This question is for road warriors: Why do you choose the same hotel chain when you travel? Do you make a choice based on service, convenience, or how the hotel treats you? Probably it is a combination of all those criteria. All who travel to earn a living know the hotel drill. A painful check-in with a reservation for tomorrow instead of today starts off your misery. Your room is at the opposite side of the complex and your rolling luggage has a bad wheel. Of course the dining room is closed—it's five minutes past ten o'clock so your dinner is something from the minibar. And finally there is no iron or ironing board in the room. A call to housekeeping gets you no sympathy. It's just another day in paradise!

One exception I noticed in Calgary was on a poster for Delta Hotels. This company is willing to put its reputation on the line with a promise—check-in in one minute or your room is free. I couldn't believe it, so I called to find out the catch. There is none. You join the free Delta Privilege Program that guarantees you a room after 3 P.M. Walk in, hand the desk your card, and they hand you a key. It's that simple. If there is a delay, you get the room free for the night plus 5,000 flyer miles. Delta Hotels is serious about keeping its properties in use.

Properties-driven companies understand the value of their capital assets. Those properties are the core of their income generation. They are the center of their universe. Because the properties are subject to daily use and abuse, great attention is given to the maintenance of the equipment. Hotel rooms must frequently be refurbished. Rental cars are rotated from low-use areas to more populated areas to even out the mileage. A new coat of paint or a face-lift is seen from time to time because the properties-driven organization knows appearance ranks close to service. Smart companies protect their investments by rewarding people for taking care of the properties. Disney World is famous for the cleanliness of its properties. The structure is highly disciplined in the care and feeding of the physical plant. Disney understands the value of image and strives minute-by-minute to protect the public's mental picture of Disney World. Even the name has become synonymous with living in a land where everything is perfect.

Another business that is properties-driven is my own—private consulting. I have three things to sell every day, 363 days of the year. (I do claim two days a year off—Christmas Eve and Christmas Day, and one is negotiable.) My first salable asset is my time, second is my knowledge, and third is my experience. Every day I sit in my office is a nonbillable day. The advantage of being an international consultant is that I can work American Thanksgivings in Canada, which I did for five years in a row. My family and I have eaten a lot of turkey outside the United States. I have a simple business philosophy—nothing gets between a billable day and me. If it means driving all night from Little Rock to Houston, which I did once to conduct a planning session when the planes were not flying, then so be it. I'm clear in my own personal business behavior that my income generator is billing every day, 363 days a year.

I've watched acquaintances get into the consulting game, lured by the perception of an exotic lifestyle, freedom from bureaucracy, and unlimited profits. The mistake that most want-to-be-consultants make is that they don't understand the need to be fully engaged. They do not have the luxury to spend excessive time developing products with the hope of selling them to an eager client. The lead time for product development kills the start-up consulting company. Cash flow or lack of it is deadly. There is no time to kick back and develop a beautiful web page, network on the Internet, and establish a plush office with administrative support. All those things are important but not critical to start or sustain a small consulting company. What is critical are billing hours, sending invoices, and cashing checks. The only way to do those three critical things is to be in the air, on the road, and at the client's location working. The path of business failures is lined with companies that simply didn't understand that having the wrong focus kills as quickly as the plague in Europe during the Dark Ages.

THE PAYOFF-DRIVEN ORGANIZATION: CATERING TO STATUS

A payoff-driven organization is one that understands the basic human need of individualism. These organizations base their products and services on some form of payoff for the users. The payoff may be many things, but I believe the central or core value is status. My favorite examples are the pens and wristwatches carried and worn by people. Take expensive writing instruments. Why would someone pay $100 or more for a ballpoint pen when the one taken from the hotel nightstand probably writes as well? Does the expensive timepiece keep any better time? I have a Rolex, so does my wife, and so do all four of our sons and daughters. We gave them as gifts for graduations from college; they are a status symbol and a mark of achievement. Each of my children has discovered the pride and pain relationship of wearing an expensive watch. All equipment needs servicing at some point. You take your car in for an oil change. Did you know you have to do the same thing with a Rolex? Sure, those little metal parts rub together. Expensive wristwatches lose time, need adjusting, and require costly servicing. Even our new ones need adjustments out of the box. Given the hassle, I've come to the conclusion that an elegant high-end watch keeps no better time than an inexpensive battery-powered model from a plastic display case at a discount store. What's my point? Status is the answer. After all, there is only one Rolls, one Randall, and one Rolex.

A payoff-driven company understands there is a market of people with those attitudes. It puts energy into the creation of status or image for the customer. In some cases payoff-driven companies are downright snobby about it. In-depth knowledge of customers' buying habits is important to a status-driven organization that designs its entire culture around elitism. If you drive our car you are above the crowd. If you wear our clothing with the little emblem on the pocket, you have arrived. If you shop in our store you must be among the most financially enhanced. And as long as people display a basic human need to be different from each other, to be unique, payoff-driven companies will continue to thrive.

When I was in Harrods in London I witnessed this dynamic at the ground-floor level. Just leaving the store with a distinctive Harrods bag was a payoff in itself, never mind what is in the bag. I left with such a bag of a few small items. Shopping for the first time in such a famous place was all that it was supposed to be.

There are other versions of the payoff organization besides the ones catering to status. The prospective members of associations are constantly asking, "What's in it for me? Why should I pay your annual dues? Is there a return for my membership?" Payoff organizations can start to build more market share if they embrace the concepts of economic value-added (EVA) or simply value-added. In today's consumer-oriented environment everyone wants to get more for their money. The problem is that many companies cannot justify or prove the value-added proposition of their goods or services. If you leave out the emotion, brand name, or status elements, how can companies justify an outrageous price for their goods or services?

Buying my last boat was a consumer's application of comparison shopping for economic value-added. I know boats, having owned a boat of some type for over thirty consecutive years. I know what features I want in a boat and what I don't want. When we made the decision to buy our boat, the *Witch Doctor*, my wife and I each listed some nonnegotiable features. She wanted some things I could live without and I wanted some things that were optional to her. Drawing up this list we quickly culled out all boats without these features. Then it was only a matter of deciding which model gave us the best value for the money while providing every feature we wanted. Consumers are getting the hang of this get-the-most-for-your-money method of evaluating their purchases.

HOW TO FIND A SINGLE FOCUS TO DRIVE YOUR COMPANY TO SUCCESS

Paying attention to the six drivers is critical to move from mission to vision. To be fully functional and get the most from the six drivers you must select one as the principal focus and relegate the other five to secondary drivers. Put the single focus in your strategic plan and save the other five for your operational plan. They are important but not the central force in your universe.

The single focus is the central organizer that drives your company to its success. I support Treacy and Wiersema's position that market leaders are those who select a single focus and go after it in all they say and do. Market leaders are those companies who have brought all their forces into a single beam of energy. They selected one driver and brought all employees into a mode of thinking that supports the one driver.

Not every organization will be number one in its industry. There will be only one. However, all organizations can use the concept of a single focus to create alignment and contribute to high performance. Many types of organizations such as London Guarantee Insurance Company, Ontario Northland, and Alcan Cable's Rod and Strip Division are using the concept to better communicate direction to employees. These companies spent the appropriate time during their planning conferences to create a distinct focus.

WHY THE CUSTOMER IS NOT ALWAYS RIGHT

The need for a single focus is very consistent with the intent of this book—to help you describe your story in congruent, authentic, and believable form. The internal integrity of your story is destroyed when you try to use all six drivers with the same sense of urgency. Your story cannot serve all six functions simultaneously. Let's say your sales team has a high customer orientation. They go to each customer with the idea of creating products or services based on customer input. It's almost a custom job shop. Traditionally this sales team lives by the motto, "The customer is always right." This battle cry from the sales force is usually an emotional argument based on some misunderstanding of what it means to have a customer orientation. The customer is not always right. That politically incorrect, unspoken thought is on many managers' minds. If the customer were always right, there would be no signs saying No Shoes, No Shirt, No Service. We wouldn't see No Pets Allowed signs posted in public places or No Smoking signs in restaurants. The customer must not always be right.

Now let's visit the production line. Here the focus is on long, record runs with minimum waste. Unit costs are important to production. Cycle times are critical. The production manager scrutinizes her entire operation to take out every possible bit of wasted energy. You could say she believes in being operationally excellent.

What happens when we put the two key management team members from sales and production into a decision process involving the choice of satisfying a customer or running a record product run? What do you, as the plant manager, tell the team? This exact case happened in a production facility in South Carolina. The sales force had carried customer intimacy to the point of absurdity. Orders were placed inside the two-week cutoff for production scheduling. Salespeople were not charging for custom color mixes and not billing back for nonstandard production setup costs. Every attempt to bring them in line was met with the stock, rote phrase, "The customer is always right." When examined, the value of many of these orders was found to be actually costing the company money. Mismanaged customer-focused orders were a drain on the plant and a principal reason the plant was slowly sinking into an unprofitable state.

The problem was compounded by the rewards system. The production manager was being rewarded for long, record runs of high quality with low-unit costs. Every time a short-run, custom order interrupted her schedule she went into lower productivity, which affected the whole production team. The sales force, on the other hand, was being rewarded for selling anything that wasn't nailed down. It didn't matter what the order did to the production line or how it influenced plant profits. The sales force got its commission no matter what the results.

The issue was resolved by an analysis of the profitability of orders covering a three-year period. Data for each order was assembled on a massive wall chart. Each was listed by rank order with less profitable orders on the bottom. The results could have been predicted. The consulting team and the plant manager suspected the outcome and here was the data as a matter of public record. There was no room for the sales force to argue. Until then it had been a finger-pointing shouting match with both sides arguing from emotional bases with no facts to support their positions. This was very similar to the situation facing Robert Duvall's character in the movie *Days of Thunder*. Duvall was trying to get his headstrong driver, played by Tom Cruise, to handle his race car differently. Only after a test case where Cruise drove the car his way, then Duvall's way, then measured the treads was he convinced of Duvall's judgment. Using Duvall's style of steering, braking, and accelerating, Cruise would keep more tread on the tires, which translated to fewer pit stops and more time on the track. Our sales force was the Cruise character. We had to show them the tires.

How to Use Focus to Clarify Your Mission

Once we had the sales force's attention, we moved on to the mission. Clearly the interpretation of the mission by each camp was further distorting and inflaming the situation. The process of mission clarification took almost three days to resolve. That session ranked as one of the most difficult of my consulting career. Getting a group of hardheaded, know-it-all, arrogant people with radically different views to agree to the interpretation of a single-sentence mission statement is close to a harrowing experience.

This is a classic story of a production plant not having clarity of its mission. Was it a custom job shop, a standard production line, or a combination of both? The story is further confused when the focus was split. The company was trying to be customer-intimate and operationally excellent at the same time, giving each focus equal weight. The only way a split focus works is in textbooks and in managerial dreams. There is no such thing as equal weight given two diametrically opposing forces. Customer intimacy and operationally excellent processes will invariably clash when they meet at your operational team level. This is because your story is incongruent. You cannot give away product and be operationally excellent. You can't deliver propane in the middle of the night and not charge for it if you are an operationally excellent company. If you are a customer-intimate company you cannot ignore your customer when she runs out of propane on the top of Bald Mountain in the middle of the winter's worst blizzard. An operationally excellent company that thought it was customer-intimate wrestled with this problem for days. It wasn't a pretty scene at the management meetings when the two opposite advocates collided.

The client had a newly hired and very knowledgeable vice president of operations who had a great deal of expertise in delivery systems. He was in the process of putting in a complex, technologically advanced routing model to achieve operational excellence when the annual strategic planning began. Somewhere from within the organization came the chant to become more customer-intimate. Naturally, the consultants picked up the rhythm and carried it right into the strategic planning meeting.

My team joined the process after the planning session to conduct leadership and managership training to support the strategic plan. At a working session with the president and vice presidents, I asked for their interpretation of how a customer-intimate organization would respond to certain business situations. My intent was to tailor specific training language and training situations to bring the strategic plan and the training into conceptual alignment. I was surprised at their answers, to say the least. All their responses were straight from an operational-excellence orientation. Pointing this out did not make me a popular person at that moment. Quickly the executive team realized that it had chased the wrong squirrel around the tree. They had just spent a week building a plan around the wrong driver. It took a few more weeks to undo and redo the plan. They were operationally excellent, not customer-intimate after all.

What do you do to prevent yourself from getting caught in the wrong dimension? You decide what is to be your primary focus and then how you plan to account for your secondary drivers. You pick one and communicate the necessary expectations of how to behave to all your employees. You may even have to teach them new behaviors in dealing with their daily activities and dealing with the customers. And you have to accept that it will be difficult for them to go from one driver to another or to consolidate from a number of drivers into a single focus.

SHIFTING FOCUS: IS IT WORTH THE EFFORT?

If you intend to change your focus, you need to understand the hidden dynamic. You must appreciate the stress you are about to create in your organization and in your workforce. Considerations must be given to the uncounted costs of the change process. You will be consuming valuable resources and your intellectual capital at an astounding rate. That's just keeping you even with the standard of performance. It doesn't move you ahead. I'm not suggesting you shy away from changing your focus. If it needs to be adjusted, clarified, or changed, then you must do so. What I am strongly suggesting is that you must carefully consider the implications of change and be prepared to offset the downside. In the end you have to answer the question, "Was it worth the effort?"

The Payoff for Finding a Central Theme in Your Story

Don't fight this issue. One single focus is the ticket to getting functional, operational alignment. Deciding the principal focus for your business quickly brings various managerial elements into a cooperative attack on your goals. Sometimes managers just can't give up the idea of being all things to all people. This is not a suggestion to pick one driver as a focus and ignore the other five. To do that would be foolish. You must maintain an acceptable level of performance with the remaining five.

Summary

You have a choice of selecting the single focus to drive from your current state to your future. In making the choice, you have six alternatives. Pick the alternative that best helps you concentrate on achieving your goals. Those are:

1. Players
2. Plans
3. Processes
4. Products
5. Properties
6. Payoff

THE KEY QUESTIONS: DEVELOPING FOCUS

Ask yourself these seven questions when you develop your focus:

1. What is the invisible force behind my business activities that creates my success?
2. What alignment problems occur as a result of selecting a single focus?
3. What can I do to remove the barriers and create a change-management process?
4. What will have to change in the rewards and recognition system to create the necessary alignment?
5. What must I do to align my focus throughout my staff or strategic business units?
6. Does my focus need to change?
7. What must be done to meet acceptable standards for the other five drivers?

THE PRACTICAL APPLICATIONS: FINDING A SINGLE FOCUS

To develop your single focus, take the following four steps:

1. Review the specific task of your mission statement.
2. Determine your focus statement. This is not an easy task. You may need to try several combinations before making a final selection.
3. Enter the single focus you selected into your 1-Page Strategic Plan.
4. Determine how you'll support the additional five drivers. Write these methods in operational terms. Put them into your 1-Page Operational Plan.

Corporate Culture: The Four Ingredients That Are Crucial to Your Company's Success

This chapter shifts attention from the components of your plan that are considered to be tangible to those parts of your story that may appear at first glance to be intangible. The term *corporate culture* is used frequently in business language. What makes up corporate culture is often in question. Many things can be and should be included in any discussion of an organization's culture. In this chapter you will develop four products for your story and business plan:

1. A set of core values
2. A philosophy statement
3. Operating principles
4. A strategic intent statement

The four represent important influences on parts of your culture and must be considered when developing the integrated planning model.

The first section on values advises you on how to build a list of values without falling into the sophomoric trap of spending all your time developing and prioritizing a list of meaningless rhetoric. The explanation leads you to developing a set of core value statements and their subsequent requirements to put the values into place while accounting for the operational values.

The second component of the culture is the philosophy statement. This statement of how you intend to do business sets a necessary tone. It sends a strong message about what is important to keep your business viable. On the other side is the implication that if you violate this philosophy you jeopardize the health and well-being of your company.

The third component of the culture are the operating principles. In this description I outline a number of filters through which you must pass your story for authentication and validation. Adherence to the principles or cross-checking your business plan against the principles provides the consistency of your story.

The fourth component, the strategic intent, is a critical restatement of where the management team intends to take the organization. It sends signals to employees and has significant influence on how they react. A military commander always signals strategic intent through the military version called commander's intent. With this statement the commander gives subordinate unit commanders advance warning that certain types of operations will follow the present tactical plan. When subordinate commanders know the intent they can better prepare to follow it. Different logistical requirements exist if you plan to continue the attack or you plan to defend the hill. Likewise, business leaders need to tell their organizations what they have in mind for the long term. For example, marketing needs to know the strategic intent so it can align its campaigns with the company direction.

THE THREE STEPS FOR DEVELOPING A LIST OF CORE VALUES

In previous years we began a planning session with work on the goals. It made sense to decide what you wanted to accomplish. There would have been no discussion of the types of soft issues now included in planning models. To suggest starting with or even discussing values would have been summarily discarded, rejected, and rebuffed. Yet we knew that values played an important part in the behavior of organizations as they moved out of a command-and-control hierarchy toward empowerment, diversity, and a virtual structure.

Today we believe core value statements may constitute one of the most important components of your story. They are different from philosophy because values define what's core to the organization's management behavior. They set boundaries on what is acceptable and unacceptable by providing ethical lines you do not cross. A simple definition of values as those things important to you is a start point, but it's not sufficient. We need to define operational values but spend the bulk of our time on the deeper core values.

The danger of introducing values into the business plan is that the concept is overworked, overused, and understated in management language. Usually a discussion around the planning table brings together a list of items such as these:

- Quality
- Teamwork
- Integrity
- Honesty

Such discussions are not only boring, they're very superficial. This is traditional list-making. Most planning teams display mild interest, but there's no astounding breakthrough at the planning session. Implicitly no one in his right mind would sit in front of peers and deny listing teamwork as a value. Not after the chief executive officer just published a newsletter proclaiming this to be the year of company teamwork.

I challenge that teamwork may be important but not necessarily a core value. It is really a by-product of another value. Likewise, we may have an emotional connection to building customer relations. Again, is this a value or something else? What happens when e-business becomes the norm and the personal component of the customer service relationship is diminished from its present form?

While these items are important to the functioning of your business, they are transitory, too. Consider the business emphasis and how it evolves and changes. In the early 1980s, a fellow consultant suggested that I change my business cards to read Total Quality Management (TQM). My response was, "Why? What will I do when that fad has passed? Change my card again?" What happens when the level of quality provided is so consistent across products and businesses that it is no longer a discriminator? This leads to another level of understanding of the concept of values and their role in the organization's story.

We need to move to another dimension of sophistication to understand values. This new level of emphasis is on core values. I didn't invent the term; lots of other people use it also. However, I do offer you a different application of values from those usually found in your planning process. The concept of core values means reaching a certain level of understanding of what is more permanent. While teamwork and quality are important transitory operational values, they do not reach deep enough into the roots of your story.

Core values are those things that probably will not change over time. These are the deep-seated fundamental lines you will not cross in spite of the circumstances. These values define the line over which you will not step in a situation where it would be easy to look the other way.

Defining the list of company values in a planning meeting is not a task to be taken lightly. Identifying your core values is really a gut-wrenching activity. By asking questions of yourself you have to thoroughly scrutinize your baseline for business behavior and determine where limits can be set.

Another important function of core values is to provide behavioral maps for business decision making. People need to know what is important to the business so they can make informed choices in decision-making situations. Values give an organization a path out of difficult situations. When a crisis occurs, it is the value statements that give stability to the chaos. Managers turn to the core values as beacons or, better still, as channel markers to see if their intended responses to the crisis are within accepted norms.

Picture a case where a manager, Susan, has reached an important junction in her project. Two alternatives are available and both are logical, practical, and make good business sense. She chooses alternative A, only to find it difficult to implement. A natural cultural resistance seems to be in effect. This is because alternative B was a better fit with the company's values system. Although alternative A was correct, it just didn't fit the norms of the organization. Had Susan known the values, had they been discussed, she could have made the more appropriate selection. Her culturally inappropriate choice caused wasted effort and lost energy, which eventually shows on the bottom line.

For the organization, values play the same role in giving direction in times of crisis. By always falling back on your bedrock beliefs or core values, you are able to be consistent in your story. There is a folk saying: "If you always tell the truth you never have to remember what lie you told to whom." If you always live your values, you never have to worry about stepping out of the ethical box. If your values are ethically in line with the societal norms of the time you should have no problems.

Step 1: Determine What's Really Important

To capture your values as part of your story, you need to have frank discussions with your team to determine what is really important to you, your team, and your business. From the discussion you need to develop a list of core values. Keep it a short list, say, around four or five items. Too many values on the list seem to dissipate the importance of the list. It becomes a tedious code of conduct for employees to remember. People seem to be able to relate better to a few core values than to a long list.

There has been research on the number of values a company should maintain and communicate. James C. Collins and Jerry I. Porras have done extensive analysis of the successful habits of visionary companies. They devote a significant amount of effort defining the role and importance of core values in a visionary company's culture. Collins and Porras found that "visionary companies tend to have only a few core values, usually between three and six. In fact, we found none of the visionary companies to have more than six core values, and most have less. And, indeed, we should expect this, for only a few values can be truly core—values so fundamental and deeply held that they will change or be compromised seldom if ever."[1] The message here is to keep your core values list limited.

If your list is of the short-term-importance type, you will spend excessive time arguing the validity of the list. In fact, there may be a direct correlation between the amount of time spent discussing operational values and the length of the list.

Don't spend a lot of time in disagreement over what should be or shouldn't be on the list. That argument is really not as important as what honesty means to the team as a core value. Don't spend any time putting the list into an order of priority. That, too, is a waste of your valuable management time. You will be considering the complete list anyway, so a priority activity is not necessary.

Step 2: Explain How to Put Each Value Into Action

Once your core list is complete, describe how you live your values. Little is accomplished in your planning if you only make a list of your value statements. They must be translated into actions or observable behaviors. There is a way to complete the value statements by making them more meaningful. Define each statement in action terms. Planners find the following format to be quite effective. Consider the complete examples provided here; they were taken from four different business plans:

We Value Profit
This means we:

1. Make a reasonable profit on every deal or we don't contract.
2. Take steps to continually eliminate inefficiencies from our business processes.
3. Spend money wisely for things we need to support our operations.

We Value Our Product
This means we:

1. Protect its image at all costs.
2. Continuously improve its performance.
3. Sell it for what it is worth.

We Value Our Reputation
This means we:

1. Safeguard our public image.
2. Require high ethical standards for employees.
3. Take swift, decisive corrective actions in potentially embarrassing situations.

We Value Our Time
This means we:

1. Don't chase contracts.

2. Don't waste time submitting competing bids.

3. Pull the plug early on bad projects.

Follow this format for discussing each of your values. Listing the actions causes your management team to achieve a more complete understanding of what the values mean to the company. I don't know of many planning sessions where this level of sophistication and meaning is attached to value statements. This format further connects the planners with an awareness of what may or may not be happening within their organizations. It is a consciousness-raising activity.

Step 3: Account for Any Gaps

When you are satisfied the list and all the action-oriented statements reflect what you want the value proposition to contain, you take still another step. Next is the gap analysis as drawn in Figure 7-1. Spend time discussing each value in terms of what you say versus what you do. Ask yourself four key questions:

1. Is there a gap between what we say and what we do?

2. If so, is it a large, medium, or small gap to my employees?

3. How important is the gap?

4. Is it critical to our short-term or long-term plan? Which or both?

Figure 7-1. You lose management credibility when you don't model your values.

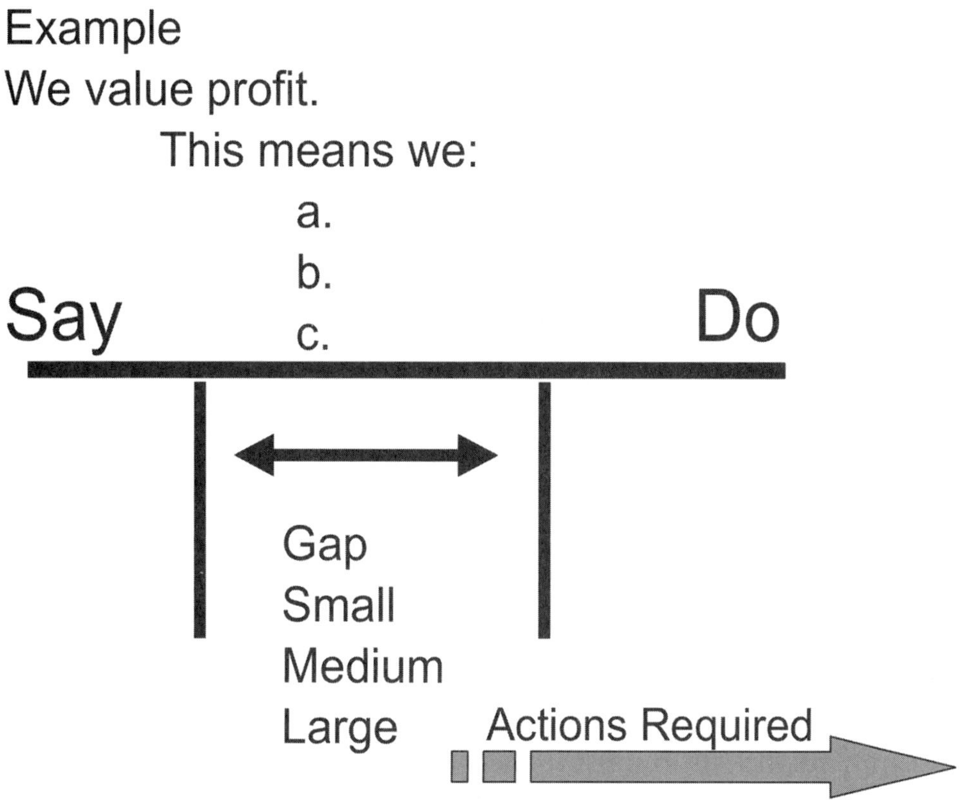

Example
We value profit.
This means we:
a.
b.
Say   c.   Do

Gap
Small
Medium
Large   Actions Required

These are serious questions that must be answered to get you to action planning. All gaps must be accounted for and closed with a definitive action. I call these your "quick fix," steps you must immediately take to protect your story. These actions are a preemptive strike on employees so you are not caught in an inconsistent story. You confess up-front to any shortfalls and present comprehensive plans to correct the problems. Never ignore or cover up identified gaps. I promise you, it will come back to haunt you one day. Think about it. If you know there is a problem, then so do the employees. And they know you know.

In summary, values are a cornerstone to your story. Careful considerations are made to define what are operational values and what are the true, core values. Separate out the short-term operational items and make them strategies or tactics. For example, teamwork may be important, but instead of restating it in the value piece, move it up to the strategies/tactics area. Then dig deep for meaning in four or five core values that drive your business's very existence. Look for things that are so fundamental to your continued success there is never any thought of violating them.

HOW TO PREPARE A CLEAR, WELL-CRAFTED PHILOSOPHY STATEMENT

Your philosophy is the second important cultural component defined in this chapter. Philosophy determines how you intend to approach your business. It signals who you are and how you will deal with the world around you. Having a well-written and communicated philosophy statement provides stability in troubled times. Working in conjunction with values, the philosophy becomes a beacon for employees and management to turn toward when the going gets rough. A clear philosophy gives you a framework for sorting problems. It also is a strong influence on how you conduct daily business. You may find the roots of your philosophy in the character or uniqueness of your business. Distinctive features are attributes that cause you to be unique. This is a good starting point to understand business philosophy. An examination of any of the following eight attributes can help you formulate your philosophy:

1. *Price.* Your philosophy may be to compete on price. Usually this means your products or services have to be priced lower than the competition. You believe you simply underprice the competition every time on every item. This is a difficult factor to manage if you are in a commodity business, such as a grocery store, that has high volumes and low margins.

2. *Speed.* Your philosophy may be built around speed of
    delivery. Pizza food chains use this standard as a major
    competitive advantage. A whole secondary wave of indus-
    tries has grown up as support facilities for these business-
    es. Selling products on the Internet is okay, but someone
    still has to deliver them to the end user.

3. *Quality.* Your philosophy may have its roots in quality. You
    may chose to be known as the best of your product line;
    however, be careful of quality because it is now a standard.
    If you don't have quality to begin with you are not in the
    game.

4. *Service Level.* Your philosophy may be to focus on service
    levels. Remember, high service also includes hidden costs.
    This means you must get your service right the first time.

5. *Quantity.* Your philosophy may be to give more for the dol-
    lar. An ice cream parlor that gives generous helpings is
    using this standard as a distinctive feature.

6. *Uniqueness.* Your philosophy may be to stand out from the
    crowd. A catchy product or perception of uniqueness
    often opens doors to customers.

7. *Brand Recognition.* Your philosophy may be to use market-
    ing to get to customers. You choose to become a recog-
    nized name in your local area, then expand to national
    recognition.

8. *Reputation.* Your philosophy may have its roots in integri-
    ty. You may choose to build your business on a reputation
    of solid products, honest practices, and reputable services.

Years ago while consuming every management book I could
find, I ran across Michael Lewis's *Liar's Poker.* Lewis was a young
stockbroker who exposed an insider's view of Salomon Brothers
circa 1989. Besides telling a great story, he had the courage to publicly state the company's philosophy statement. "Screw the customer, they have a short-term memory" is very revealing of the

arrogance of some brokerage houses. It seemed that customers only had so many choices, so the traders didn't worry about how their clients were treated. The business circle was small, so the clients would have to return sooner or later.[2]

Let's examine another case of a poor philosophy and its resulting implications. Picture an automobile dealership in the 1960s. Recall buying a new car from a dealer across town or out of town and trying to get it serviced? Much to your dismay you were told to take it back to the dealer where you bought the car. What prompted that behavior was the philosophy of "one car, one customer, and one deal." Car dealers saw the market as a never-ending stream of customers so captivated by the big American car mystique that the buyer was in fact helpless. The result of this philosophy was that dealers didn't want you back in the dealership for maintenance and warranty work. In fact, you were a nuisance. Selling the product in a one-transaction relationship was the name of the game, so service was poor to nonexistent.

Then something changed. Better quality foreign automobiles began showing up on the market. Less maintenance, less downtime, and less fighting with the dealers for simple service had instant appeal with the consumers. This began a wave of buyer behavior that got the dealerships' attention. Not only had the automobile manufacturers been forced to make better-quality cars, but another economic factor kicked in to further punish the dealership. Someone realized how much money a person spends in a lifetime for automobiles. The one car, one customer, and one deal philosophy was costing a fortune in lost revenue.

Dealerships had to not only revise their products, they were forced by the economics to rethink their business approach to customers. The product was no longer the driving force. The customer's buying capacity became the central focus. If a dealer wanted to achieve a multiplier effect with repeat customers, customers' children, and all their friends, something had to change. How about changing the philosophy? Perhaps a philosophy statement that reads something like "A customer for life." Clearly the deals had to have a customer attraction. What would get the customer back in the door? It certainly wasn't the product—that could be bought from around the corner or across town or from a competitor. It certainly couldn't be price, because underselling the competition has an end price point. If the price is not right, the customer will simply move down the street until he finds the price he is looking for. Service became the door opener and saving feature of the dealerships. Now great stories are told about high-contact service, such as cars being picked up at the airport and taken in for maintenance. And you even get your car back washed and vacuumed. Outstanding dealers follow up with a call to see if you are satisfied. This is a far cry from the treatment you and I received with our new cars back in the sixties. Sadly, it took economics to get car dealers' attention. But isn't that always the way?

Tips for Developing Your Philosophy

You need to spend the same quality time defining your philosophy as you did with your core values. Ask yourself questions such as these:

- What is the one thing about our business that sets us apart from everyone else?

- When the situation is bleak, profits are down, and things look hopeless, what is the single belief we turn to for survival?

- What belief has been the bedrock or foundation of our success?

- What theme will ensure success if we follow it faithfully?

From this thinking should come a single-sentence statement that captures the essence of your philosophy.

In Chapter 6, I listed people (i.e., players) as one of the business drivers. In the example I cited Rosenbluth Travel as an employee-driven organization. Logic would dictate that a natural philosophy for that company might be, "Take care of employees and they take care of customers." See how the philosophy fits nicely with the concept of a player focus? This is an example of the close fit and similarities of parts of the integrated planning model.

Other examples of good, solid philosophy statements taken from actual business plans illustrate the range of philosophy statements:

- Give people simple software that they can use.
- We will serve no wine before its time.
- Nothing gets between a billable day and me.
- Build it and they will come.
- Cash is king.
- We don't give away our services.
- We believe in understated elegance in our designs.
- Our products will overperform a customer's requirements, every time.

The importance of a well-crafted philosophy statement is that it puts pressure on both the management and employees. First, managers must take care of all the hygiene factors found in business. If you think I'm talking about clean rest rooms, then you are off base by miles. I'm talking about all the little irritants that seem to distract employees from full-time focus on taking care of customers. Enough distractions exist to interfere with getting the job done.

Employees also must buy into the philosophy statement. If they have other ideas then problems occur. A propane company cannot survive if its employees have the philosophy that the company is rich and can afford to give away tankloads of products. One of the reasons the philosophy is captured in print in the business plan is to ensure everyone understands, buys into, and executes business in line with the intent of the philosophy.

MAKE SURE WHAT YOU SAY IS WHAT YOU DO

When you have determined your philosophy statement, you must analyze the concept to determine if a gap exists between what you say and what you do, as shown in Figure 7-2. As with the value statements, this gap is subjectively labeled small, medium, or large. Determine the size and then the importance. It may be large but not important. Or it may be large and very critical to your organizational well-being. Once the gap is identified you may need to design actions to correct the problem or problems. These actions become part of your quick-fix plan. Finally, the actions must be communicated to employees in an appropriate manner to prevent a backlash in your story.

Figure 7-2. The foundation of your story is in danger when a gap exists in your philosophy because your story loses operational alignment.

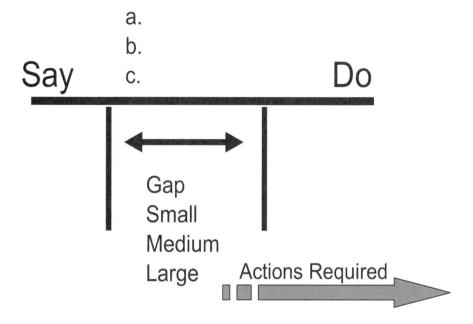

Example
Our philosophy is to get it right the first time.
          This means we:
                    a.
                    b.
Say   c.   Do

                    Gap
                    Small
                    Medium
                    Large   Actions Required

THE SEVEN KEY OPERATING PRINCIPLES THAT GUIDE SUCCESSFUL BUSINESSES

Another key piece of the soft side of your story is your principles. These are "laws of business" by which you must operate as a business. All organizations must operate from a set of guidelines or principles. They are the governing forces in the business universe. Principles become the benchmark through which you pass the plan before it is published for your employees (see Figure 7-3). This promotes consistency and provides one more way to validate the authenticity and believability of your story.

Figure 7-3. Principles are the cross-check you filter the business plan through to ensure nothing is missing.

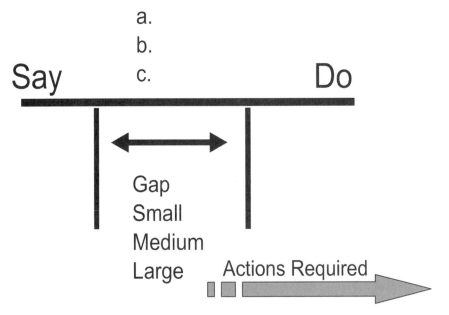

When I went into private practice in the early 1980s, a client asked me for a copy of the business principles taught in graduate school. In other words, what was the textbook solution? As we started digging though the literature on what we thought should have been an easy task, we found many examples of principles but no consolidated list of the fundamental principles of how any organization must function to survive. As I began examining the few client documents I again found no consistent theme or list. What I observed were statements such as, "A principle of selling is to stop selling when you've made the sale." That is great as a sales principle, but what about the higher-order principles that govern the basic functions of the business?

As a subsequent task my clients and I began to develop a list of principles common to any business. We approached the task using a large system theory. Over a ten-year period I had asked the same question of 125 presidents, hundreds of management teams, and thousands of managers in management seminars. These represented a cross-section of organizational levels and industries. I asked the same question in at least ten countries. The question was, "What principles do you use to guide your business?" Here is the consolidated and refined list of the seven principles that emerged:

1. *The Principle of Products.* You must have a steady stream of viable products, goods, or services.

2. *The Principle of Profit.* Except for unusual situations, all organizations need financial viability.

3. *The Principle of Customer.* You need a constantly replenished customer base.

4. *The Principle of Direction.* You need some form of path to travel.

5. *The Principle of Structure.* You need an organizing force for your resources for mission accomplishment.

6. *The Principle of People.* Most organizations need human elements to make them work.

7. *The Principle of Ethics.* You must operate with the laws, rules, and norms of the society of the day.

The Principle of Products: Know What You Are Selling

All organizations, no matter their status, must honor this principle of having something to sell. To conform to the principle of products, every organization is faced with the same problem. You must have products that have some value in some market segment.

As discussed in Chapter 6, some organizations build their whole business around their product or products. Even if you are a customer-intimate organization, without something to sell, rent, or barter you are out of business. Products go back to the root of all business. What is your business reason? What is your output? What will customers pay for what you can provide?

To conform to the principle of products, every organization should be able to answer this question: What goods or services can we provide that people are willing to buy? A related problem is the question of product diversity. Two alternatives seem to be the answer.

One product-driven organization may follow the strategy of developing one product as the best in the business. The company may elect to keep the product line very small, offer continuous improvements, and promote a quality image of the single product. This allows the company to focus on a limited number of efforts rather than being spread too widely across a number of offerings. The choice is made to be very, very good with a few things.

Another company may choose multiple lines to stay healthy. This company is constantly adding to its product line to attract more customers. A breakfast cereal company knows the jaded attitude of its markets and constantly seeks to bring out new lines. The simplest illustration of this approach is the movie theater business. Long gone are the days of a theater operating with only one screen and one movie per day. Multiple offers must be made to the viewing public or the enterprise cannot stay economically healthy. It will not draw enough participation.

The Principle of Profit: Money Matters

If you don't make money you don't stay in business very long. Even not-for-profit organizations must pay attention to financial issues. This flaw became evident to me when I consulted to a prestigious university and teaching hospital combination. The doctors and professors were totally uninterested in the concepts of managing money. They worked hard to get grants, but after that it was back to their classrooms and research labs. Discussing how money was to be managed was too pedestrian for their learned minds. Often researchers in corporate situations are totally ignorant of the concepts of fiscal responsibility.

Another of my observations is that few employees understand the concept of profit. Even management teams get this requirement out of context. A simple test is to ask how the pricing of a product is done. What is the relationship between what it costs to make and deliver the product and the price customers are willing to pay you? The difference is profit.

This cost versus profit is usually unknown by upper management. How can one company sell propane for 99 cents a pound and make a handsome profit when a company down the street prices it for $1.13 and complains of low margins? Many organizations have gone out of existence because they didn't know the costs of their goods and services. The reason is simple. They couldn't possibly know the selling price and therefore couldn't establish the profit margins.

I once discovered a regional division hidden among the folds of a large international corporation that had not made a profit in twenty years. Profit wasn't in their business language, either written or spoken. The company had lived for twenty years on handouts from the corporation. Every year the division lost money, yet the president seemed to always wrangle enough from the board of directors to pay bonuses. A new president took over from the retiring executive with a dedication to turn the situation around. He did many good things to demonstrate professional management and expert leadership. Key to his actions was to put profit into the value statements and strategic goals. He also began to communicate the actual financial situation of the division to the employees. Everywhere he went, he spent time with employees educating them about the realities of their business state and what was necessary to turn the situation to the positive. In four years the division went from losing $10 million annually to a profit of $37 million. It was quite a scene the day they rolled out the yearly performance numbers and passed out the bonus checks.

The Principle of Customer: Continually Replenish Your Base

You need a constantly replenished customer base. Customers come and go. Often they are assisted in leaving by poor customer service, overpriced products, and the difficulty of buying from you. As you go about your life for the next month, I challenge you to observe how difficult we make it for people to give us their money. We make them stand in line, give them a hard time with processing their transactions, and hurriedly send them on their way. If customers are hard to find, why do we treat them this way?

Customers also have their own peculiarities. They tend to wander off. As a business you need to keep a close eye on your customer base. That's where the rule of "staying close to the customer" was born. A great deal of organizational time is spent trying to keep up with customers. I describe it as herding cats. Customers also leave your products and services out of curiosity. Again, like a cat, a customer will look at another offering just because it may look different, be a little unusual, or have some sort of mysterious appeal. Other times customers simply get bored with you and your products. They decide to try something different just to spice up life. All these things cause you to lose customers, so you should never let one out of your sight.

One of the worst examples of this behavior I ever observed was in a computer store in Baton Rouge, Louisiana. I was sitting at a demonstration machine when a young man approached the lone storekeeper. It seemed the potential customer had located a computer he wanted at the New Orleans store and had been able to save the money to pay cash. His problem was that he didn't have a way to drive the eighty-five miles to pick up the computer. Did the salesperson think he could have the computer shipped to Baton Rouge? Seemed like a simple request. The sales clerk replied, "I don't have the authority to make that decision." "Who does?" asked the young man. "The store manager, and he is out on a service call today." "Will he be back tomorrow?" the customer asked. "No, he's on service calls all day tomorrow." No alternatives were offered. The customer mumbled something in bewilderment and wandered out of the store with his check in hand. I sat there dumbfounded at the exchange I had witnessed.

A real businessperson would have dived across the counter, grabbed the check from the customer's hand, and told him to be back at five when the store closed. Together they would drive down to pick up the computer. Where have all the businesspeople gone, long time passing? The point of the story is simple: Don't ever let a customer with money out of your sight.

The Principle of Direction: Know Where Your Organization Is Headed

Organizations that know what they want to do, communicate that intent to their employees, and proceed in that direction do better than those that follow the Cracker Jack approach. The Cracker Jack approach is when you open a box and find a prize at the bottom. Some organizations live from day-to-day, digging in the box to find the prize. Often the results are cheap novelties and offer no real substance.

Consider the case of a Louisiana-based company that considered itself to be opportunist or entrepreneurial. This company was rapidly expanding, acquiring small businesses left and right with no plan. During an interview the CEO was asked, "Where are you heading with your effort?" Stretching back expansively in his chair, he enlightened the interviewer with his sage wisdom. "We just look for opportunities. That's our strength. We see a good deal and we jump on it—anywhere—everywhere. Right now we are looking at a marina. Last month we bought a chain of theaters. We just seize the opportunity." Within a year they were bankrupt.

For several years now planning and its subordinate topics of strategic thinking and vision have been under fire. Micklethwait and Wooldridge are not kind to the planning community.[3] They slam-dunk Alfred Sloan, the late chairman of General Motors, and chastise Alfred Chandler of the Harvard Business School. They work right up to the most-recognized names of the present generation by stabbing George A. Steiner, the strategic thinker, and pot shooting Michael Porter, the competitive analysis planner. Their criticism of a huge elaborate planning machine is justified. But it still does not negate the fact that an organization must have direction.

Properly conducted planning works. I've used it too often to discount the process. I've worked with too many companies that would be in serious trouble today if they had not buckled down to serious planning.

Let's consider the planning for Operation Desert Storm. Did it make a difference that the planning staff had a clear mandate, clear mission, and specific goals? How differently would the operations have been implemented if the commanding general had said to each of the services and agencies, "Folks, we are going to have a little war over in the Middle East. Don't have much more information for you at this time. Just show up as soon as you can, bring what you've got, and we'll get started." This may seem like a silly example, but I assure you many businesses approach their operations in much the same fashion.

The Principle of Structure: Provide Comfort and Stability

Structure has been with us since the first cave people banded together to fight a common enemy, hunt for food, or protect their tribes. Structure provides comfort and stability, inbred requirements of the human race. It creates a unified body of energy to be applied to the task at hand by focusing resources. Over time, prehistoric humans found that banding together gave them more power. Slowly an understanding developed that power was not effective unless it was coordinated. Organizations and organizational structure began in this fashion. It has evolved into an important business element, a force to be reckoned with in creating your story. Because structure as an organizing force is a critical element of your plan, Chapter 9 is devoted to this topic.

The Principle of People: Don't Ignore the Human Factor

Most organizations need human elements to make them work. Except in some specific cases, humans are the delivery component of the equations that breathe life into a system. Robots can run a production line, but they cannot make business decisions (yet). That's why your businesses need people. General Motors tried to get rid of people in the 1980s by investing nearly $80 million into factories and robotic equipment only to have it fail. Henry Ford had complained many years earlier, "How come when I want a pair of hands, I get a human being as well."[4] I doubt we'll ever reach a stage where robotics completely usurps the human input.

The original television series *Star Trek* had a huge following of cult proportion. One reason I believe it was so popular was that when the final crisis was faced, Captain Kirk and his team always prevailed over technology or adversity. The subtle message was that the human spirit conquers.

Another issue with the people principle is that quality people are in short supply. There may always be a bountiful supply of medium or average managers and workers, but where do the brightest and best hang out?

The problem is severe, with talented people hopping from one technical job to the other based on what the next company can better offer. One company issued an unofficial directive to its recruiters and managers to look for only "average people." The fact was that the company couldn't retain the brightest for very long. In another situation a principal at one of the largest consulting companies said the firm didn't pay signing bonuses for newly minted MBA graduates. When asked how the company stayed competitive, the answer was startling and frank. The company targets the B-grade graduate schools and picks up what the other companies don't want. In both of these examples, the two companies are sending a strong message to their workforce. We are content to work with the second string and you are it. And because you are second string we don't have to pay you as much. The other scary point is that the two companies will always be behind in intellectual capital.

The Principle of Ethics: You Will Get Caught

You can cut corners, but eventually you are "found out." If you are violating the ethics, laws, and norms of society in the era in which you are living, you need to take heed. It is only a matter of time before you get caught. It may take decades or generations, but you will get caught. You can take that to the bank, as the saying goes. A fundamental behavior of systems is that they tend to purge themselves of bad participants and bad activities over time.

At the individual level, take a look at two examples from our highest office, the presidency of the United States. Look at those who want to be and those who achieved this honor. John F. Kennedy's escapades came to light even after he was assassinated and his memory became legendary. The House of Representatives charged Bill Clinton's troubles as a pattern of inappropriate behavior and impeached him in December 1998. Eventually your buried past comes back to haunt you. Those small deals you made on the side are found out. All things eventually come to light. Recall the names Gary Hart, the possible presidential candidate, or Kelly Flinn, the first woman B-52 pilot, or Jimmy Bakker, the television evangelist, just to name a few. They found out the system eventually works.

The system gets even in the long run. Al Dunlop's problems at Sunbeam are an example of payback by the system. Think of how many times the corporate killers have unnecessarily destroyed careers, lives, and futures in the name of shareholders' equity and profitability. This behavior is so bad *Newsweek* devoted a whole issue to the subject and named the top offenders. Slash and burn long enough and someone will return the tactics.

A longer-term problem is that companies sometimes get caught in a paradox. They obey the norms of the times only to find themselves being penalized fifty years later as the rules changed. The inhuman working conditions of the steel industry in Pittsburgh come to mind. Child labor in the mills is another example. Thankfully, as workers' rights and human decency applied to business situations became more sophisticated, the public view of these conditions shifted. After a century of perfect 20/20 hindsight, we would never consider operating with those conditions. Thankfully, our national and international laws will not let us do it. Furthermore, we are bringing pressure on those countries that do not fully honor human rights.

Today we connect the dots between the past and the present and catch some international companies in a squeeze. The example in South America between the government of Ecuador and a well-known American oil company is a case in point. For fourteen years the company was making unknown millions of dollars in profit from Ecuador. When they left the country, they turned the business over to a national company that had owned a majority of stock all along. When the government changed and the practices of the American company were brought to light, a major lawsuit erupted. Anticipating the bad press the company paid $40 million in cleanup costs. A spokesperson never flinched on national television, repeatedly stating that they had operated within the laws of the country at the time. Nevermind that the laws were reported to be poorly written and totally naive. The company was knowingly using techniques in Ecuador reportedly banned in Louisiana and Texas as early as 1924. Never mind that their majority stockholder partner was probably a sham with the American company calling the shots.

Here is the point: Companies operating in underdeveloped countries think they can whip in and take advantage of the lack of sophistication or plain ignorance of the host country. They can take out for years, but sooner or later they must give back. The French found this out in Indochina (later known as Vietnam). Stripping natural resources from an underdeveloped country is getting more difficult with each decade.

In a more modern case, consider the unlawful-practices lawsuit against Microsoft. Isn't it interesting that in the same year Microsoft was listed as one of the world's most admired companies in the world it was defending itself in court against charges of bullying and intimidating the Internet market? Where is the line drawn for a powerful company between its aggressive strategies and its ethics? Seems to be good strategy for Microsoft to keep Apple and Sun apart. How Microsoft did it would be the ethical question. Is the Microsoft controversy really about assertive or even aggressive capitalism directed toward beating the competition, or is the whole case about arrogant, manipulative behavior by a company that enjoys strong consumer backing? Companies do reach a point where they feel invincible to the point of thumbing their nose at their own government.

There is another point on ethics that falls into the gray area. When a product defect is found and the company doesn't recall the product, is that a business strategy called calculated risk? What ethical responsibility does the producer have to protect the consumer? There are many court cases on this subject with results that are decided in both directions. Is one lawsuit less costly than the recall? Pay now or pay later, because the principle of ethics catches up with offending companies sooner or later.

So far in the planning process you have generated many activities that go into your final action plan. However, some things will not wait until the plan is complete and formal implementation begins. They need to be dealt with on an immediate basis. These issues stem from issues you identified during the examination of your philosophy, values, and principles. I strongly suggest you develop a short-term or quick-fix action plan. A suggested template is provided in Appendix J.

THINKING LONG TERM: HOW TO COMMUNICATE YOUR STRATEGIC INTENT

You need to inform your organization of your executive intentions. This is another of those subtle pieces of planning that is missing from most models. In the military it is used for every operation and viewed as a critical element of every campaign. The strategic intent is not the same as the vision of the company. It is close but not the same. The difference is that the vision is a description of where you want to be in the future whereas the strategic intent is the concept of how you plan to reach the vision. It defines what you are going to do to put the plan in place. Understanding strategic intent is tricky to those managers and leaders who have not actually used the tool. Sullivan and Harper do a thorough analysis of strategic intent and how it fits the schema of planning. They state, "The intent translates the vision into very specific terms that can guide your actions. In articulating the intent, the leader stretches the organization, both pushing and pulling toward success. It is important to understand that intent seldom leads directly to realization of the vision but carries the organization in the direction of the vision."[5] I interpret the last sentence to mean that strategic intent is the energizer that gets the organization moving toward the vision. It is the public commitment from the leadership to get on your feet and moving in the right direction.

Several payoffs come to mind for ensuring your company understands your view of future actions. First, your employees can help strategize for the future and appropriately allocate resources to make sure the future occurs. Second, knowing your intentions helps them make personal career decisions.

To help your management teams better prepare for the future you need to develop a short, succinct statement about what you intend to do. This forces you to commit to your plan and your story. Not many managers have the courage to stand before the company and declare their intentions in such a definitive way. The normal language is about vision and the future of the company. Goals are always discussed. Presidential intentions are almost always missing. This is a chance for you to establish leadership and communicate that you are fully committed to making the future happen. It is your personal stake in the ground.

Strategic intent statements can be short. They may be simple or complex. Here are examples of short intent statements:

- I intend to grow this business and pass it down to the children of your children.

- We intend to buy our biggest competitor and anchor ourselves as the leader in this field.

- I intend to take this company public within three years.

- My intentions are to establish us as a rock-solid company with long-term security for all employees.

- Our management intention is to be the best-managed company in the world, freeing employees to get on with their jobs.

- I intend to create fifty-two new millionaires within this company in three years.

Here is an example of a longer, more definitive strategic intent statement developed as part of the planning process. The text was made available to the membership in the written business plan, through marketing and publicity documents, and electronically.

Strategic Intent Statement

The Arkansas Forestry Association [AFA] will examine and refine the organization's mission and develop a cohesive strategic plan to guide and grow AFA in the years to come. Although AFA will continue focusing on issues that have been vital to our community in the past, it is time for the organization to adapt and prepare for new challenges and opportunities.

With five full-time staff members on board, AFA is well equipped to accomplish great things on behalf of the forestry community for many years to come. In addition to administering AFA's established programs, more staff time can be dedicated to developing and implementing new ideas and activities.

A strategic plan, talented staff, and dedicated board of directors will take the association a long way toward achieving its mission. The rest of the effort, however, is up to each member. Together, we represent an essential element of the state's economy and environment. Therefore, we must show the public that Arkansas's forestry community is doing its part to ensure healthy, productive forests and provide abundant forest products, today and in the future.

We can do this many ways, including strictly following voluntary Best Management Practices, implementing forestry aesthetics, and, most importantly, promoting sound environmental education in our schools. Actions speak louder than words, so we need to act accordingly.

THE NINE KEY ACTIONS TO INCLUDE IN YOUR STRATEGIC INTENT STATEMENT

A number of things can be included in your strategic intent statement. These elements were extracted from the actual strategic intent statement just cited. Obviously the key actions do not capture the spirit, emotion, or energy of the complete statement. Please do not take the items out of context.

1. Refine the organization's mission to stay current.
2. Develop a cohesive strategic plan.
3. Focus on vital community issues.
4. Prepare for new challenges.
5. Administer existing, established programs.
6. Develop and implement new ideas and activities.
7. Follow Best Management Practices.
8. Implement product aesthetics.
9. Promote sound education in schools.

The second major function of a presidential strategic intent statement is to allow subordinate managers to "read the tea leaves" and make personal and professional decisions. Not everyone will like your vision, goals, and the overall direction of your plan. The strategic intent gives them an opportunity to weigh their own potential contributions and possible shortfalls against the company commitment. This is where you start to align individual goals to organizational goals. Tell people what you intend to do in plain language and let them decide if they want to participate. Some will, and some will not.

One of the most cowardly or unethical things a president can do is to declare a strategic intent while secretly working a deal in the opposite direction. I picked up this example by following newspaper and business magazine articles on one of America's most famous "corporate killers." The new president, Mr. X, assumed his current position after a series of similar positions where he had downsized companies to the point of anorexia. Within six months of assuming his new job and after a significant downsizing, Mr. X grandly announced to the remaining employees that his wandering days were over. He had finally found his home. He was prepared to stay forever, making this company his last resting place. Here he could do all the good as a president, turning this company into the perfect model of how a business should perform. At the same time he was secretly negotiating to sell the company as soon as the restructuring, reengineering, and downsizing brought the stock to a certain level. When the stock triggered the sale, he announced the deal, took multiple millions, and moved to another company. All this took place within eighteen months.

How intentions are stated produces different results. A CEO who says, "We want to make the numbers look good because I intend to sell the company within the next two years" will get a different reaction from one who says, "I plan to grow this company for the long term." Either way is okay. It is your management choice. The point is that employees have a different comfort level when they are clear about management's intentions.

SUMMARY

You build your culture around many things, but there are four key ingredients. As a result of working with this chapter you should have developed five distinct products for your story and business plan:

1. A set of values statements
2. A philosophy statement
3. A set of operating principles
4. A set of action items to close identified gaps
5. A strategic intent statement

Each defines and communicates its own unique contribution to the story. Look for deeper meaning with the core values and avoid superficial lists. Write a philosophy statement defining how you intend to operate as a company, and then benchmark your story using principles as the filter. Finally, develop action plans from the gaps you identify. These actions become quick hits necessary to show progress until you get the plan in place.

THE KEY QUESTIONS: DEFINING YOUR CORPORATE CULTURE

As you define your corporate culture, ask yourself these five questions:

1. What is important to my team, my company, and me?
2. Are gaps in our values, philosophy, or principles creating a disturbance in our story?
3. How difficult will it be to change unwanted behaviors that are causing our story to be incongruent?
4. What good principles of business are we violating?
5. What affect do these violations have on the bottom line of our performance?

THE PRACTICAL APPLICATIONS: DEVELOPING CORE VALUES STATEMENTS

These thirteen steps will help you develop the written parts of the materials:

1. Conduct a group discussion with your management team about what is important to your business. List keywords from the comments.
2. Fashion a short list of items you label as values. Do not be concerned with priorities. To spend time rank-ordering the values is nonproductive.
3. Write out the values in behavioral terms. Use action words for the descriptions. Example: We value customers. This means we respond to every call within one hour.
4. Conduct a gap analysis for each value statement.
5. Define actions necessary to close identified gaps.
6. Discuss your business philosophy.
7. Write a philosophy statement.
8. Conduct a gap analysis for the philosophy.
9. Define activities necessary to close identified gaps.
10. Discuss your operating principles and develop a list.
11. Conduct a gap analysis for the principles.
12. Define actions necessary to close the perception gap.
13. Write your strategic intent statement.

As a result of working with this chapter you should have developed five products for your story and business plan.

1. A set of values statements
2. A philosophy statement
3. A set of operating principles
4. A set of action items to close identified gaps
5. A strategic intent statement

8

How to Build a One-Year Operational Plan That Improves Performance

In this chapter you move from the strategic view to the operational applications. Here you separate the strategic from the tactical, the global from the specific, and the long term from the short term. This is where most management energy is focused for execution.

The 1-Page Strategic Plan generally spells out where you intend to take the organization while the operational plan defines how you plan to make the trip. Yet getting to a practical application of a business plan seems to always get lost in the planning process. Earlier you defined the goals, objectives, and tasks necessary to give you three levels of definitions. Now let's examine your business plan up close by defining what must happen next year. This is called the operational plan (see Figure 8-1). The content for the plan is developed during the initial planning conference. All the information for the operational plan can be extracted from the original planning process. This is mostly true for the other plans as well. The real task becomes putting the information into the right portion of the 5-Page Business Plan. In lay language, we call this "getting it in the right bucket."

Figure 8-1. The operational plan sets the direction into motion. It is how you plan to work the next year.

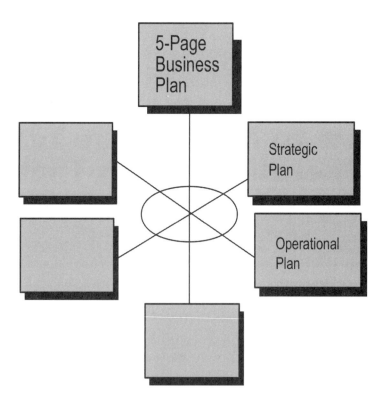

The operational plan usually extends out one year (see Figure 8-2). It is always the first year of your strategic plan, which automatically makes it the first year of your business plan. Although some companies elect to use two or three years, one year is more practical and best fits accepted business reporting standards. One year fits with the quarterly concepts and the annual budget cycle. This permits you to look at your performance on a frequent basis and make annual adjustments if necessary. One year is also about all the detail you can plan without becoming overwhelmed. Do not spend a lot of time, if any, trying to develop the details and numbers for subsequent years because they will be adjusted as you work with your plan over its life span.

Figure 8-2. The operational plan is cut out of the total ten years.

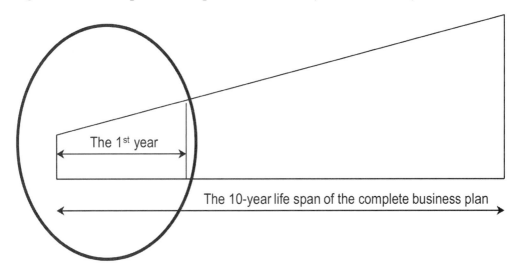

SITUATIONAL ANALYSIS: THE BRIDGE BETWEEN THE STRATEGIC PLAN AND THE OPERATIONAL PLAN

To get from the strategic view to the operational view you must do very detailed thinking. Situational analysis is the middle or second step of the backPlanning process (see Chapter 3), with strategic thinking and operational execution being the first and third steps, respectively. At this stage of planning you must do a reality check. In strategic thinking you examined what you wanted to do in the long term. Now you must carefully consider what can be done in the short term in light of the realities of the business environment in which you must act.

To conduct a good situational analysis, you must consider eight criteria:

1. Analysis of company performance
   a. Current
   b. Historical
2. Analysis of competition
3. Analysis of market share
4. Analysis of mission
   a. Implied tasks
   b. Mission capability
5. Analysis of existing resources
6. Analysis of your business's drivers—excluding, at this time, your primary operational focus (i.e., single focus)
7. Analysis of existing structure
8. Analysis of reference information
   a. Customer satisfaction survey
   b. Employee satisfaction survey
   c. Others as identified

Analysis of Company Performance

As part of the planning model you must conduct self-evaluations. This means taking a hard look at your last year's performance and a second look at your overall performance from a historical view. Usually there is no shortage of charts and graphs depicting how well you did financially for the past year. The analysis usually includes one or more previous years, depending on the size print and complexity of the chart. It always includes actual performance against projected performance. Usually these are just numbers drills.

To be truly effective you need to have some lessons learned. You need to know why the numbers went up or down. Thought must be given to why spikes occurred in your performance. A poor showing cannot be written off as the result of a bad economy or an unexpected downturn. These are simply excuses for mediocre management performance.

This analysis is where you start to sort out the serious planning session from the weekend at the golf resort session. Often managers are unprepared to talk specifics of the current business situation of their industry at a planning session. This can only mean these people came to the meeting unprepared. At your next planning session have your principal attendees give a short briefing to the team on the status of their portion of the business. This can be assigned as homework in the preconference briefing.

The best team I've ever seen do this is Cedarglen Homes in Calgary. The two principal players really know their business. Robert Bezemer and Scott Haggins can talk for hours about the back corners of the industry in Calgary, Alberta, and all of Canada. That is because they are out every day dealing with the details of what it takes to run a successful building company. This means they are doing more than just building houses. Both executives are involved and have a genuine interest in how their company fits into the social fabric of the community. They spend a considerable amount of time with customers, other builders, and the trades. This pays off with a multiplier effect.

Analysis of Competition

Many planners want to start the initial planning process with a SWOT (strengths, weaknesses, opportunities, and threats) analysis. I disagree. While this is critical information to validate the planning content, it is the wrong starting point. To be creative and bold in planning the team must start with the future and work back-ward, so I advocate the backPlanning approach. This future orien-tation removes the inherent limitations placed on the thinking process. Once team members decide where they want to go, they can test the validity of their decision with the situational analysis to determine the plausibility and practicality of the plan.

If you are dead set on starting your planning process with a competitive analysis flavor, think about these two points. First, the more time you spend in competition the less time you have to accomplish your own goals. Second, why do you care about the competition, anyway? If you are accomplishing your goals, which you freely set, why should you have more than a passing interest in the competition? You need a healthy respect for your competitors and should honor them as legitimate players in the market, but don't overdo it.

What I've observed is that competitive strategy actually should be called competitive obsession. Management consultants have led us astray in this area by building large, complex schemas for strate-gic thinking and planning based on intricate formulas for compet-itiveness. This approach appeals to the macho tendencies often found in the upper levels of management. You don't need a lot of competitiveness except toward one thing—your vision and its asso-ciated strategic goals.

Analysis of Market and Market Share

What is your market and who is your customer? Don't tell me everyone! Someone once asked Willie Sutton, the famous American bank robber, why he robbed banks. His answer was very insightful. "Because that's where they keep the money." A danger is to not know where the money is kept. Are you guilty of selling or servic-ing every customer with no real knowledge if it is a profitable sale or not? When was the last time you did a careful screening of your sales to decide which customers should be dropped?

Some companies think any sale is a good sale. That is simply not so. You may be robbing a convenience store after-hours instead of a bank on payday. It's hard to turn down an order when your people are not busy or your machines are idle. The normal justification for marginal to nonprofitable sales is to exercise the equipment, keep the plant running, and pay for overhead. Well, that has a downside, too. I'm not suggesting you turn down work or turn away orders. What I am suggesting is that you look at work to see if it is profitable.

Define your market and, specifically, who is and who is not your customer. The latter is just as important as the former. When EZCertify.com developed its business plan, the management focused like a laser on this issue. After careful market analysis they determined exactly who they were attempting to reach with their product. By first defining the market and then the profile of the actual customer within that market they were able to develop realistic annual targets. Without this information your operational planning targets are going to be guesses at best and badly skewed.

Analysis of Mission

Give your mission statement another look during the planning process. Make certain that you fully understand the implied tasks of the mission statement. This gives you coordination points for activities that cross boundaries between staff functions. Ask these five key questions as a validity check:

1. What am I being asked to do in the mission statement that is not spelled out in the text?

2. Are there implications of those tasks that may or may not be fully understood and appreciated?

3. What resources are going to be implicated when the hidden tasks are brought to execution?

4. Have we coordinated those implied tasks among the management team?

5. Are we fully committed to the range of tasks?

Another reason to revisit the mission statement is to confirm your mission capability. That is defined as your ability to carry out the requirements. In the plan that means you must be able to hit the targets you are setting for the first year. Not only is mission capability a planning issue, it has leadership implications as well. Too often managers set targets, objectives, or goals that are beyond the capabilities of the management team. Test your reality by asking several hard questions. Start with the following six about your team and their ability to fulfill the mission:

1. Does my team have the management maturity to complete the mission?

2. Do they have the wisdom, experience, and judgment to be successful?

3. Are they willing to commit the time, energy, and effort to accomplish the mission?

4. Can they complete the mission or operational tasks being set within the time frames being established?

5. Are we giving the team the right tools and equipment to get the job done?

6. Will they have enough information to properly do their job in the spirit in which intended?

Analysis of Resources

You must review the resources requirement from two perspectives: strategic and tactical. (Later, in Chapter 10, we look at the complete resources plan by addressing strategic resources in more detail.)

For tactical or short-term existing resources supporting your operational plan, you must be ruthlessly analytical. A great danger of planning is to overcommit tasks and targets without adequate resources for support. Consider these ten items when looking at your existing resources base to support the operational plan:

1. Time

    a. Have we distributed the tasks over the right time frame by quarter?

    b. Is the time frame realistic for the task at hand?

2. Information

    a. Do I have the right amount of information on hand to make short-term decisions?

    b. What additional data must I gather to support my decisions?

    c. How will I manage the volume of information currently flowing through the system?

    d. What are obstacles and barriers to overcome for effective communication of information?

3. Staffing levels

    a. Do I have the right amount of people in place to accomplish the tasks?

    b. Are the right skills represented among the workforce?

    c. Will I be able to find and hire against my job skills shortfall?

    d. Can I afford to pay for the core competencies I need?

4. Facilities

    a. Do we have adequate facilities to get the work done?

    b. Are conditions in the offices, plants, or facilities conducive to effective work?

5. Tools and equipment

    a. Do we have the right items on hand to properly do the job?

    b. Can we afford any upgrades or replacements required?

    c. How soon will we be able to get the tools and equipment needed?

6. Technology

   a. Will our existing technology be able to keep pace with the action plan?

   b. Can we afford to leapfrog technology?

   c. What will be the implications of working with outdated technology if our competitor is state-of-the-art?

7. Relationships

   a. Do we have the right partnerships, alliances, and outsource partners for the mission?

   b. How difficult will it be to put a relationship in place to meet mission deadlines?

   c. Are there old relationships that must be renegotiated or dropped?

8. Intellectual capital

   a. Do I have people with the willingness to share experiences for a synergistic effect?

   b. Do we have a formal database of lessons learned to draw from along the way?

9. Financial

   a. Do we have the money to support the annual plan?

   b. Have budget considerations been included as an internal part of the planning process or are they an add-on feature?

10. Image

    a. Will our brand recognition help or hinder us from reaching the intended annual targets?

    b. How must marketing be cranked up to support the plan?

    c. Are there customer or community activities that need to be renewed or revisited?

d. How can we make the most of our good name and reputation?

Analysis of Drivers

In the planning conference you examined six key business drivers and initially selected a single business driver as your focus. The single focus creates alignment. Now you must account for the remaining five drivers. You need to ask specific questions of your operations to make sure none of the other five have been neglected. Case in point: Although Wal-Mart is not a customer-intimate business, it certainly doesn't mistreat the customer. Regardless of which driver you select as your focus, you must maintain an acceptable level of performance with the other five. Ask these questions for each driver:

Players

1. Am I taking care of my employees? Does my plan facilitate the employee component of our business, or is it a punitive document?

2. Am I solving my customers' problems? Have I looked at what is at the center of my operational focus—customers or things?

Plans

1. Are we operating in a planned way, or are we living from day to day? Is the span of time for our plan long enough, or have we been too limiting in time?

2. Are we disciplined about how we do business? Do we have accountability measures in place to make sure the plan is followed? Do the rewards and compensations match the desired results of the plan?

Processes

1. Are we operationally efficient? Do we have a plan for controlling overhead?

2. Do we pay attention to our business process? Are we upgrading our ways of doing business or just continuing to do business the same old way?

3. What is our level of heat loss? Do we know how much money is draining out the bottom through inefficient processes? What is our plan to fix the loss?

Products, Goods, and Services

1. Are we single-product focused with no alternatives? What would be the implications of additional products? Have we let go of obsolete but emotional lines of goods?

2. Where do we make our money? Is our attention and focus in the right place?

Properties

1. Are we using our intellectual capital database as well as we should? Is teamwork required of our people?

2. Are we protecting and preserving our capital assets? Are we willing to invest money to make money with our facilities and equipment?

Payoffs

1. Why should our customers buy from us? Have we made the connection to our customers worth their effort?

2. Why should people work for us? Are we realistic about what it costs to court and retain labor? Are we willing to be top-of-the-line, or do we choose to be second string in matters such as benefits? Can we afford it?

Analysis of Structure

To implement your operational plan you need the proper structure. This topic has two halves and will be addressed in two places. The big picture structural issues will be discussed in more detail in

Chapter 9, in relationship to the complete business plan. For the annual activities, let's examine what we need to do from an organizational viewpoint. You need to look at your plan from three perspectives:

1. Organizational charting

    a. Do you have the right teams in place to carry out the mission?

    b. Are the reporting relationships lean and efficient?

    c. Is the organization structure as flat as possible?

2. Soft infrastructure

    a. Have you defined the right authority levels to facilitate immediate implementation of the plan?

    b. Have you communicated your expectations of responsibility for execution of the plan?

    c. Have you defined the accountability and how it will be exercised in the first year of the plan?

3. Hard infrastructure

    a. Are the physical facilities set up to support the mission?

    b. Do you have the right equipment spotted at the right locations?

Analysis of Reference Information

There is a wealth of information available to you for a situational analysis. You may have a customer satisfaction survey that provides details on a range of vital items. Use this information to cross-check your goals and supporting tasks. The key questions to ask are as follows:

■ Are we satisfied with the current customer satisfaction rating? If not, what must we change?

■ Does the plan allow for improving the customer relationship?

■   How does the customer fit into the total picture of the plan?

You may use an employee satisfaction survey to determine the culture temperature of your workforce. The data may or may not be translated into a goal. In all cases the purpose of gathering reference information is so you can apply it to the development of action items to close identified gaps. For your situational analysis you should know the answers to these questions:

■   What is the employee feedback telling us in relationship to the plan?

■   Is the plan too ambitious or too conservative in relationship to our employee base?

■   What roles are specifically designated in the plan?

■   What actions are necessary to close any employee satisfaction gap?

THE KEY COMPONENTS OF AN EFFECTIVE OPERATIONAL PLAN

The operational plan is a busy document, containing a number of important components. They are:

■   Annual targets

■   Quarterly target(s)

■   A comprehensive tasks list with respective accountabilities, authorities, and responsibilities

■   Tactics

■   Coordinating instructions

■   Concept of operation

The operational plan is where you start to get very specific about things to do for the next year.

Choose Annual Targets

From your planning process you need to scale down the numbers from the strategic goals and select numbers for one year out. These become your annual targets, which are critical to your fiscal health and well-being. This is what the stockholders and Wall Street grades you on. Everything you do for the next year should focus on meeting the annual target you set.

To set annual targets review your goals and objectives. Examine one objective and determine how much you can accomplish next year. Apply realism to the target based on the previous description of the situational analysis. Repeat the process until targets are set for the remainder of the objectives.

Avoid the twin dangers of setting the targets too high or too low. The first danger of shooting too high comes from the inherent enthusiasm found when planning. It is easy to sign up for more than you can do based on the adrenaline high from the process. To avoid this danger, apply the situational analysis measures and make a determination.

Setting targets too low is equally a danger because not enough will be accomplished to put you on the correct climb for your strategic goals. Frequently a low target is set for the first year then repeated the second and third years to produce a hockey stick performance figure (see Figure 8-3). The management rationale is to stay relatively flat for several years to get systems in place or ramp up the activity. This may or may not be valid. I've worked with several CEOs who will not allow a flat model of any type. Their thinking is that a hockey stick model permits continued mediocre performance rather than demanding improved performance from the plan. Interestingly, each CEO has been able to get the company to rise to the occasion and make the numbers over sustained periods of time.

Figure 8-3. The hockey stick model allows an organization to get by for several years with less than satisfactory performance. As the flat spot is extended year after year with only small growth, the real target is identified.

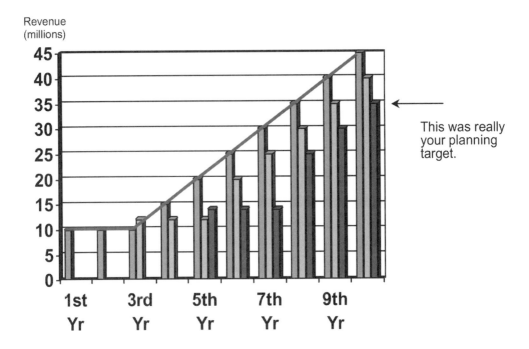

Set Quarterly Performance Measurements

Waiting a full year to see how well you are performing against your annual targets is not good business. You need interim measurements. These are usually done on a quarterly basis. Business is based on quarterly measurements, so there is a need to be consistent across quarters. It is common to rely on one single quarter to pull out your numbers for the year. This is a traditional but dangerous way to work. Look carefully at the distribution of your sales, cash flow, and other measurements to see how they can be equally spread across all four quarters.

Measuring against quarterly performance has both an upside and a downside. The positive aspect is the fact that you are controlling the work and results on an incremental basis. The downside is that you may tend to overcontrol if the quarter is not exactly on target. A planner must exercise great care when the plan doesn't make target in the first quarter. The tough question is to decide whether the plan is off because the original number was bad or because of the zigzag deviation of normal projections. To oversteer the plan will cause an erratic performance. To wait too many quarters before taking action can be equally dangerous because you are too close to year-end to make up the shortfall. Judging how and when to make course corrections is one of the toughest calls in planning. Use judgment and trust your original thinking before you change targets. Make corrections only when you see new, additional, or contradicting data that suggests an error in your original thinking.

Concentrate on Key Tasks

Earlier we moved from goals to objectives to tasks. These tasks are the operational end of the "what" you have to do, the end of the action chain. They are at the opposite end of the goal. Be careful in defining tasks because they can overwhelm you. Again I suggest you create a master task list and translate them to processes. Cut out all extraneous tasks and stick to the few things that must be done for mission accomplishment. Each task must have assigned times and responsibilities. Who will do the task by when? A common document found in planning and useful to the implementation of the plan is an action plan. This is nothing more than a control sheet to list the particulars of all the tasks. The action plan can be as simple or complex as you like. The intention of the document is to be able to see all the actions and related information in one place.

Define Tactics

Review the list of tactics you developed in conjunction with the strategies. Make sure they are reasonable in view of a one-year time frame. Remember, tactics require resources and you will need to make allowances for those requirements.

Coordinate the Operational Plan

You will need to be specific in your operational plan as to who must coordinate with whom. Sadly, managers cannot be left to their own initiatives for coordination. Spell it out. Make them cross organizational boundaries and climb out of their stovepipes to coordinate a task. Hold them accountable as a team for a result. This will force people to work together.

Summarize the Short-Term Plan With a Concept of Operation

A technique used to create operational alignment is to present the total concept of what you will be doing but in a thumbnail format. Write a short paragraph defining how you will be approaching the first year. Be as specific as necessary with strategic business units and staff sections to ensure they understand the total plan and the part they are playing. Consider this a mini-executive summary.

Now you have the components of the operational plan in place. This gives you a good summary of the status of your current reality. Building the short-term plan required you to be brutal when examining your present performance and the potential capacities. From this point you need to complete an additional level of analysis to determine where your plan may fail.

HOW TO IMPROVE YOUR OPERATIONAL PLAN EFFICIENCY

Have you ever had a good operational plan and it just didn't seem to work? No one big thing killed your projections. No matter what you did, how hard you tried, or how diligent you were to the market, the numbers just didn't materialize at the end of the year.

That's because there is a hidden force within your organization that takes away your profits a little bite at a time. On close examination some are found to be big bites and some are small, multiple bites. This organizational inefficiency is called heat loss and will defeat your annual targets.

Heat Loss: The Hidden Force That Chips Away at Your Profits

It does little good to generate more annual revenue if the profits are being drained out through the cracks in your organization's performance. This heat loss stems from many sources (see Figure 8-4). An example of a big savings is Nortel Networks outsourcing its information technology services to Computer Sciences in August 2000. Along with five other outsourcing pacts, the company expects to save approximately $300 million a year. That is recovery of a big bite of heat loss.

But heat loss is not recovered just from outsourcing $3 billion of IT services to Computer Sciences over seven years. Millions of dollars a year are found in the combined little losses. This is called the death of a thousand cuts—an old knife fighter's metaphor. Examples of these small cuts are plentiful in the business world around us. Here are nine of them:

1. Telephone tag with someone who left a message, "Please call me."

2. Merchandise returned with no information or return authorization.

3. Lateness to meetings accepted as part of the cultural norm.

4. Receipt of 283 e-mail messages in three days, of which only eight were important.

5. Money spent to complete a project and the materials, programs, or products are never used.

6. Annual strategic planning conferences that are never completed at the employee level.

7. Training seminars that are not connected to the business plan that become an education, skill, or knowledge shortfall.

8. Seminar participants who are not held accountable by management for integrating and implementing training.

9. Participants leaving conferences and seminars early.

Figure 8-4. It does little good to develop more business while your profits are draining out the bottom due to operational inefficiencies.

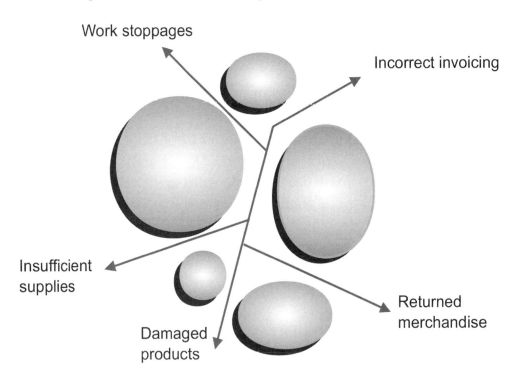

If you want other good examples of these small, annoying, and destructive cuts, ask your employees. They can probably give you dozens. A young manager was asked to identify his greatest loss of efficiency. His answer was almost instantaneous. It was in the area of time management. The manager is David W. Rector, Jr., formerly the North American Operations Manager for the Industrial Products Division of Taconic in New York State. David said, "People don't understand the value of a manager's time. They don't seem to get the fact that it is a resource that cannot be replenished. This is a fundamental error on their part. I struggle with it every day—people coming in late for meetings, events not starting on time, participating on unnecessary committees. These just drain my ability to get my job done in an effective manner."

Four common business behaviors trigger heat loss. They seem to occur in large organizations but are not restricted to them. Small organizations usually cannot afford the inherent heat loss so they intuitively fix the problems. There may be a loose correlation between profitable, medium to large organizations and those who have higher degrees of heat loss. The four behaviors are as follows:

1. Most organizations think they are well run and don't realize the profits draining out the cracks in their operations.

2. Most organizations have no idea how much the dollar values of their heat loss amounts to each year.

3. Most organizations don't understand the fastest way to recover resources is to eliminate waste in their business processes.

4. Most organizations don't have disciplined methods to recover the heat loss.

After a daylong ride with a driver delivering propane, we gathered at the yard to prepare the trucks for the following day. I casually asked the drivers, "Well, did we make any money today?" The answer: "We must have because we sure pumped a lot of propane." Yes, but did we pump it to the right accounts in the right amounts should have been one question. A second question should have been, did we do it in an efficient manner? The answer to the second question would have probably been no. One of the greatest challenges facing the vice president of operations was to get drivers to adjust to efficient routing by the computer instead of door-to-door sequential deliveries. It seems logical to a driver with years of experience to catch the next house down the street. Yet when the operations staff ran cost data to demonstrate the compared efficiencies of the two models, the drivers still disbelieved.

Heat loss takes on many forms. These forms cause the organization to function at less than maximum performance levels. It can be overt or it can be subtle. The loss of organizational effectiveness can be small or large. In all cases, taking out wasted motion is important to your story because it improves the bottom-line profits. To find these central pools of loss, look closely at two areas:

1. Islands of power (where power in many forms is being used in an unproductive fashion)

2. White space (places in your organization where the lack of assigned responsibility and accountability are creating losses)

Islands of Power: When Control Is Lopsided

Islands of power occur when someone or some group has a need to control another to the level where a disproportional ratio of power exists. This can be in information, money, or other resources (see Figure 8-5). Heat loss occurs when you find lopsided power ratios.

Figure 8-5. Heat loss starts when the company doesn't work in a coordinated team fashion.

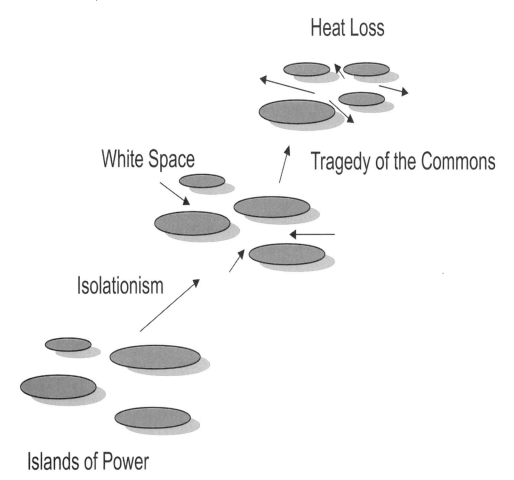

There is a folk saying, "Absolute power corrupts absolutely." When one staff section has excessive power over the other functions, abuse begins to occur no matter how pure of heart people try to act. The primary reason this is dangerous to your organization is that bad and often costly decisions are made. When quality information is discouraged or rejected by those in power, the company is cut off from vital facts and figures necessary to make informed decisions. Bad decisions waste resources that ultimately can reach the bottom-line profit levels.

Islands of power exist at other levels above the internal staff functions of your organization. Just as one power broker in your organization affects your bottom line, the same influence is felt in an industry, a nation, or an international situation. One island of power that is difficult to understand is how land developers have been able to bully and intimidate the building industry in Calgary. Canada is one country that has no shortage of land. Its population base is small compared with the acreage in the country. Fly into Alberta and look at the vast stretches of land adjacent to Calgary. Yet if you wish to build a house in Calgary you will pay homage to the land developers.

Another example at the world level has been the control of the diamond industry by De Beers. Historically, De Beers has been able to control the sources, dictate terms to the dealers, and set the price for diamonds. South Africa is not the only country in the world to produce diamonds. Russia has a huge quantity of large, gem-grade stones available and is giving the monopoly a difficult time. Canada is rich in potential diamond sites with one mine in production and a number of potential sites ready for development. Both Winspear Diamonds, Inc. and Darnley Bay Resources Ltd. are Canadian diamond forces to be dealt with. Arkansas has a reportedly large diamond site, yet it was immediately placed within a national park shortly after the find was made.

Information also can be used as a power source. For centuries people have known that to control knowledge is to control the population. Dictators like to keep people uninformed. By controlling the information that people receive through the media the truth can be distorted to an advantage.

Remember when only a few people had all the knowledge of hardware and how software controlled computers? These chosen few lived on their own floor of the building where it was cold enough to hang meat. They wore white coats and talked in a funny language that us neophytes couldn't understand. Any simple request for computer support was answered with a lengthy explanation of why you didn't want that, it couldn't be done, or it would take a minimum of six months to program. The antidote for this behavior was the invention of the personal computer.

White Space: When No One Is Held Accountable

What islands of power eventually lead to is a breakup of the integrity of the organization's operating processes. As communications shut down, political warfare rages, and mission-essential energy is deflected, the gulf between and among the staff functions widens. This creates a vast area called white space, or spaces between the operating behaviors that are ignored or neglected. Nonresponsibility and accountability for common items also create white space across the organization's operating requirements.

A huge amount of organizational heat loss occurs when there is default in controlling or managing the resource, the problem, or the situation. In all organizations there exist common grounds used by all participants but assigned to no particular staff agency. What happens is that everyone uses the resource but doesn't maintain the property. An ecologist, Garrett Hardin, first identified this concept. He defined what he called the Tragedy of the Commons to be " . . . situations where two conditions are met." He further explained the two conditions as follows:

> *[1] there exists a "commons," a resource shared among a group of people, and [2] individual decision makers, free to dictate their own actions, achieve short-term gains from exploiting the resources but do not pay, and are often unaware of, the cost of that exploitation—except in the long run.*[1]

For a simple explanation of the concept, think of a village that owns a pasture where all families could graze their flocks. When the pasture was overgrazed, who could be held accountable?

The oceans of today are a prime example of the commons. Who has responsibility for the fisheries of the ocean? Countries have tried to extend territorial waters to protect those rights. Often this is seen as imperialism instead of protectionism. Canada is so concerned with the ocean fishing industry's status that it fired a shot across the bow of a Spanish trawler to stop what it considered illegal, harmful fishing. This incident is an act of war—firing on another country's ship on the high seas. A world court later vindicated the Canadian forces.

A business example of the commons is the area of morale. Who is responsible for morale in a company? When we speak of leadership and people issues we often think of the human resources department. The correct answer is that every manager and supervisor is responsible. Then what about the saying, "If everyone is in charge, then no one is in charge"? Morale is not something that can be designated as a staff responsibility, yet someone has to answer when morale is lacking or low. Thinking that it is the responsibility of human resources is an absurd avoidance of management responsibility. The U.S. military has a clear stand on the issue. The unit commander is responsible for all her unit does or fails to do. That sums it up.

Business Process Mapping: A Practical Tool for Eliminating Corporate Excess

This section explains how to conduct process mapping as an activity to get momentum going for your operational plan. Instructions for more detailed process mapping for the complete business plan are presented in Chapter 12. Do not attempt to process map during the initial planning conference. The volume of work is too large and you do not have all the right players at the conference. Wait to do this as an operational activity.

Process mapping your operational requirements has five payoffs:

1. To present a tool to better understand your current working processes

2. To learn a process approach to reducing visible inefficiencies

3. To solve current process problems using the team approach

4. To measure improvements for quarterly and annual targets

5. To provide specific performance benchmarks for daily behavior

Here is the fastest way to set up a process map activity:

- Identify two or three critical processes that you suspect to be a source of recoverable time, money, or effort. If you don't have several candidates, ask your firstline supervisors or people who are directly in contact with the work processes. They can give you an extensive list.

- Assemble a team of people around a large, long table that is covered in newsprint or plain paper. A long roll of brown "butcher" paper works well. Provide a quantity of assorted colored sticky notes.

- Map out the problem.

- Connect the expected result of the improved process directly to the operational plan at the quarterly target points (see Figure 8-6). This gives you a way to measure the progress of your plan and to check the results of your mapping efforts.

Figure 8-6. Your operational plan should contain well-defined quarterly targets for responsibility and accountability. As illustrated here, the targets will not necessarily be equal across quarters.

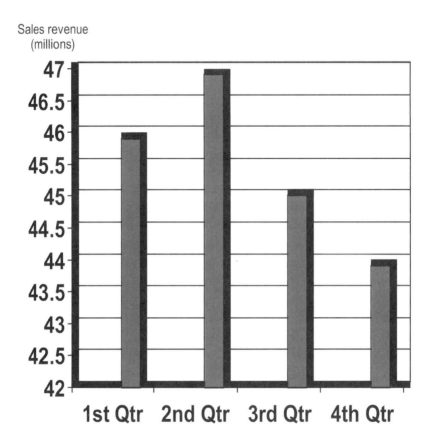

THE PAYOFFS FROM ELIMINATING ORGANIZATIONAL INEFFICIENCIES

The payoffs for being efficient are staggering. In the projections for Nortel Networks, they run into the hundreds of millions of dollars per year. For the average-size company the payoffs can mean equally important savings, especially when extrapolated over the life span of the plan. Here are a few examples from a wide range of industries:

■   A manufacturing company saved six week of downtime for annual maintenance on its big machines. By replicating the process and modifying the procedures, the manufacturer found similar savings with the medium and small machines. The results were machines turned around and back in production six weeks faster.

■   A hospital saved approximately $295 per patient by examining its patient appointment notification package. By looking at the purpose of the package, the hospital trimmed the contents and total costs to approximately $5 per patient.

■   A propane company found it cost approximately $1.2 million to process new customer records. By eliminating all unnecessary information requests and consolidating the screens from twenty to two, it brought the cost down to $300,000.

■   A chemical company found $500,000 of stainless steel drums not being effectively used. By removing the customer names (a marketing tactic) and recycling the drums, it put $500,000 of assets back into play.

■   An automobile company cut 100 weeks out of a 146-week cycle for precision parts tooling. Although the company spent a whopping $16 million, it found repetitive annual savings of nearly a quarter-billion dollars.

Paying attention to your operating losses can have a significant influence on your annual operating plan. By setting realistic targets and removing inefficient processes you increase your chances of meeting annual targets.

SUMMARY

This chapter has presented the left side of the business plan, the immediate year, or the operational portion of the five plans. Items found in the operational plan are usually more familiar to a planning team because they are the more common elements. This means an operational plan should be comfortable territory for both the planners and the implementers.

THE KEY QUESTIONS: WRITING YOUR OPERATIONAL PLAN

Use the following nine questions to stir creativity around your operational element of the planning cycle:

1. Do we have solid annual targets?
2. Can those targets be translated into more manageable quarterly targets?
3. Is the task list of everything that needs to be done as complete as necessary?
4. What tactics must be used to make the operational plan a success?
5. Did we cross-coordinate all the implied tasks from the mission statement?
6. How truthful is our assessment of the current situation?
7. Did we properly identify who should and should not be in our target markets?
8. Did we match our products, goods, and services to the financial numbers to see if we can achieve our annual target?
9. What steps were taken to plan for, or eliminate, barriers and obstacles to the operations plan?

THE PRACTICAL APPLICATIONS: IMPROVING OPERATIONAL ACTIVITIES

As a result of this chapter you should have developed the following two items:

1. A 1-Page Operational Plan

2. A set of process maps that directly improve your operational activities

9

Structuring Your Story: How to Develop an Organizational Plan

This chapter examines the third of the five types of planning you must develop for a complete business plan, as seen in Figure 9-1. You'll discover how to break away from the traditional forms of structure and explore new ways of looking at organizing work. The chapter also includes information for you to integrate an organizational plan into your overall planning model.

Figure 9-1. The organizational plan is the platform from which you structure resources and control work.

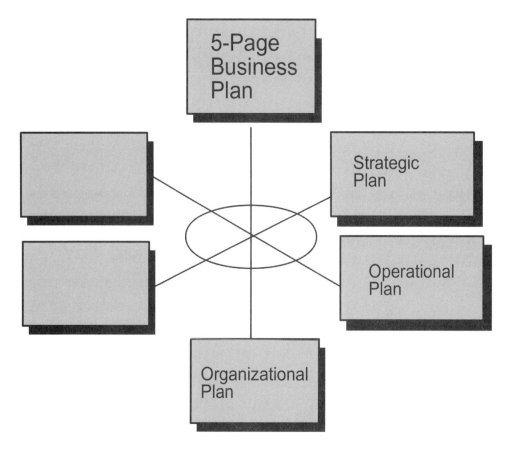

THE FIVE KEY FUNCTIONS OF AN ORGANIZATIONAL STRUCTURE

The five purposes of your organizational structure are to:

1. Organize work.
2. Provide a resource vehicle for the implementation of strategies.
3. Match headcount to responsibilities.

4. Create a place for employees to experience belonging.

5. Control costs.

Let's look at each of these purposes more closely.

Organize Work

Structure (as opposed to no structure) provides a framework or template to accomplish a number of functions within your business. Organizations work better than mobs. Since the first people banded together to fight saber-toothed tigers, they came to a realization that working together has more rewards than independent actions. By coordinating the task at hand, more efficient use is made of the mob's total resources. From the concept of division of labor came the next logical step. Those groups of labor must be coordinated in some fashion. The hunters must be coordinated with the gatherers who must be coordinated with the camp watchers. Thus, the primitive functions of organizations began.

Alfred Sloan of General Motors is given credit for being the first to really perfect the concept of the corporation as an organizing institution. He did for organizing management what Henry Ford did for organizing the production line.[1] His idea of decentralized work under semiautonomous operating units, but with rigid and formal command and control, became the standard of business. Sloan's concept of having a group of managers formally directing workers, while cold and impersonal, was quite sophisticated for its time.

Provide a Means to Implement Strategies

Organizational structure provides an important service as the implementation activity of your strategies. Without a structure there would be no intelligent assembly of resources to carry on work. Julius Caesar understood the concept of organization and structure in fighting the Celts in northern Europe. He observed that the Celtic warriors were fierce individual fighters who could be overwhelming in the first rush of battle. More important, he recognized that they were not organized as a cohesive fighting unit and their energies dissipated as the engagement continued. His strategy was to hold in place and survive the onslaught of the first contact. This was accomplished with tight formations of troops with an almost impenetrable structure called the "box formation." This structure and strategy combination permitted Caesar to use inferior numbers to defeat much larger forces.[2]

Match Headcount to Responsibility

A third function of your structure is to match headcount to responsibilities. This means you use the talents and efforts of all your people and resources. A properly built structure avoids duplication and fragmentation of essential tasks. In fact, an economy of effort is achieved because you have enough people to match the tasks and the right people with the right skills. There should be a form of linkage between who is assigned and what is required. This means your plan and your operational behaviors are in step.

Create a Place Where Employees Feel They Belong

The fourth purpose of structure is to provide identification, order, and stability. People can identify with your structure. That's why companies go to great lengths with logos and symbols for internal and external recognition. A few years ago people didn't display their company symbols on their personal items. It was not cool to be known as a company person. In fact, some people were not very proud of their companies. Now it is very popular to carry a briefcase with your company logo discreetly embossed on the side. A good company has no trouble getting its employees to wear articles of clothing displaying its letters or logo.

Structure gives a comfort level of order to what could be confusion. People like to know where they stand in relationships, power bases, and the general pecking order. Where this got out of hand in the traditional structures was the corporate ladder and the need to climb to the top. My father worked for Gulf Oil for thirty years. His sage advice to me was, "Son, go to college, get your degree, and go to work for a big company. They will take care of you for life." What he meant was, work hard, climb the corporate ladder, and retire somewhere near the top with a cup of Kool-Aid, a gold watch, and a good retirement package.

My father's intent was for me to play the corporate game for thirty-five to forty years. Climbing the corporate ladder was the standard or accepted practice to get ahead in his time. Now my children have no need to play the corporate ladder game because the ladder is rapidly becoming a step stool. Organizations are tending to flatten out with fewer and fewer layers. There is no ladder to climb. How, then, does a structure attract and encourage young supertalent? We know it is not with promises of rewards based on tenure. The attractions must be in the quality of work and the potential for individual contributions.

There will always be a segment of the workforce that has a need for a structure that is the encompassing place to work—everything is accounted for and controlled. Dad was a product of Texas in the early 1900s when times were tough. He knew what it was like to have holes in the bottom of his cowboy boots. To him, a large company was a refuge where he could work hard and be rewarded. His future was secure as long as he remained loyal to Gulf. That was the mind-set of his generation and how he saw corporate life.

Planning must have been easy in traditional work situations. With workforce stability a manager of yesteryear could plan and project the company structure to infinity. It was a simple formula of growing and doing more of the same. There was no need to tamper with the organization's structure except to make it even bigger.

That norm of endless continuity is dead. Today my children would laugh at their grandfather's advice. They see themselves moving around in their professions and careers as frequently as necessary to achieve whatever they wish to achieve. One of our daughters is a computer engineer. When she talks about her career and her challenges, it doesn't include tenure with her present company. She freely admits expecting to change companies every two to three years with no qualms about moving. Her comments to me about loyalty seem to sum it up: "Dad, these companies have no loyalty to their employees. They use us, so why shouldn't we use them? I know what I'm worth on the market, so why shouldn't I move on to use my talents and enjoy the rewards?"

I don't know if there is a moral judgment to this conversation with my daughter. I do know that managers who build their business plans on the assumption of a stable workforce with a fixed structure are in serious trouble from the beginning. No longer can organizational structure be based on the loyalty factor. Once it could be used as an emotional tie by management to the employees. Today, companies are reaping the fruits of decades of employee abuse, mismanagement, and poor relationships. If they want loyalty from these new whiz kids who know how to make computers talk, then the loyalty is measured in what rewards, compensation, and pay are offered.

Control Costs

Your structure should help you determine financial status. While organization cost control takes many forms, the most simple is the employee/profit ratio. By clearly accounting for all employees and matching headcount to profit, you determine a cost or profit ratio. In simple terms, each employee is worth how many dollars in profit. This is one simple method to determine how you are doing at the macro level. By changing the number of employees you can raise the ratio in either direction. Add more people to do more work or add more people who become costly overhead. Reduce people and your profit goes up.

Profitable companies are catching on to this trick and cutting out layers of management and employees in the distasteful process called downsizing. This practice has sociological implications far beyond the short-term increase in profitability. Downsizing gets great responses from Wall Street because it looks at short-term profitability. Downsizing, however, has a serious effect on employees' morale.

Many years ago a colleague wrote about the concept of the informal contract. Dr. T. O. Jacobs described a tacit understanding between employees and management.[3] That understanding was summed up as follows: There are no layoffs when we are profitable. For decades, management honored the unwritten rule. Modern management is ignoring this informal contract and reducing the structures and headcounts during record profit times. A twenty-first-century case in point is Standard Charter PLC, a bank with 33,000 employees based in Asia, the Middle East, and Africa. In August 2000 it announced a cut of 20 percent of the workforce. This was in spite of improved first-half economics where revenue increased by 9 percent, pretax profit doubled, and forecasted GDP growth was well over 5 percent.

This example of breaking the unwritten rules leaves employees to question the ulterior motives of management. Employees see greed as the management driver with no loyalty to the people who created the success and subsequent wealth. It further deepens, widens, and anchors the distrust chasm between management and employees. Employees distrust companies that downsize in good times, quickly projecting what will happen when times turn bad.

While reducing structures does reduce overall costs, care must be taken to avoid repercussions in other areas. One example of a trade-off in reducing headcount by downsizing is the loss of institutional memory. There is no way to calculate the damage done to organizations by the excessive downsizing and subsequent loss of intellectual capital. Don't make the same mistakes. If you plan to restructure, then do it wisely by carefully thinking through what you stand to gain or lose.

A CAUTION WHEN DEVELOPING STRUCTURE

Today it is mostly a shell game of revitalizing organizational structures. That's because during the planning process managers simply move boxes around on the organizational wiring diagram. This doesn't change the core way they support their businesses. If your structure is not matching strategy, then the structure is out of alignment. Don't make the fatal mistake of changing the strategy to meet the structural requirements. That is definitely a tail wagging the dog approach. When you develop your business plan, ask tough questions, such as:

- Will this structure accomplish my vision?
- How much of this structure is applied to goal accomplishment?
- How much of this structure is to maintain overhead?
- How much of this structure is dedicated to long-term development?
- How do I need to modify my structure for the short term?
- What do I need to do to position my resources for future structural requirements?

Another false start at organizational restructuring is thinking that improving the processes solves all problems. Improving processes may simply mean improving a bad process that actually should be removed. Let's not take our businesses through another generation of reengineering. Most astute managers are aware that reengineering is a dismal failure as a management concept. It is synonymous with getting rid of people to bring up the stock prices. It is usually done in one functional area at the expense of other functional processes or the total business. I doubt if we could find a handful of companies that looked at reengineering the total organization from top to bottom in one strategic move. Instead of reengineering your company, scrutinize your structure and look for answers to these questions:

- Has duplication of effort been eliminated?
- Is there fragmentation of tasks?
- Is the right person doing the work?

- Is all work being done that should be done?
- Is any unnecessary work being done?

THE SIX CRITICAL PARTS OF A SUCCESSFUL ORGANIZATIONAL STRUCTURE

We need a template for organizational structure that answers to certain traditional values yet stays modern enough to be viable in the new millennium. The model must answer tough questions and concerns businesspeople bring up during the transitional period of business chaos. The future structure must accomplish several things to make it acceptable among businesspeople, especially those hard-line managers who have seen it all over the years.

There are at least six dimensions of the template that the structure must support:

1. *Control.* Allow management, who is ultimately responsible, to have some form of control over the business processes and the expected results.

2. *Accountability.* Someone must ultimately be accountable. Don't say teams, because that just doesn't happen. Empowerment can be used for the mass of employees, but eventually a single manager must be held accountable to the system.

3. *Rapid Response.* Long lead times are not acceptable. Organizations must become accustomed to playing by the rule of first on the scene with the most value wins the medal.

4. *High Performance.* There will always be low-, medium-, and high-performing companies. That's the nature of statistics and the law of averages. If you want to be a world-class organization, your structure must be designed to deliver above and beyond the norm. It must be geared to high performance.

5. *Correct Decision Taking.* A future structure must permit all levels of people to make decisions at points in time necessary for the situations. Decentralized decisions become the norm of the day.

6. *Accurate Analysis.* A business case or competitive analysis that must work its way from the bottom of an organization to the top, survive multiple political edits, and be influenced by managers with vested interests in the findings is no longer acceptable in real time. Managers must be able to access information, sort the load, and do impeccable analysis of their business situations. To have lag time because of systems or structural reporting causes an organization to be noncompetitive.

THE SIX FACTORS THAT SHAPE HOW YOUR ORGANIZATIONAL STRUCTURE OPERATES

Most people don't know the difference between a fairy tale and a war story. The former begins with "Once upon a time. . . ." The latter begins with, "No joke, there I was surrounded by all these bad guys." I'm going to tell you a war story to illustrate the requirements for any future organizational structure to operate in a fast-breaking manner.

During the middle of 1967, my Infantry company was extracted from an ongoing battle on the Saigon River and flown by helicopter to a free-fire zone in the southern part of Vietnam, far outside our normal operating zone. The local friendly forces were in pursuit of a large unit of enemy bad guys. The plan was to use my unit of about 110 soldiers as a blocking force while the enemy regiment was being pushed south.

We moved into position and coordinated with the commander by radio in the middle of the night. The next day, as the battle continued, the enemy didn't retreat in a southern direction as expected but instead repeatedly turned inside the maneuver box.

The battle area covered many square miles, so we attempted to channel the enemy's movements. My company was committed to being dropped immediately in front of the enemy forces to keep them from turning in the wrong direction. This is much the same as cowboys herding cattle, except we were moved around by helicopter instead of horses and the cattle were shooting back.

This movement by helicopter is known in military language as a combat assault. One such assault a day can be physically demanding, especially depending on what happens when you jump out of the helicopter. If it is a cold landing zone (a term for no action on the ground when you are dropped off), it's not so bad. It becomes a different matter when the landing zone is hot. We made nine such combat assaults in one day. Sometimes they were hot and sometimes they were not. In three days we went from over a hundred soldiers to fifty-six.

During that time we didn't have the luxury to regroup, rethink, and refit the organization. There was no time. I briefed my platoon leaders in the air and on the way to the next set of grid coordinates, which was only a spot on a map. Often those subordinate leaders were not the same people who were in the leadership position from the last assault. They may not be on the radio the next time either, so continuity of planning and thinking would be lost.

What is the organizational structure message learned from this story? How can a combat company carry on its mission with a steady attrition of its leaders and its men? At what point does the commander lose combat effectiveness? How does the commander restructure to keep the mission going when dealing with seemingly impossible scenarios?

I never want to do that story again, and I doubt you will ever be faced with nine business situations of that nature in one day. However, from this compressed example we should be able to extract lessons learned and make observations for business applications. I identify a minimum of six key factors that influence and guide a business leader in shaping the structure and carrying the mission in this situation:

1. *A Common Enemy.* A well-known leadership technique is to find a rally point or common enemy for the company to rally against. Steven Jobs knew this when he walked out on the stage at meetings with a sweatshirt that read, "Beat Big Blue." A common enemy is what forms the challenge. The enemy doesn't have to be a person. It can be overwhelming conditions, difficult situations, or impossible odds. A common enemy eliminates petty issues between and among structural elements and causes them to work together.

2. *A Dangerous Situation.* Complacency is fatal. Lethargy sets in to create bad management habits. Perhaps a little tension is needed to rally the organization. In stress management, we know that some stress is good. It is called eustress as opposed to the bad stresses—hypostress and distress. Perhaps we need a little eustress superimposed over our structure to make it function more cohesively. When a company faces an outside threat that could be dangerous to it as a whole, the tendency is for the structure to become more cohesive. Teamwork becomes the norm as long as there is danger from outside.

3. *A Trained Workforce.* A deteriorating structure requires a group of well-trained people. In times of reengineering, downsizing, and cutbacks, intellectual capital is lost. This is not good for the long term because certain institutional memories and requisite skill sets are lost to the organization. Time needed to reacquire those basic functions is costly in terms of immediate expenditures and potential dollars lost. A trained and skilled workforce is necessary to maintain fiscal health in times of an organization's structural fluctuation.

4. *A High Level of Trust.* Leaders only lead because of a certain level of trust, which works both ways. As a leader, I must trust you to get the job done if empowerment is in effect. On the other hand, you must trust me as a company

leader to always do what is in the best interest of the company. In traditional structures high trust was not necessary. Managers directed and employees performed. In the new way of looking at structures based on relationships, trust becomes the foundation cornerstone.

5. *A Clear Set of Expectations.* This is clearly trust and communications rolled into one package. For any structure to work properly there must be a two-way exchange of what is expected from all parties. I need to know what you expect of me in a management role. In reverse, what can you do for me? Often we find structures that don't work because of miscommunicated expectations or even unreasonable expectations, which never seem to be met.

6. *A Clear Set of Defined Roles and Responsibilities.* This means all parties know what to do and accept full responsibility for their duties. This can be accomplished in the planning process at the task level when names are attached to tasks and functional requirements. This is commonly called an action plan. Further identification of roles and responsibilities is found in the process mapping activities.

RELATIONSHIP AND APPROXIMATION ORGANIZATIONS OF THE FUTURE

The opposite end of the traditional structure (shown in Figure 9-2) is the model built on relationships instead of things. A quick read of contemporary works reveals very interesting names for these new structures. *Virtual, network, holographic,* and *snowflake* are some of the more catchy terms. Try selling a snowflake business model to a veteran businessperson in this time of cynicism toward management theories!

Figure 9-2. A traditional structure is graphically represented by a pyramid. Regardless of the labels put in the boxes, it still represents high control, fixed lines of communications, and definitive responsibilities.

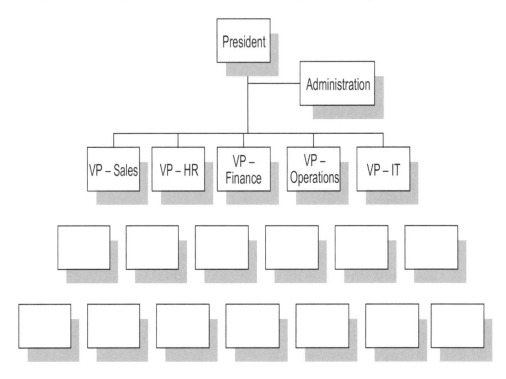

For all of their cleverness, the names for new structures do have commonality. The theme of these concepts is consistent with the shift in thinking about order and structure. We are definitely moving from rigid command and control to a new model with relationships orientations.[4] The theme for the future must be a structure based on a combination of approximations and relationships (see Figure 9-3). In plain language, this means everything in the world has an approximation and relationship with everything else. This is not out of line for a business environment. Consider the following:

- No business exists without a customer.
- No sales can be conducted without something to sell.

- No employee will work without some form of compensation.

- No product can be manufactured without raw materials.

- No warehouse is necessary unless there is inventory.

- No computer will work without software.

Figure 9-3. Organizations of the future will be fluid and flexible with an open architecture that permits free flow of information.

STRUCTURE WITHOUT VISIBLE STRUCTURE—A PARADOX

A virtual organization is characterized by its constantly shaping and reshaping itself. Its form fits its requirements. This fits nicely with a relationship orientation because the organization is in a constant flux. It is evolving as the requirements are dictated by the situation. It is a fluid organizational diagram with parts and pieces added or subtracted as necessary (see Figure 9-4). The structure may be anchored with a core team of management overseeing the business. It is supplemented by administrative support as needed. Customers are included inside the organizational structure as a necessary part of understanding the business requirements. No longer are they added at the end of the transaction. The final piece of the fluid organizational structure is the relationships. Using an outside source permits the business to overcome many of the problems

Figure 9-4. An organization can reshape itself by using strategic alliances, strategic partnerships, and outsourcing.

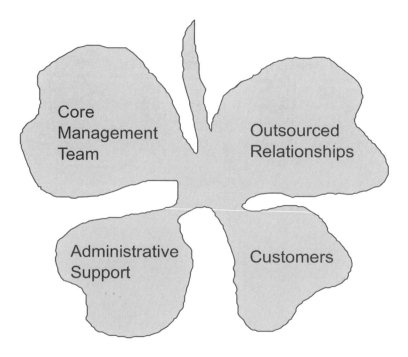

inherent with resources. While there are downsides to strategic partnerships and outsourced work, the advantages are evident to those companies that successfully use the technique.

The virtual organization approaches its work from a different perspective. Its targets may be short term, with the resources coming together to complete the task then fading into the background as another shape evolves to take its place and continue the mission. A movie production is an excellent example of this theory. All the resources are assembled for the mission then dissolve at the end. The core stays in place and reassembles another team to complete the next movie.

While in Alberta, Canada, on the annual hunting trip I make with close friends, Bob Stone, a retired Canadian businessman, and I discussed many issues and management theories over the course of a week. It was a real education for me to compare notes with him, since he had recently sold his successful business. One specific moment comes to mind and is appropriate in a discussion of organizational structure.

Just at sunset one evening, Bob and I were watching a flight of thousands of mallard ducks trying to decide where to land in a field for their evening banquet of peas. At first it was a few ducks, maybe in the hundreds, circling overhead. Other scattered groups gradually joined them until they numbered in the thousands, forming a bridge across the sky. As the lead ducks in this huge flock would get close to the ground looking for food, the control would shift to the other side of the formation as other ducks took the lead. The visual effect was a huge mass of birds shifting leadership from one side to the other, circling and climbing, only to dip down again at some point. It was organizational structure in chaos. Yet watching the birds we could see a pattern in their leadership, structure, and movement. Would the evening feeding been better served with an organizational wiring diagram? I don't think so. Maybe this is an example of a true virtual organization.

Choosing Your Structure: The Beautiful Solution

I like simple solutions. My business plan has a value statement around understated yet elegant solutions for all our work. Over the years I've tried to use that theme for both my personal life and professional work. That same approach could be used for building your business structure.

So far we've been laying the groundwork for you to construct an organization that best fits your needs. To do so requires a number of considerations. Perhaps the best way to build your structure is to use a fluid method of constructing the diagram instead of trying to make it fit into a preexisting format. To start, you must account for seven elements:

1. *Targets.* First, you need to be absolutely clear about what you are trying to do with your organization. This comes from the mission, vision, goals, objectives, and task components of your business plan. Those were clearly defined.

2. *Strategies and Tactics.* Next you must revisit how you are going to accomplish the "what" portion of the business plan. This is the conceptual portion of the "how."

3. *Forces.* With the "what" and the conceptual "how" in place, you next prepare your employees to accomplish your end state. In military terms this is called tailoring your forces, which is a standard practice before any engagement. In this step you look at exactly what personnel are required to get the job done given the task at hand. It is critical that you ask specific questions during this step, including:
   - What types of skills are required?
   - What education levels are required?
   - How much experience is necessary?
   - How many people are needed?

- How do I group the people into effective work units?
- How will these work units be led and managed?

4. *Resources.* For employees to do their jobs effectively, proper resources must be designated.

5. *Communications.* The structure must facilitate communications across, up, down, and outside the organization to be effective. Make sure your design doesn't have bottlenecks in the communications flow.

6. *Decisions.* Decide early how you plan to handle decision taking. You may choose to centralize or decentralize, or you may adopt a combination of the two. The latter is probably the best solution. There are some things that should be centralized for the benefit of the structure as a whole. An example would be the vacation policy. There are other things that are best decentralized. An example is the local purchase of common supplies. Figure out which decisions need to be retained and which can be delegated. Hint: There is more to be delegated than you may first think.

7. *Command and Control.* Unfortunately, these two words, *command* and *control*, have connotations of authoritarian or dictatorial. My argument for using them as an element of structure is that an organization cannot be allowed to be a free spirit; someone has to answer for the performance. No matter what structure, pyramid or flat, circular or horizontal, or relationship or approximate, there is still a need for discipline and order. Make sure your structure includes methods to protect authority, responsibility, and accountability.

Your final organizational plan must include three parts:

1. *An Organizational Chart.* This is a wiring diagram that shows reporting relationships and how groups of people

are formed to do work. This document is one of the most important pieces of literature you produce for your plan. It provides a wealth of information to the user. Names, titles, phone numbers, and business functions are helpful to anyone trying to understand and contact people within an organization. The organizational chart provides a sense of stability, order, and security to the system. Lastly, the organizational chart defines the power and influence designated to individuals and groups within the plan.

2. *The Soft Infrastructure.* This is the infrastructure needed for communications flow. It is the map of how information flows through the system. It defines the flow of decision making along with the information. By default it also defines the de facto leadership of an organization. After all, the people who make the decisions are the ones seen as leaders.

3. *The Hard Infrastructure.* This is the infrastructure needed to support the plan. It may be in the form of annexes to support the business plan. For long-term or strategic thinking, it may include a facilities utilization plan or an equipment utilization plan.

The final test of your organizational plan is to examine what the structure does for you. It must be facilitative to accomplish your vision and long-term goals. You will want your existing and future structure to:

- Use the full talents of all people and resources.
- Aid coordination among the critical staff and business unit functions.
- Make communications between and among the work units easy.
- Facilitate the development, motivation, and retention of key people.
- Achieve minimum costs.

- Provide logical growth and succession of the management team.

- Facilitate coordination of special project teams within a formal structure.

SUMMARY

This chapter has been about developing your 1-Page Organizational Plan. Not a lot of time was spent defending traditional or conventional structures. These served their purposes well at the right moment of history, but we need to move on. Several companies are venturing into the brave new world in transitional or contemporary fashion. They are trying to make new concepts work in a sea of instability, which sometimes is proving difficult. Yet despite all the setbacks, the movement away from a traditional to a more relationship orientation is gradually descending upon the business communities. Will we ever reach the age of virtual or futuristic management structures? Probably. It is just a matter of when. The new theories will advance then retreat. We will regress to find a norm. Perhaps the future structure will not be as radical as first thought but rather will combine designs that feature the best of all we know about how to organize for work.

THE KEY QUESTIONS: CREATING YOUR ORGANIZATIONAL STRUCTURE

Use the following twelve questions to stimulate your thinking about organizational structure. A helpful tool would be to have your existing organizational wiring diagram available. It may be beneficial to do this work in a room with an easel and newsprint or a whiteboard so you can sketch out some of the existing and future relationships.

1. What is your existing structure? Describe it as:
   a. Traditional
   b. Relationship
2. How well is your existing structure working for you?
3. When was the last time you made major modifications to your structure?
4. How well does your structure act as an implementation vehicle for your strategies?
5. Will your structure get you to your vision?
6. What currently is influencing your structure?
7. If you need to switch models, what resistance points will be encountered?
8. How can you assertively overcome resistance to structural changes?
9. If you flatten out the corporate ladder, how will you reward people?
10. Does your new structure provide the correct levels of:
    a. Authority
    b. Responsibility
    c. Accountability
11. Does your old structure provide the correct levels of:
    a. Authority
    b. Responsibility
    c. Accountability
12. Does your new organizational structure have understated elegance? Is it beautiful?

THE PRACTICAL APPLICATIONS: DEVELOPING YOUR ORGANIZATIONAL PLAN

From this information you should develop the following three tools:

1. A 1-Page Organizational Plan
2. A structural analysis of your organization
3. A review of authority levels, responsibility assignments, and accountability tools

10

Pulling It All Together: The Resources Plan

This chapter outlines the requirements for developing the fourth of the series of the one-page business plans (see Figure 10-1). The resources plan is the document that pulls all the requirements for supporting your business plan together in one place. This approach goes beyond the traditional view of people as the sole resource. Resources are more than the human element. They consist of all things necessary for you to accomplish your goals. There are at least ten items for consideration when building a resources plan. Each is discussed in detail in the following sections.

Figure 10-1. The resources plan helps you determine both short-term and long-term requirements for core competencies in addition to other prerequisites needed to accomplish the plan.

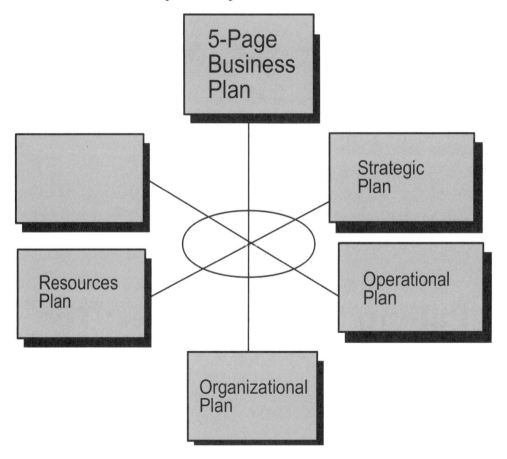

Probably our ancestors' major concerns when hunting a woolly creature were, "Do we have enough resources? Maybe we need a few more hunters. Are the spears sharp enough? What will we do with all the meat? How do I get it back to the village?" Today we don't hunt woolly creatures to survive but we do hunt in the jungles of the corporate world. Businesspeople are daily asking the same questions as they go into conferences, prepare reports, or hold meetings with customers.

THE TWO MAJOR RESOURCES PROBLEMS FACING PLANNERS TODAY

Two major resources problems face the planner today. One has to do with people and the other with dwindling resources. First, there is a shortage of people—good people, that is. You can always hire a body to put into a position, but can you hire a quality person for the specific job requirements? People who know this business will tell you that to replace a lost employee costs between $18,000 and $35,000 apiece. That is recruitment costs and doesn't count lost capacity as the job sits vacant for months. Multiply that times your turnover rate to see what your annual recruiting is costing the company. In conclusion, there are not enough good people to go around and they are expensive to replace.

The business community has tried to put on a good face about how it deals with its most valuable resource. To attract and retain qualified people, many gimmicks have been tried. These range from signing bonuses to sleight-of-hand name changes. Remember when people who worked for a company were called employees? Now they are associates. Historically humans were called personnel, now they are human resources. I sometimes wonder if that shift didn't actually do more harm to the way people are managed. I'm not so sure that the term *human resources* isn't as depersonalizing as any other. Attempts to personalize the individual may have been lost in the activity itself.

Once in Vietnam, while watching a buffalo herder gathering his thirty charges for the return to the village late in the afternoon, our paths crossed and we stopped to exchange greetings. I asked if the herd belonged to the village or the families. I was told that each buffalo belonged to a family and was considered their most prized possession. Then I asked if they were kept in a common corral at night. "No," the elder herdsman chuckled, and said he dropped each animal off at each owner's place. That puzzled me. I didn't know how he could do that because they all looked exactly the same. When I asked how he knew which one went to which family, he asked with a polite but embarrassed laugh, "Major, do you have children?" I nodded. He continued, "Can you tell them apart?" Point made.

Organizations want to treat employees as individuals but instead view them as I did the buffalo—as one indistinguishable herd. Employee satisfaction studies tell organizations it is important to treat employees as people. Historically there have been many humanistic movements to put the *P* back into personnel or the *human* back into human resources management. Attempts to have meaningful inclusion of employees in company management tend to fail. Calling employees by any other title still means they are employees. No one is fooled. Putting popcorn machines in the break room is no substitute for changing ineffective core management processes. A relaxed dress code doesn't add to the employee paycheck.

The second problem is the overall shortage of resources. Vast quantities of resources once available are no long in such abundant supply. Look at natural resources as examples. Timber, coal, and water all have histories of abuse. Think of all the virgin timber that has been cut in North America sometimes in slash-and-burn efforts to clear land for farming and urban development. Think of how our great rivers have been polluted in some cases to the edge of destruction. The Great Lakes in North America come to mind when we think of how pollution has created dead bodies of water. Imagine how shortsighted it was for the city of Toronto to dump its garbage in Lake Ontario for years. Decades later the city is paying the price to dredge the garbage out and handle it properly.

Management has also plundered natural resources of organizations. Consider what separates you from your competition. It's not money, because that has a limit. Neither is it technology or information because everyone can acquire those. These resources have boundaries or finite limits. The one resource that has no boundaries, is unlimited in size, and is basically free for the asking is intellectual capital. People's brainpower is your only differentiation. Ironically, companies are busy downsizing, giving away the very resource that makes the difference.

Traditionally the American solution was to throw more effort and resources at a problem until it was overwhelmed. That is a brute-force solution in times of plenty. It works if you have unlimited resources. What happens when you have a limited supply of people, materials, and money? How do you still make your plan work? Once a Canadian president asked me if I saw a difference between Canadian executives and U.S. executives. The answer for me was easy. Canadians seemed more thoughtful when approaching a task. They ask what are they going to get for their effort. Because they have limited resources, they cannot afford the luxury of ready, fire, and aim.[1] In the United States, executives tend to expend resources like there is no limit. Of course I'm generalizing, but it does seem to be a truism.

BUILDING YOUR RESOURCES PLAN: THE TEN KEY ELEMENTS

Your resources plan should include documentation of what has to be marshaled to support your operational and organizational plans. One purpose of a taking a systemic look at resources is to glean every edge you can develop to make your business plan fully operational. The company-level resources plan is developed in conjunction with the other parts of the business plan during the planning conference. At least ten components are identified for the resources plan:

1. Staffing levels
2. Information requirements
3. Facilities

4. Technology

5. Dollars

6. Untapped potential

7. Time

8. Relationships

9. Image

10. Leadership

Some of these elements are hard-core mechanical things the resource planner must consider. Others may be new to the planner and are sometimes overlooked as resources. The ten elements are presented here in detail but not necessarily in any priority.

Staffing Levels: How to Work at Peak Efficiency

How many people will it take to carry out your operational plan? How many are required to achieve your strategic plan? These are two basic, critical questions to ask when considering the personnel required to support your business plan. It is called staffing levels because it considers how many bodies are required to fill out your organizational structure.

The organization I know to best manage the issue of staffing levels is the U.S. military. Three factors play a part in their management of people numbers. First, every day, every unit in the U.S. Army submits a headcount. Unit leaders account for every person assigned to them no matter what is happening. This is done even in wartime conditions. A Morning Report (MR) is filed by a certain time each day. This document becomes an official record of how many people are located and where they are located in the vast Army system. The second management technique is a document called the Table of Organization and Equipment (TO&E). This means every unit, no matter what the type, has been scrutinized to determine exactly how many people and what type equipment are needed for the unit to carry out its formal mission. Somebody has to give a lot of thought to determine the force requirements. This leads us to the third tool. Somewhere in some headquarters, probably the Pentagon and all major commands, is a complete staff section whose task is to determine future force requirements.

It would not be too far-fetched for civilian organizations to take a few notes from the military.[2] Remember, though, militaries have had several centuries to learn how to keep up with their headcount and make their organizations work at peak efficiency. Contrary to the stereotype portrayed by some media, the military is a very well run institution.

Information Requirements: How to Gather, Decipher, and Apply Information Effectively

Today's information requirements are quite different from those of the past. The problem is not gathering information. Rather, the problem is sorting what information we have immediately available. Remember going to the library to do research for a school paper, or turning to the encyclopedia to look up a topic? In my grade school in Baxterville, Mississippi, the encyclopedia was considered the center of all information and the fountain of all knowledge. Everything I needed to know was in that one set of books. Think how different our research is today. The problem is not finding what we need; it is sorting through massive amounts of information to pick out the kernels of information we need.

Your ability to gather, decipher, and apply information in a timely, effective manner is a strategic tool. In fact, it may even be a weapon to get you to the market first with the most preparation. Training may be necessary to improve the analytical skills of your key decision makers. Their competencies must be in rapid analysis and forming sound decisions from information. You may have to teach people skills, such as how to set priorities when analyzing these volumes of information and how to manage the stresses that result from overload and that can hamper the making of effective decisions.

A second take on information as a resource relates back to the structure. Cross-check your communication channels to determine whether your organization's structure supports easy communications. Eliminate any obstructions or activities that conserve information flow and that do not facilitate two-way communications. Be very clear with managers that withholding vital information from other staff sections won't be tolerated.

Your resources plan should give careful consideration to how you move large amounts of information around within the operating systems. This is where the value of your information technology staff (IT) comes into play. Large blocks of information are necessary to maintain and sustain the vital operations of your business. This information is considered the lifeblood of all your actions, but it must be managed. Without information management, you could not run a business. In resources planning for information management, you must consider:

- Existing computer networks
- The next upgrade of your software
- The next upgrade of your hardware
- Interoperability of software systems

Information management seems to be a major source of frustration for all sizes of business, but small businesses have a distinct advantage over their larger kin. A small company can totally replace its computers or upgrade its software faster than a large company and at a proportioned cost. A case in point is IBM. Some elements of its Global Services Consulting division were not Windows 95 operational until February of 1998. Even though the company owns Lotus Notes, not all business units had been brought online for a long time. Software standardization is another frustrating factor in information management. An example is a New York–based employee having trouble communicating with a colleague in England. The American sends an e-mail attachment prepared in Microsoft Word over Lotus Notes. The receiver isn't allowed to use

Microsoft Word. These two people are in the same company, working on the same project, but in different countries.

Big companies are definitely at a disadvantage when it comes to changing and upgrading information systems. The costs are prohibitive. Yet the danger of not switching or upgrading is evident to anyone trying to dial in to a computer from an outdated facility. I had that experience on an international trip for a client. For two weeks my team of three consultants, using three different laptops, was unable to dial in to the client's global network from five different locations. We were effectively shut down and shut out except for face-to-face contact and the use of the telephone.

Facilities: Too Much Versus Too Little

The resources plan must also consider physical properties such as office space, warehousing, and other site locations. With facilities, there always seems to be too much or too little. A common problem in rapid-growth companies is the lack of office space. Many company office buildings are so crowded I wonder how much effective work is done in a single day. When I worked in the Pentagon, I had a desk jammed between two six-foot-high dividers and space for my chair. Stories of people having to share desks are common in many company facilities.

One solution to expensive office space is the home office. Some employees find working from home can be quite effective, given their job requirements. These mobile employees work out of their home base but spend most of their time at the customer's location. Or the employee works from a computer at home in the same fashion as would be done in a company office. The only major differences in working from a home office are the length of time it takes to get to your desk and your dress code options (you can work in your pajamas).

At the other end of the scale is the problem of excessive space. Vacant warehouse space is costly. Should your company keep the extra space in anticipation of growth? If you need a new manufacturing facility, when is the time to buy the land and break ground? How far out should you project growth to be able to properly plan your facilities requirements? This is a case where the need for a longer time span in your business plan becomes self-evident.

For a resources plan to be complete, projections of facility requirements must be matched to the business plan. This is a point in the plan where accuracy of forecasting is critical. The numbers and support requirements found in those big stretch goals become even more magnified. To get the projections and targets wrong by even a little bit has serious consequences. Since resources are committed against these numbers, they need to be right the first time.

Technology: How to Keep Your Competitive Edge

Present and future technology must be considered in the resources plan. What technologies are you using today, and are they about to change? Consider the cost of changing to new technology. Think about how your competitive edge is lost if you don't embrace the new technology. How much will you have lost by the time you get around to changing?

On March 8, 1862, an event occurred about ten miles from where I now live that changed the world and demonstrates the sudden introduction of technology. On that day the Confederate ironclad, CSS *Virginia*, steamed from her berth at the Norfolk Navy Yard to sink two major warships of the Union Navy. The Union blockade near Old Point Comfort on the James River was not prepared for the appearance of an ironclad.[3] As a result of the first battle between a true ironclad warship and wooden-hulled adversaries, all wooden warships around the world became obsolete. The entire British fleet of nearly 300 ships moved from being the most powerful war fleet in the world to second-class status. The strongest navy on the seas had no involvement with events that created its own demise.

Wireless communications is an example of technology that will someday replace the majority of hardwired communications. Consider the limits to landlines. Think how freeing the wireless concept could be to a mobile society and a fast-moving business community. We already see the impact in daily use of the telephone. Everywhere you look people have a cell phone stuck in their ear while on the move. Computers can talk to handheld devices with infrared technology, eliminating computers. Even the mouse has gone cordless. These may seem small or trivial examples, but they have serious implications. What is the long-term downside for companies that put in cable and hardwire office equipment?

The message from this example is that technology can kill you overnight with or without your direct involvement. With the introduction of a new way to do something or a new piece of equipment coming online, you can be at a serious disadvantage. Watch carefully where this technology originates. Consider disruptive technology. Someone outside your field may invent or discover something that has a spin-off application to your industry. The danger of disruptive technology is that you don't know where it will come from. While you are watching your conventional competition, someone in another industry kills you.

The influence of technology must be considered in the assumptions of your business plan and written into your resources plan. During the planning conference, the management team has examined the status of technology and calculated that into the overall planning framework. If this issue has not been discussed there is a serious flaw in your thinking process, so revisit the assumptions about technology.

Dollars: Three Significant Behaviors That Affect Your Business Plan Finances

This is the most sensitive area of the resources planning. Everyone seems to be mystified by money and those who speak the financial language. This intimidation sometimes gets in the way of effective decision making by the executive team. Three significant behaviors must be considered when planning to finance your business plan.

Watch Out for the Hockey Stick Approach

When longer-term plans are used there is a tendency to believe you have all the time in the world to make your strategic goals. Complacency or lethargy may occur around the first two or three years of the plan. As the associated numbers are fed into the plan, there is a tendency to produce flat performance for several years. There is logical, rational thinking for getting things in place before you ramp up your activities. When flatness continues year after year, the growth is in reality only a creeping model. There will always be reasons to justify not making the numbers or staying flat. This management behavior can be played out for years. If you are the chief decision maker, you have a choice to push the curve or accept a reasonable hockey stick approach. Make the call; that's why you get paid the big bucks.

The real danger from either planning creep or the flat hockey stick approach is the ramp-up energy you'll need to ultimately meet your goals. The closer you get to the end date the more energy, resources, and activities are required to meet the goals because the ramp is steeper. This is another justification for using the backPlanning approach. By establishing long-term goals, you have a better incremental chance of accomplishing targets and making the goals than if you used a short-term, intense approach (see Figure 10-2).

Figure 10-2. Three approaches give you different results. Planning creep produces mediocre results. Planned action gives you desired results. The hockey stick does not produce your full potential. Notice the "ramp up" effort required in line A–B.

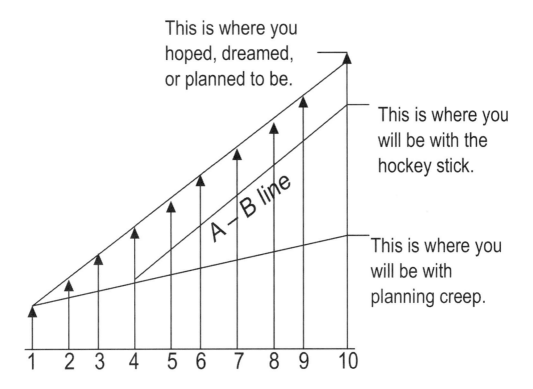

The Tail Wags the Dog

Another misuse of financial resources in planning is in the decision-making process. The tail cannot wag the dog. A single staff section (finance—the tail) shouldn't have control over the whole company (the dog) during the planning process. The financial people are simply advisers at the conference on money matters to the executive team. They don't dictate, run the show, or call the shots for the whole executive team. If they do, then the financial staff is in control of your company, not the designated president. Listen to the advice of your financial advisers, but make your own decisions when it comes to the final plan.

Preventing Post-Planning Veto

Financial people have a habit of negating the complete planning process by publishing the budget. An executive team can spend days preparing a logical, thoughtful plan only to have it significantly altered by the finance section. How can that be allowed to happen? If your plan is altered after the fact, then you have failed as planners. It is not supposed to be that way, and shame on you if you let it happen. The solution is simple. The chief financial officer or vice president of finance should be sitting in the planning conference and working the numbers as the goals are developed. There should be no kickback after the fact. If there is default, then the president is not giving good initial guidance and mentoring to the vice president of finance.

Untapped Potential: Making the Most of Employees

The people who work for your company are one of your most important resources. They, not your product, will be the key to your organization in the future. Let's examine how you can maximize your employees' potential to the organization's benefit—and their own.

Corporate Culture Adds or Subtracts Resources

You have available to you, at no extra expense, a vast source of power and energy. This energy can be unleashed in a focused manner to achieve your business plans and gain your future. It can also go unrecognized and lie dormant. In many cases this energy is even turned against you and actually prevents you from accomplishing your strategic goals and objectives. This force has the potential to catapult companies into greatness or break them after decades of success. The name for this organizational force is corporate culture.

Too often the culture of an organization is not recognized or connected to the strategic planning process. Yet we know it is the energizer, the electricity that runs through the system to support or deny what needs to take place. Corporate culture was presented in part during the development of the soft side of your plan and your story. The value statements, the philosophy statement, and the principles are all part of the corporate culture and your untapped potential.

The Company IQ

Intellectual capital may have been a term invented by Wall Street to put a dollar value on the worth of a company that doesn't show up on the balance sheet. We know that reputation is valuable and can bring more to the sale price. How smart your company is in terms of solving problems and generating revenue is equally as valuable. That organizational intelligence quotient (IQ) shows up when looking at an organization's accumulated knowledge. Think about how we approach intellectual capital. Most organizations think of intellectual capital as the information that's recorded in a computer database of lessons learned and other documentation of activities. Intellectual capital is not documentation. It is the new knowledge that comes from people putting their heads together to solve a problem. It is also how people learn—from each other. When an employee asks another employee how to work a piece of software, that's intellectual capital. If you give away people you lose your ability to generate those interactions, which puts you at a disadvantage with your competition.

Energy Sources

Nodes are small pockets of dormant energy. Imagine your company as a system with thousands of these "hot spots" waiting to be energized. I suggest you have an infinite number within your culture waiting for use by management. How many times have employees commented, "I knew a better way to do it, but nobody asked me." It is a sad state of affairs when management is not drawing on its resources. Even sadder is the culture that doesn't promote, permit, and encourage employees to volunteer solutions.

Triggers must be found to release the energy contained in the organization. The following four triggers may be the most important ways of getting into the energy sources:

1. Creating individual and organizational story alignment

2. Applying the first rule of psychology—people work for themselves first

3. Hooking the employee on learning

4. Shifting the roles of the employee in your story

Story Alignment

Perhaps a key to creating the equivalent of a critical mass of energy release in a company is alignment. Labovitz and Rosansky believe power is unleashed by getting all the elements of the organization heading in the same direction at the same time.[4] There is great practical merit in talking about alignment of goals and ways of working. There should and must be synchronized behavior. Yet, with all that has been written about alignment, it doesn't seem to work as well as it should. Perhaps alignment activities are too psychologically cold. I think alignment is far more than the mechanical side of the business plan. Maybe we need to approach alignment differently.

I believe the real payoff is the alignment of the two stories: the individual's story along with the company's story. That's why the vision is so critical in the business plan. It sets the condition for the alignment of stories. The purpose of the vision is more than dictating the direction of the company. Its most important function is to allow every company member to see his or her role in the future. This gives them an opportunity to look to the future and determine how they can add meaning to their lives today. Alignment means individuals can see their story within the company story. People feel okay with work because there is an intuitive feeling of comfort with their place in the story. There is no feeling of being shut out. Contributions can be made and a purpose for being is identified.

People Work for Themselves First

Managers need to be careful in assuming they know the foundations of alignment. James Lucas calls these false assumptions. He states, "We can't assume that those who work for us always have our organization and its interests as their number-one priority. To believe this, to be deceived by people's surface excitement, is truly a fatal illusion."[5] The first rule of understanding people is to understand they work for themselves first and the company second. The sooner businesspeople come to grips with this fact the easier it becomes to figure out how to set conditions for motivation.

All people work for themselves first. Everyone has a reason for behaving the way they do. To the outside manager this reason may not be readily visible or understood. This puts management into a double bind. A first requirement is to decipher what motivates the employee. The second requirement is to provide gratification of that reward within the constraints and confinements of good business. If that focal point can be identified and provided, then alignment of stories occurs.

Creating Employee Excitement Through Learning

There's a trend developing. I've observed it with the four young adults in our family and in others I've interviewed around the world. Recently we conducted interviews with employees of a multinational company while visiting six countries. There was a consistent message at an unconscious level: "What can I learn from this job that will prepare me for my next job?" This fits very well with the schema of employees who see employment with any one company as a transitory step in their career progression. To be competitive in the move from company to company, they must do skills stacking, which can only be accomplished through learning and experiencing as much as possible along the way.

The Shifting Role of the Employee in Your Story

The employee, not your product, will be the key to your future organization. Business writers present a one-sided story about modern employee demands of the organization. Books are replete with examples of better work/life balance, better management behavior, and increased reward systems. These are all traditional views of the employee/company relationship as seen from the employee side.

There is a storm on the horizon. Let me take the company side of the situation for a moment in an attempt to present a balanced view. Someone better alert the employees that a new age of relationships is dawning. The tempo is not going to slow. Requirements are not going to be reduced. Resources will never be abundant. And it is going to get worse. As the business plan puts all the pieces into place for authority, accountability, and responsibility, there will be major shift on who picks up the pieces. The new organizational structure will place certain demands on the employee never before experienced in business. The employee will act as the core from which all activities revolve, and this carries inherent responsibilities.

A fast-tracking company and client of mine put an even more powerful and aggressive business plan in place over a three-year period. Then the company brought up the skill and competencies requirements for all three levels of management and supervision to match the strategic requirements. Over time individual managers fell by the wayside. Some didn't have the ability to grasp and apply the concepts of the new business models. Others chose to remain in the relatively catatonic state of mediocre performance, thinking the efforts were just another management fad. The message here is critical to the resources planner. Employees will be lost in this tough business planning process. There is no room for people who cannot perform. Be prepared to have different people at the end of the planning cycle from those you started with. There will be personnel changes.

As these organizational shifts take hold, employees will also need to shift their behaviors to keep up with the increasing tempo. Here are some prime examples:

- *Career Development.* No longer will the human resources division design and develop training for the individual or company in the blind. Any scheduled training will be goal-oriented. Here is the major difference: Instead of blanket required attendance, individuals will be responsible for self-selection of training programs based on their own needs. There will be no notices sent out to attend a special training program as part of career development. In future relationships, employees are responsible for identifying their own shortfalls in job performance and soliciting help to fill the gap. The reward for the individual is called job security. If they don't stay current in their required job skills, their colleagues will bypass them to get the quality jobs.

■ *Core Competencies.* Showing up as a set of arms and legs will not be acceptable in the future. Every employee must have a demonstrated set of core competencies to bring to the job. As the movement continues to shift away from industrial jobs to knowledge jobs, organizations want people with the ability to think as well as execute. Future teams will be asking what skills a person brings to the project before the person will be allowed on the team.

■ *Individual High Performance.* Future requirements are for higher levels of performance from every single person in the company. This is going to cause a problem when communicated to employees. Currently many people see themselves as overworked and underpaid. They put in long hours, work hard, and give a lot. What are they getting in return? Now management asks them to do more. This causes inconsistency in the plan. Several things contribute to this inconsistency.

First, there may be a self-belief that employees are working hard; it is the management squandering the profits. Good point. It is embarrassing to ask people to work longer and harder when their efforts are being offset by dumb management decisions. Before you ask of others, clean up your own act.

Second will be the compensation issues. Financial returns are a sensitive subject. Don't suggest that management is presently not getting a full return for its money. The folk saying, "a full day's work for a full day's pay" can be interpreted from two views. Management thinks it is getting a 60 percent return while employees see themselves working at 110 percent. Both are right.

■ *Loyalty to Profession.* In the future more employees will be returning to the days of being professionals. The loyalty will be to the skill and not the company. We see this today with the IT community and the frequent movement of people in the IT workforce. The individual loyalty is to the skills of being a good computer professional who can work for any company.

■ *Specialist Versus Generalist.* In the future the employee will have to be like a member of a Special Forces team. On these elite teams each person is trained in a primary skill. People have to be a specialist in one area. They are also trained in other areas to the point that they can fill in for a member who is incapacitated. This is cross-training at its perfection. Civilian organizations don't have people trained in this specialist and generalist model. There is frequent rhetoric about cross-training people, but it never happens. The sad truth is people are usually so poorly trained in their primary job there is no time or money to provide additional training.

Time: Choose to Squander or Choose to Save

Time is an equal resource for everyone, even your competition. There are 168 hours in a week and 8,736 hours in a year. You cannot make more time, so you have two choices for using time as a resource. The first choice is to continue to squander time; the second choice is to use it more wisely.

The race to use time more wisely is not a new one. In the manufacturing business it's a very sensitive issue. With the industrial revolution, businesspeople quickly discovered the need for speed on the assembly line. The sooner the product reached the consumer, the sooner the company made money. Henry Ford invented the term and the implementation methods of mass production.[6] The stories of his perfecting interchangeable parts and inventing the moving assembly line are legendary when considered in terms of time saved. Through a series of designs, Ford was able to achieve a cycle time of 1.19 minutes. That is a far cry from the time required to build a car by hand. The assembly line got so good that it "eventually spewed out a Tin Lizzie every twenty-four seconds."[7]

No work on strategic planning or business processes would be complete without referencing W. Edwards Deming and his contributions to both Japanese and American industry.[8] While Deming is usually considered a quality guru and continuous improvement expert, his work has application in this portion of your resources plan. What is the objective of process improvement? It is about getting to market faster—read that as improved time management. By studying the methods of Deming you achieve triple benefits. Your quality goes up as your processes improve and you save time overall.

The Japanese took Deming to heart and applied his concepts of continuous improvements. Their work in automobile production is well known in terms of quality and cycle times. One of the keys to their success was the ability to achieve a higher standard by doing many little things better.[9] They call it kaizen, which has been loosely translated in American business language to mean continuous improvement as a way to reach quality.

Since quality is an overworked subject known and pounded into every manager's head for the last decade or so, I will not revisit the concept except to make a few observations. My first observation from firsthand experience working to improve performance is this: Quality is not free.[10] It is a very expensive cash flow issue. This is contrary to popular belief. I have never found quality improvement activities like apples on a tree ready to pluck. They require hard work, dedicated management, and money up-front. When planning for quality you need to allocate resources for investing in the quality efforts. Quality is not a strategic leverage. It was at one time, but now quality is such a given requirement by the customer that it no longer provides an advantage. It doesn't matter what the product or what the cost, customers expect and demand quality for their shopping dollar.

This reminds me of an incident that happened a few years ago. I ordered an inexpensive piece of software to do text editing. After spending considerable time following all the instructions I just couldn't get it to work, so I called the publishing company. After explaining the problem to the customer service representative I was stunned at the reply: "Well, what did you expect? It only cost $20. We have a really good program that's about $200." My response was that "I would have liked it to work at least $20 worth. It doesn't work at all." People want their $20 worth and more, so don't think of quality as leverage. It is a customer expectation.

But let's not fall into the trap of talking about manufacturing when it comes to time as a resource. Phillip Thomas, a cycle time expert, believes that "60 to 90 percent cycle time improvement will occur outside the manufacturing area."[11] What would be the payoff if you could get a new product to market sooner? How would your company be influenced if the top team had more time to devote to the strategic plan? Would your company be financially better if all wasted motion were eliminated for all the business processes?

When you look at saving time as one of your principal resources, don't just consider reengineering, continuous improvement, and process mapping of the manufacturing facility. Look at every single thing you do as a business. Start with the major activities first and work through the list.

Relationships: How Strategic Alliances Spread the Workload

Your strategic alliances, partnerships, and other devices for collaboration are also important and necessary resources. As your organizational structure flattens, there must be some way to let go of control without losing control. Instead of the favored vertical integration, where all the work is done in-house (a model common in some big corporations), there may be another way. Why not give up some of the control and profits through shared work? Why not form relationships with vested interest in mutual success? In a rigid structure this may be hard to do, but given the need to add and subtract work units, this model fits very nicely with the relationship organization.

Nortel Networks practices the model of downloading responsibilities by outsourcing. Nortel has extensive relationships to perform urgent but not important activities, leaving the core team to do those things that matter more to the company's well-being. Here is a list of some of Nortel's strategic partners and the functions each handles:

Company	Function
Computer Sciences	IT services
PriceWaterhouseCoopers	Human resources
Solectron	Circuit board making Computer-aided design
STMicroelectronics NV	Semiconductor wafers
Perot Systems	IT services
C-MAC Industries	Electromechanical parts

Source: *Canadian Business* (August 3, 2000)

A good resource is your competition. In the old model of seeing the world, the competition was the enemy to be met and defeated on the business battlefield. Today we have many examples of how organizations thought to be enemies are now working together to achieve even greater returns. Twenty years ago who would have thought IBM and Apple Computers would be working off the same platform, or that BMW would be building cars in Alabama (known in slang language as "bubba beamers"), or that Honda would be making cars in the United States.

Explaining the Inconsistency to Your Employees

A word of caution is in order. When you move to new ways of working and develop new business models, there will be confusion by those who must execute the changed processes. Part of why your story is confusing is that you send mixed messages. For example, in yesteryear the name of the game was to beat the competition at every turn, by every means. Sometimes that competition even got out of hand to the point of being unethical, unprofessional, and illegal. Now you are telling employees to work in harmony with the competition; that the company's once fiercest competitors are now its new best friends. Write out that speech. What are three or four logical explanations for these new relationships and alliances? Practice your speech in front of a mirror until you believe it yourself. Congruency of your story is important in this situation.

Image: How to Capitalize on It for Your Company's Advantage

How you are viewed by the world is important—very important. That image influences what you can and cannot do. Image is a resource on its own merit.[12] It can be shaped, managed, and manipulated. Probably the best use of company image is as a springboard to attract more customers and generate more profits. For example, if you are an American, what comes to mind if you read or hear the name Burberry? Americans immediately think of $800 raincoats with special plaid liners and the metal loops on the belt that trigger the alarms at airport security gates.

The image of status doesn't seem to stop buyers. In fact, it seems to attract a certain market segment. Admit it. Don't you flash back to the movie *Casablanca* every time you put on your gabardine trench coat? Are you willing to pay the price to be connected to a certain image?

Image, as a resource, is a perfect fit if your focus is to be a pay-off-driven organization. If your focus is something else, you still must account for your image. Either way, your image can be used as a strategic tool. Capitalize on it with customers, employees, and the general public. Make image part of your story.

Leadership: Your Number-One Priority

If I had to put a priority on the ten elements of resources planning I would probably opt for leadership for the number-one place. I have, however, put it at the end of this discussion to reinforce a powerful message.

There is a major leadership void in companies across North America. Although there is steady improvement in management techniques, real breakthroughs are not keeping pace in the leadership side of the equation of managership and leadership. Let's look at a multibillion-dollar, international company that is well managed and easily recognized. It is making billions of dollars in profit each year and its stock prices are still good. The managers of the company are doing well at managing. They push paper through the system, watch the billable time reports, and track the dozens of administrative things their people must do every day. They focus on one goal—to make the revenue they are told to make by year-end. But are they well led? Sadly, from my observation the answer is no. Do they have mediocre performance because of this lack of leadership? They make the numbers, but the potential they waste is incalculable. They have unhappy people—excellent people who simply keep a low profile, collect their annual bonus, and wait for enough tenure to move on. The real tragedy is that this is a good company with good people. The fatal long-term flaw is that they are looking at the stock prices, and, as long as they remain high, they think they are also well led. I've talked to hundreds of their employees who tell the same story.

For the resource planner a look into the untapped leadership area will pay great dividends. By creating better leadership skills at the executive levels the culture will be enhanced exponentially. Then move to the middle levels and finally to the lowest levels of supervision. Vertical integration of skills is a requirement of the planning cycle. This means the skills found at the top must be pushed to the bottom. Executives must be able to coach people. So should firstline supervisors. The top team of managers must be excellent decision makers, so should the bottom tier of managers. Whatever leadership is demanded at the top must also be demanded at the bottom.

THE FOUR QUESTIONS FOR COORDINATING YOUR RESOURCES PLAN

Proper coordination of a company-level resources plan requires the planning team to use a formula consisting of four parts:

1. Who
2. What
3. When
4. How

Answers to these questions are necessary to make sure the business plan is fully integrated, that it is complete, and that it is communicated to the bulk of the company.

Who Is in Charge?

The principal owner and coordinator of the resources plan should be the vice president of human resources. Why was this function chosen? The human resources function is the one that has more universal contact with all parts of the company than any other. This may vary company by company, but usually human resources is a strong communications link in a company.

Serving as the coordinator has another benefit to the particular staff function assuming this role. A by-product of developing the strategic plan is the need to fully understand the complete business planning cycle. Since knowledge is power, this gives someone an incentive to become the planning guru for the company.

What Resources Are Needed to Make Your Plan Work?

The resources plan is more fully developed after the planning conference as staff sections develop their requirements. This demands close coordination and cooperation between and among major functions, business units, and operational teams. The information is consolidated and cross-checked to make sure it fits the requirement of the company planning team by the resources plan owner/coordinator.

When Will the Resources Be Available?

Coordination for the resources must begin during the actual planning conference. A great deal of work will be done on the topic when discussing goals, objectives, and tasks. Major resource requirements should not come as a surprise to the planners of the subsequent plans. A reasonable amount of time should be allowed for all parties to develop their resources wish lists and submit them to the resources planner/coordinator. Remember, these resources have to be matched against the budget requirements.

How Will the Plan Be Communicated to the Company?

Finally, the resources plan must be incorporated into the business plan and communicated to the entire company. What works well is to develop a set of actions that communicate as much information as far downward as possible. The target recipient should be every member of the organization. Some companies call this a communications plan, but in reality it is the action plan derived from the business planning process.

SUMMARY

This chapter has been about how to fully support your business plan. We have examined a number of resources requirements to make your plan active at both tactical and strategic levels. There are ten of these requirements with no specific priority. All are important to some degree—though leadership is most likely the number-one priority. Be careful in assigning resources because a small error here will magnify in the long-term plan. Once again you must cross-check your assumptions to make sure they are valid. Finally, you must communicate your resources requirements across all functions of the business.

THE KEY QUESTIONS: SUPPORTING YOUR BUSINESS PLAN

Ask yourself these questions:

1. Are you using a hockey stick to develop your performance numbers?
2. Can communications flow freely between and among the people who need the information?
3. Is your planning process being held captive by the budgeting cycle?
4. What do you need to do to realign the thinking of the financial staff to better support the plan?
5. Do you have the tail wagging the dog (i.e., finance dictating operational terms)?
6. What core competencies are needed for the long term?
7. What long-term skills should be developed?
8. What is the status of your IT processes?
9. What is the status of your computer support?
10. What is required to bring your computer support up to date?
11. Is there technology you need to adopt to be competitive?

THE PRACTICAL APPLICATIONS: DEVELOPING A RESOURCES PLAN

From this chapter you should have developed three items:

1. A 1-Page Resources Plan
2. A resources development plan that ties directly to education, development, and training
3. A communications tool or action plan to get the business plan to all levels of the organization

11

Contingency Planning: How to Prepare for the Unexpected

Contingency planning is the fifth of the five types of business plans (see Figure 11-1). While it is very important, it is also one of the most neglected elements of a business plan. Because so much energy is put into the basic strategic and operational plans, planning teams seldom give attention to a portion of the total plan that could put a company out of business. This chapter presents two types of contingency planning. The first is long-term, true contingency planning that is designed to counter deviations from your business plans when your assumptions fail. The second is more common and comes quickly to mind. This is disaster planning or crisis management planning, both of which are in vogue with current business and social trends.

Figure 11-1. The contingency component triggers when alternatives to the basic plan are needed.

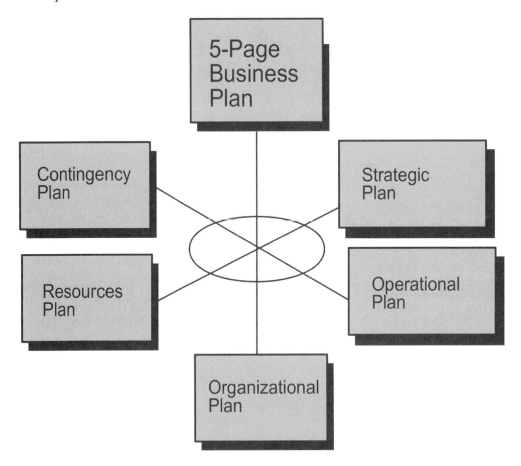

For those planners who would tend to stop reading at this point, let me emphasize again the need to be prepared for the future. No one can predict the future but we can be prepared for it. General Norman Schwarzkopf had this to say about prediction: "The future is not always easy to predict and our record regarding where we will fight future wars is not the best. If someone had asked me on the day I graduated from West Point, in June 1956, where I would fight for my country during my years of service, I'm not sure what I would have said. But I'm damn sure I would not have not said Vietnam, Grenada, and Iraq."[1]

Like all thinking executives, the general didn't sit around unprepared. Over a long and successful career he perfected his skills as a leader, a manager, and a warrior. When the day came for his country to call upon his services he was prepared. His execution of Desert Storm places him in the history books with five-star colleagues such as "Black Jack" Pershing, Dwight D. Eisenhower, and Douglas MacArthur.

Contingency Planning: Preparing for an Unpredictable Future

Contingency planning is being prepared. It is actually that simple. Philip Crosby said it with a little more eloquence: "The centurions will have to learn how to manage so that they can deal with whatever happens, and at the same time, anticipate what is coming. They will have to be in a permanent situation of awareness in order to tell the difference between fads and reality."[2] One of the earlier strategic planning gurus, George Steiner, also uses a simple but elegant explanation. He defines contingency planning as ". . . preparations to take specific actions when an event or condition not planned for in the formal planning process actually does not take place."[3] If we listen to Steiner, anything that falls outside the conditions or goals of your strategic and operational plans should be considered a condition for contingency planning.

This business planning model goes one step further. Contingency planning is not outside your planning process. It is a critical component found inside the planning process to position your plan in case of deviation. "The fundamental purpose of contingency planning is to place managers in a better position to deal with unexpected developments than if they had not made such preparations."[4] Without this preparation managers are always in a reactive mode.

THE FIVE KEY TERMS USED IN CONTINGENCY PLANNING

Early in this chapter we need to sort definitions to ensure we are not talking at cross-purposes with definitions. There are a number of terms to be used when writing about activities that cause deviation from the plan. Some of them and their definitions are:

Term	Definition
Contingency planning	The overall activity that looks at the complete situation and plans accordingly.
Contingency plan	The documentation of contingency planning, it is the hard copy of your thinking and intentions.
Crisis management	Actions you take to manage the total environment when facing a disruptive situation.
Crisis intervention	Actions taken to correct a developing situation. As the name implies, there must be an entry into the process of the situation.
Disaster plan	A step-by-step plan of action available for immediate implementation in times of crisis or disaster.

THE TWO COMMON WAYS THAT PLANS RUN AMISS

This business planning cycle and model uses contingency planning as the overall umbrella term to describe what has to be done. The range of contingency situations you'll face can be broken down into two categories, each of which seems to be connected to the time period involved. Trend deviation is connected to the strategic portion of your business plan whereas the crisis element seems to be connected to the tactical or operational plan because of its short-term orientation. A full range of the model is shown in Figure 11-2.

Figure 11-2. The map of different contingency situations can help you tailor your responses.

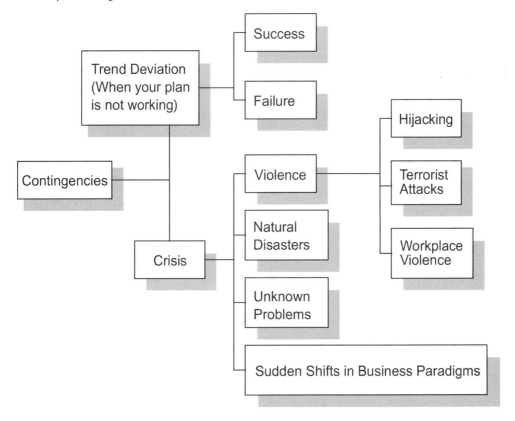

Trend Deviation: When You Miss the Mark

One type of deviation is experienced when the results of your planning are not developing as you expected. Bluntly speaking, you are missing the mark. You may not be hitting your sale goals because of internal company behavior; maybe management is not performing. Another reason could be due to outside influences. Still a third reason is that the market is moving in a different direction from what you assumed, expected, or planned for. In any case your plan is in trouble.

Crises: Circumstances Beyond Your Control

A second major type of deviation is the abrupt or sudden disruption of your plan because of circumstances or events usually beyond your control. These crises are usually related to natural disasters and catastrophic events. These situations are usually the ones that come to mind when we think of disruptions and dangers to order and stability.

THE NINE CRITICAL COMPONENTS OF A SUCCESSFUL CONTINGENCY PLAN

The 1-Page Contingency Plan must have at least nine basic components (see Appendix F). Certain considerations are important when facing a deviation from plan over a longer period of time; others become especially important when in a crisis mode. These nine components must be reviewed in a contingency situation no matter what triggered the requirement. In developing your contingency reactions, ask the following questions:

- *Facilities.* Will you have enough physical support? Are your warehouses and offices located in the right places?

- *People.* Will you have enough people with the right core competencies to carry on the work? What will be the burnout time for people who must work around the clock?

■   *Information.* Do you have enough facts to make decisions? How risky is it to initiate actions on what information is available? Are you able to get the information you need?

■   *Time.* How fast must you react to the situation before it gets even worse?

■   *Image.* What must you do to protect the public perception of your company during the situation?

■   *Technology.* Can you leverage technology as a replacement for time or people?

■   *Tools and Equipment.* What special tools are needed to carry out your mission? Is any special equipment needed? Where and when will the tools and equipment be needed?

■   *Leadership and Managership.* What leadership and managership behaviors are needed to instill the confidence of the public in your company?

■   *Assumptions.* What assumptions have failed, requiring you to take action? What is the antidote for these best guesses you have made about your business?

THE TWO TOUGH QUESTIONS FOR TARGETING POTENTIAL PROBLEMS

When preparing a contingency plan the management team must consider all possibilities and potential target areas, then cut the list down to what is reasonable, realistic, and practical. To start the review, the team asks itself two very hard questions:

1.   *What is the one thing that could put us out of business?* Every organization has a weak spot or area of potential danger. Look for the one thing considered the most dangerous to your operation. Account for this happening in your contingency plan. If you work in the software business, a new code or program could put you out of business.

2. *What is the one thing that could seriously damage our business?* There are other events that will not bankrupt you but can nonetheless do enormous damage to your ability to conduct business. Each of these must be accounted for in your contingency planning. Write specific situations and actions for these variations. An example might be when funding for a project is not approved by the board of directors.

A good technique is to conduct a think tank or "blue sky" session to get the management team to examine the problem. A weekend retreat in a nice creative environment would be a way to get the creative juices flowing and out-of-the-box thinking to occur. Think how powerful a two-question agenda could be for the participants.

THE FIVE AREAS THAT ARE VITAL TO YOUR COMPANY'S WELL-BEING

Next the team determines where the answers to the two questions are found in the following list of five conditions. From this list, develop actions to form your contingency plans:

1. Business conditions
   a. What things are changing in your business that you see as trending patterns?
   b. What things are changing in your industry that you see as trending patterns?

2. Social conditions
   a. What influences are changing social conditions having on your business behaviors?
   b. What management behavior from the past is no longer considered socially acceptable?

3. Political conditions

   a. What kinds of government influences are you experiencing that are different?

   b. How have the conservative or liberal government positions influenced your business?

   c. How have the conservative or liberal government positions influenced your industry?

4. Economic conditions

   a. What global economic incidents have influenced your bottom-line profits?

   b. What are the general economic conditions for your industry as compared with other professions or businesses?

5. Environmental conditions

   a. What environmental issue could put you out of business?

   b. What compliance situations are getting so restrictive that they endanger your operational behavior?

The Six Conditions That Can Trigger the Need for a Contingency Plan

To effectively sort out the possible deviations from a well-written business plan, there must be some logical grouping of information into more detail than just two broad crisis or trend types. I identify six kinds of events:

1. Natural disasters
2. Violence
3. Sudden shifts in business paradigms
4. Unknown problems

5. Known potential problems that are ignored

6. Excess growth

In this section, let's further define what creates the need or conditions for you to write a formal contingency plan.

Natural Disasters

Pick up the newspaper or turn on a news channel on any given day and it appears the weather world is in total chaos. El Niño dominated reports for a major portion of 1998. Every disturbance, natural or unnatural, seemed to be blamed on that one phenomenon. The fall season brought hurricanes and extensive damage to parts of the eastern coast of the United States. Texas experienced floods. In December 1998, Virginia was locked into a serious ice storm that left tens of thousands of people without power for several weeks. Tempers were frayed but sanity and order prevailed as the Christmas season came and went by in candlelight for many families.

With some time and effort, reactions to these natural disasters can be planned and implemented. The problem seems to be that planners are misjudging the scope and scale of the natural occurrences. The hurricanes that wiped out the Mississippi Gulf Coast and did extensive damage to Louisiana in the 1960s and 1970s were not predicted. There have always been floods in the Houston area, but did anyone expect the extent of the one in 2001? The Amite River has always flooded the town of Denham Springs, Louisiana, but no one expected the two or three floods in the early 1980s that set new 100-year flood levels. The message for the disaster contingency planner is to think big, then think even bigger. If the flood is smaller, your excessive planning is okay.

Violence

Unfortunately, violence in the workplace, both on-site and off-site, at home and abroad, is more than a headline in the newspapers. It is a sad reality for many organizations and thus should be a part of your contingency plan.

Hijacking

D. B. Cooper set the stage for what has become a major threat to commercial vehicles, especially those that carry passengers. He boarded a commercial aircraft, held it hostage for a huge ransom, then bailed out over a remote mountain range. Although fragments of the money have been recovered, no trace of the man has ever been found. The story still rates as the most intriguing vanishing act of modern day with D. B. Cooper becoming a sort of folk hero.

Hijacking of boats, trains, and planes has become a pastime for some people. Terrorist groups have elevated it to a fine art. The fear of hijackings has left the world tied in knots over security procedures. Contingency planning for such incidents includes extensive preventive measures prior to departure and onboard aircraft.

Returning from Vietnam on September 8, 1970, I hand-carried an SKS carbine, a K-54 Chicom pistol, and a Randall six-inch blade fighting knife. These were all duly registered, legitimate war trophies that I declared. I carried them from Saigon to Baton Rouge, Louisiana, onboard military and commercial aircraft. It was perfectly normal at the time. Just entering an airport with a weapon of any type today could get a traveler a quick set of metal bracelets courtesy of the security police.

Contingency planning to prevent a hijacking is difficult at best, but it is getting better. Technology is a great assistance. However, the bad guys simply move to other targets or wait until the vigilance wears off to strike again.

Terrorist Attacks

Terrorists can and do strike at will. No amount of contingency planning can totally stop dedicated terrorists from striking somewhere at a time and place of their choosing. These can be attacks planned for months and implemented on a timetable, or they can be random acts of retribution. The bombing of Pan Am Flight 103 over

Scotland required extensive preparation. The Oklahoma City bombing was a deliberately planned incident with a great deal of effort on the part of the terrorists. On the other hand, a power company reportedly experienced acts of sabotage at the access entrances to its nuclear power plant during an ice storm in December 1998. Devices were scattered on the roadway that caused a large number of flat tires on vehicles moving up and down the roads. Management considered the incident dangerous enough to declare it a terrorist act and put all employees on alert. Was it a "terrorist" act by the popular definition? Probably not by lay standards, but nuclear power stations view such incidents in a no-nonsense fashion.

Workplace Violence

"Going Postal" is slang term that is a tragic commentary on the state of affairs in some businesses. Over the past decade, the U.S. Postal Service has had a number of incidents leading to deaths and injuries in the workplace. The slang term developed as a direct result. That's sad on two accounts. First, the fact that any deaths and injuries occurred is the ultimate tragedy. Also tragic is the global tarnishing of the reputation of one of the finest postal systems in the world.

But the post office is not the only business that has to contend with violence in the workplace. This is a serious new set of developing behaviors that must be countered with contingency planning. There are consultants and consultant companies expert in the area of workplace violence. They will tell you strict protocols for prevention and swift actions when incidents occur are necessary to survive with any sort of respect, dignity, and support.

Sudden Shifts in Business Paradigms

Sudden changes in business patterns can also be disruptive to your organization. Your contingency plan should take them into account. Two examples are disruptive technology and bad mental models.

Disruptive Technology

Two ways to counter disruptive technologies are to constantly rein-vest in your own research, always looking for new ideas and ulti-mately new products, and to continuously improve the products you have. By looking outward you are keeping a finger on the pulse of what is happening in other industries. The approximations to your business become apparent if you pay attention. If you reinvest in your own research, you may find the solution first or you may become the disruptive influence for another industry. Finally, by reinvesting you make it difficult for the competition to enter the market by setting the standard for the product. Make the cost of entry so high for competitors that it is not worth the effort.

Bad Mental Models

Often businesses are forced into contingency planning because they have been operating with bad mental models. Peter Senge first brought the concept of mental models to the general public aware-ness.[5] The same concept applies to how a company does business. It is a bad sign when emergency actions are required and there is no plan. An unplanned emergency situation comes from a company with lethargic management. Several things may be happening at one time.

One thing to watch for is discounting or downplaying the pos-sibility of danger. Management teams sometimes discount the pos-sibility of a serious situation ever happening to their company. It will always happen to the other company. Not so. Downplaying or underestimating the problem is equally dangerous. The rule of thumb in business is that a problem doesn't go away. It only gets bigger.

A contemporary example is the Bridgestone/Firestone recall of 6.5 million tires in August 2000. Tire tread separation is not a new problem, having been identified years ago. Only after nearly fifty deaths, more than 200 accidents, and government interest did the company take decisive action. The company dragged its feet for three months until intense publicity forced recall of three tire models. The company further downplayed the danger, blaming weather, roads, and tire inflation as the problem. This denial is not acceptable to a public who has access to information and can rally a worldwide resistance to a product.

Another thing to watch for: History is replete with examples of creeping into progress. Today many appear humorous after the fact. We laugh at the shortsightedness of the business thinkers of the day. Western Union turned down Alexander Graham Bell's invention to carry voice by wire when offered for sale. When it realized the mistake a year later, it was too late. The inventors of Corian sat on the technology until it was sold for a small sum to DuPont, which now uses it in high-grade countertops. The U.S. Army saw no need for the airplane, thinking it of little military significance and relegating it to mail service. The concept of the first computer was a mechanical device designed to help accountants and bookkeepers do calculations. It was turned down because it was seen as a threat that would put them out of work instead of a tool to do work more efficiently.

We can see examples of creeping technology even today. Think about the travel agency business. About 33,000 independent agencies existed in the United States in 1999. These were considered a nice, modest, and respectable way to earn a living. The Internet changed this industry by racking up $4.2 billion in online sales transactions that same year. The number is expected to quadruple by 2002. What happens to the independent travel agency that doesn't quickly adjust to the Internet model of doing business?

The Antidote for Bad Mental Models

Unfortunately, it takes a significant act of nature or a condition with a big impact on the bottom line to change many mental models. Lee Iacocca writes with great emotion about coming to grips with the mass firings at Chrysler. "At one point in April 1980, we cut our white-collar ranks by 7,000 people, a move that saved us over $200 million a year. A few months earlier, we had laid off 8,500 salaried workers. These two moves alone cut out $500 million in annual costs."[6] While it was painful to Iacocca it was also necessary because of the bad mental models in place at Chrysler over an extended period of time.

If you are going to plan for change, make it a big change, then make it bigger. Don't wait for events to force change. Do a preemptive strike on the problem before it becomes a problem.

Unknown Problems

You will always be blindsided by events over which you have no control. Guesswork could be done, but it would be just that—guessing. For example, no one could have predicated or planned for the disaster of TWA Flight 800 over Long Island. Even the best engineering couldn't help another doomed flight that went down near Halifax in 1998. Those are mechanical accidents that even the best minds in the engineering profession cannot protect us from.

Another category is the unpredicted problem. A business cannot account for every single possibility—only the major things likely to happen. A case in point is the first crash of a Concorde, which happened in France. A catastrophic mechanical failure was suspected to be the source. More investigation indicated that a tire failure may have been the originating fault. Later work points to the possibility that a stray piece of metal on the runway may have damaged the tire, which triggered the chain of events that brought down the plane. Accidents such as this will happen no matter how diligently the runways are checked or the operations monitored.

Other "unknown problems" fall into a gray area. Although they are not expected, with some creative thinking they could be identified as possible situations requiring contingency or emergency actions. Jack in the Box didn't expect contaminated meat to cause its restaurants a major problem. On the other hand, why not? After all they are in the food business and contaminated food causes people to get sick and die. Should that have been a surprise? Union Carbide didn't expect a major death toll in India with a plant problem, but why not? Chemical plants blow up, catch fire, or spew ugly stuff into the air that kills people. Are these two cases examples of the "it can't happen to us" syndrome? The *Exxon Valdez* incident was not intended in Alaska's Prince William Sound, but there was no contingency plan. Why not? More than 1,800 ships have been lost in the Chesapeake Bay and its tributaries between 1608 and 1978. Many of these ran aground in the shallow waters off Cape Henry, Cape Charles, and the Middle Ground Shoals.[7] Did Exxon think ships stopped running aground in later years or that ships don't have accidents on the West Coast?

Known Potential Problems That Are Ignored

The computer industry knew about the Y2K problem for years. With the turn of the calendar to January 1, 1999, the news channels were filled with even more stories of the countdown. The problem had even been personalized with its own acronym and slang label, the millennium bug. Management reaction to the problem over the last decade ranged from ignoring the problem to investing tens of millions of dollars to solve it. On New Year's Day 1999, CNN carried a special report titled *The Millennium Bug*. It reported the U.S. government would spend $6.4 billion on the problem with the total cost of corrections reaching $1,000,000,000,000. That's a lot of zeros. And to think the problem was created by shortsighted programmers trying to save a little code space years ago. For those of you who are still not convinced that planning should be a long-term exercise, I hand you this problem. How much heat loss did the entire world experience because of shortsighted planning?

Another example of a problem that is someday going to bite an industry is propane tanks that are out of certification. Thousands of tanks are sitting across the country with expired certification for use. In some cases the ownership of the tanks is unclear or unknown. In other cases the certification inspections and required paperwork are just not completed. Everyone in the propane business knows this situation but no one talks openly about it. Someday a string of incidents involving these tanks will call national attention and action.

Is yours one of those companies playing the odds? What if your product has a built-in liability just waiting for an incident? What is the ethics of gambling that no injuries or deaths will bring it to attention? Is one accident worth the profits? Is it worth the trade-off? Some companies think so. A few million dollars reserved for out-of-court settlements is cheaper than a massive recall or discontinuing the product. You have to make your own decisions. If you decide to play the odds, you need a contingency plan to cover the probability of a class-action suit.

Excessive Growth: Too Much, Too Soon

Not all contingency plans are for bad conditions and bad times. There needs to be thought given to what happens if you exceed your targets. Too much growth can kill you more quickly than slow growth. With the latter case you just hang on until eventually your business dies. With excessive growth the demise is much quicker. Rapid growth has significant implications when it comes to resources. Where will you get the resources to fill all the new orders or the one large order that came from nowhere? Your contingency plan may include giving up some work to save the company. One example of fast growth challenging a company is AOL's trouble scaling its servers for all kinds of new users in the mid-1990s.

THE EARLY WARNINGS THAT CAN HELP KEEP YOU ON TRACK

There is a firstline alert for implementing a contingency plan should an emergency situation begin to evolve. These are devices that allow you to self-correct before having to implement a contingency plan. A trip wire must be in place to give you early warning about correcting the deviation before it requires contingency-level action. For a business plan you might consider the strategic goals.

For example, if there was a long-term goal of reaching $100 million in revenue, dependent upon a 12 percent growth each year, there is a yardstick in place to measure progress. If you miss the growth target two years in a row on a ten-year plan, what is the signal?

Look for specific indicators along your goal path that will tell you whether you are on the right track. When a pilot is landing an airplane there is a calculated glide path for properly descending and touching down at the correct spot on the runway. If the pilot is off course, there is a warning and a recommended correction. A business is no different. There is a path to the strategic goals and a sufficient number of warnings along the way. Planning teams must watch for the signs, listen to the cues, and respond to the signals that their plan is off course.

THE SIX STEPS TO DIMINISH THE NEGATIVE IMPACT OF A TROUBLED SITUATION

Several actions are necessary if you have to initiate a contingency plan in the deteriorating situation. Here are six of them:

1. *Review all information to make a determination of the accuracy of the data.* Is what you are seeing fact or fiction? Make certain that it is not a market reaction or some knee-jerk reaction by local management.

2. *Revisit the plan to see how the developing data matches or mismatches your plan.* Are you on your goal path or off? If off plan, how much is the deviation, and is it really a problem or a nonproblem? This is where it gets tough. Every card-playing gambler knows there is a time to hold and a time to fold. Do you continue on your course (hold) or do you make a course deviation (fold) and do something different?

3. *Review your assumptions.* Did you miss your assumptions or have conditions changed that legitimately required

alteration of your plan? Remember that assumptions are a trip wire for your plan. If they change you will have to either go into a revision of your plan or implement a contingency plan.

4. *Recalibrate your goals if necessary.* You may have to scale them back.

5. *Communicate your revised plan to the company.* Make sure everyone understands the conditions for change and what has triggered the new numbers.

6. *Implement strategies and tactics.* These steps should have been established during the planning conference. A crisis situation is not the time to be making up the rules.

How to React Quickly and Decisively to Disaster Situations

A crisis situation often requires swift, decisive action. The next sections discuss how you can best be prepared for acting under crisis conditions.

Decision Making in a Crisis

The most important thing to be attended to in a contingency situation is a clear set of rules for decision making. Who makes what decisions should be established well in advance. This should be part of your standard operating procedures (SOP). If uncoordinated decisions are communicated, the situation will only be made more confusing.

Damage Control

There must be an organized plan to contain the damage caused by the unhealthy situation. This may be in customer relationships, public trust, or confidence in the product. Basic questions of who, what, when, where, and how give the planner a good framework to build a workable response to crisis conditions. Let's go through the specifics.

- *Who Should Be Involved.* The most senior person in the company should be directly involved in the situation. If it is a response to a crisis, then the senior person should be highly visible. If it is business planning deviations, the president should be leading the planning revision. When natural disasters happen the state governor is always involved and visible to the public. The senior official needs to be supported by a crisis management team. This designated team may or may not be the executive leadership team. The composition depends on the nature of the situation. There must be problem experts on hand to give expert witness and take charge of the technical content of the problem.

- *What Should Be Managed.* The answer is simple: perceptions. Faith in the company must be maintained. The integrity of the story must be reconfirmed. The story must be authentic, congruent, and believable by all parties. This faith in the retention and restoration of the story falls into five areas:

  1. *Company.* Faith of employees needs to be maintained. They will be concerned with the viability of the company. If a fire has just destroyed a plant, job security will be an immediate concern.

  2. *Public.* Faith of shareholders is critical to the immediate fiscal health of the company. If there is a sudden loss of confidence your stock prices drop as people dump their holdings. During a crisis situation you don't need a run on your stock.

  3. *Customers.* The people who buy your goods and services need to be reassured. They are looking for faith in the products. Will they be harmed if they

continue to buy the goods? Are they getting their money's worth? Is the product still effective?

4. *Competition.* A crisis situation is a good time for your competitors to make moves on you or your market. You need to reassure your competition that you are still a strong player and not to count you out of the game.

5. *Regulators.* Give regulators and other governing bodies faith that you will be in compliance with all necessary rules and regulations. Remember that their perceptions of how you respond could influence your future. Act in an unprofessional manner and watch them start digging. Don't give anyone with this kind of power any reason to start probing.

- *When You Should Act.* One thought comes to mind. You should immediately respond. The senior company person should be on the scene as soon as possible. The CEO of Exxon sat in his office for three weeks after the accident in Alaska. Congress noted this response and it was not a good impression.

- *Where Management Is Located in a Contingency Situation.* Get as close to the incident as possible. If a plane crashed in Chicago, then go to the location and direct contingency operations from that city. Work from a mobile facility at the scene so you are readily available.

- *How to Respond.* Act in a professional manner at all times.

THE SEVEN RULES FOR SUCCESSFULLY MANAGING A CONTINGENCY SITUATION

A few rules are in order to successfully manage a contingency situation:

1. *Stay calm.* Everyone needs the leadership to be steady in a crisis. Coolness in times of crisis builds stability to the situation. Yet sometimes the attempt backfires. When General Alexander Haig took immediate charge after President Reagan was shot he said something to the effect, "Stay calm, I'm in charge here." What the general was doing was reacting from his military training that requires the senior person to assume command until the crisis has passed and the normal chain of command can be restored. However, the press had a different reaction.

2. *Study the situation to get a working grasp of the facts.* Information early in the situation may be sketchy and confusing. Be careful what you say because it may come back to haunt you. Whatever you do, don't make it up as you go. Ad-libbing can be dangerous to people in front of a news camera.

3. *Act in a responsible manner.* The public takes great comfort seeing someone take responsibility. The later repercussions will be diminished if senior management steps up and takes charge of the situation without finding blame or shifting blame. In fact, taking responsibility during a crisis is counterintuitive. A company's stock usually goes up afterward.

4. *Speak with one voice.* This means the story coming from the company should be consistent. To ensure one message is delivered, any and all press releases must be delivered by a team of two people working from a single reference source. A good plan is to have the senior person make an overview statement and show commitment. Then the actual designated media spokesperson or team who provides the details supports the lead contact. Secretary of Defense William Cohen used these standard techniques in the December 1998 briefing of Operation Desert Fox. Secretary Cohen would initially face the press, then turn the detailed briefing over to a team of experts.

5. *Maintain congruency.* The fastest way to get into trouble with anyone listening to your story is to be incongruent. Discrepancies stand out. Information reported as facts that doesn't seem to fit observations causes people to question your sincerity. This whole planning model is built on your telling a congruent, authentic, believable story. Doesn't lose the game now in the contingency stage. A good technique, suggested by Dr. Larry Barton, a crisis management expert consultant, is to get clarity about your goal, your message, and your audience.[8] Think through your goal. What is the outcome of your contingency plan? What message do you want to convey while executing your contingency plan? Keep your audience in mind. Who are you trying to reach? Cross-check every angle of your story to look for breaches of continuity.

6. *Be prepared.* A number of tools can be developed to help you manage perceptions and control damage during a crisis. They include:

    ■ Press kits

    ■ Video news releases

    ■ News conferences

    ■ Documentation

7. *Practice for perfection.* Prepare for the real thing by practicing as close to reality as possible. There are two scenarios for rehearsals:

    ■ *Business Situations.* Put together a team and practice simulated situations using scenario scripts. This is a technique that has been around for years. It is highly effective to get teams to think and practice how to respond to specific conditions found in contingency situations.

    ■ *Crisis Situations.* Rehearsals for crisis conditions are critical. I have firsthand experience with alert procedures and the necessary actions to get an organization on the move in a compressed time. My first duty assignment in the Army was as a platoon leader with an Infantry company in Berlin, Germany. I remember hearing a lecture at the new personnel in-briefing that got my attention. If the Russians attacked the city we would not be reinforced or relieved. We were on our own. The major command in Heidelberg must have figured they couldn't get to us across the Russian-controlled sector of Germany and the allied forces would have enough to do on their own fronts. Our plan was to create as much rubble as possible and hold Berlin with a combat-in-cities strategy. The tactic was to fight from building to building, making it costly for the enemy to gain ground.

To accomplish this strategy we had to get combat units to certain predesignated locations within the city. This meant a flawless alert system and an efficient procedure for drawing weapons and equipment. Other features of the alert system that could be relevant to any contingency planning effort included:

- A current alert roster with phone numbers of all off-post personnel
- A faultless system of command and control
- A clear set of assigned roles and responsibilities

The key to this alert procedure working as planned was rehearsals. Did we rehearse? Yes, we rehearsed, and we rehearsed, and we rehearsed until our responses were automatic when the alert siren went off.

SUMMARY

This chapter has been about being prepared for the unexpected. The mechanics of your preparation is called contingency planning. Templates for two types of contingency plans were presented. One is for business plan deviation and the other for crisis management.

If you don't take the time to adequately prepare a formal contingency plan, at least learn the six rules for behaving when a crisis does happen.

THE KEY QUESTIONS: PREPARING A SOLID CONTINGENCY PLAN

The following questions are important to your developing a solid contingency plan. They are intended as triggers to stimulate your thinking about what could help or hinder your plan:

1. Where does danger exist in my business situation?
2. Will my management team be willing to go the extra steps for contingency planning?
3. How can I make contingency planning exciting and not a fearful exercise?
4. Is my team mentally tough enough to survive a crisis situation?

THE PRACTICAL APPLICATIONS: DEVELOPING YOUR CONTINGENCY PLAN

As a result of working with the information in this chapter you will have developed two items:

1. A 1-Page Contingency Plan for either a long-term plan deviation or a crisis situation
2. A methodology to implement during a contingency situation

CHAPTER

12

Implementing and Sustaining Your Business Plan

This chapter describes how you implement and sustain your business plan. It suggests how you can assemble the plan from different levels, initiate the plan, and provide sustaining activities. These are the third and fourth steps in the four-step plan (see Figure 12-1) that began with preplanning and planning activities. Included in the implementation phase are suggestions for measuring the performance of your plan.

Figure 12-1. The implementing and sustaining phases must work together in a seamless flow to ensure execution of the plan.

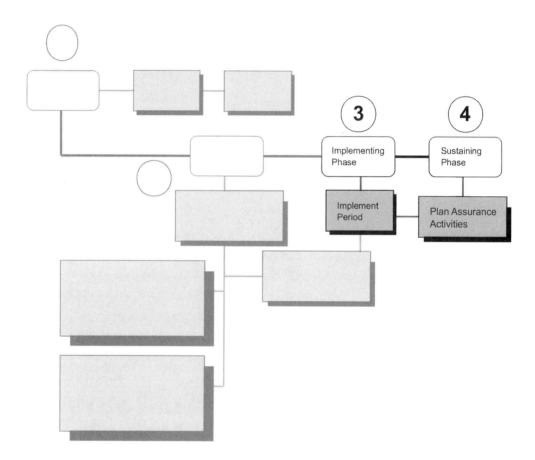

One of the key steps for implementing the plan is the removal of heat loss or organizational inefficiencies inherent to any system. This chapter provides the steps for you to successfully map and correct any deficiencies.

The chapter concludes with information on conducting organizational change activities, along with suggestions on leadership and managership skills development. For the plan to succeed it must be implemented by people with the basic skills of leading and managing the workforce.

HOW TO IMPLEMENT YOUR PLAN

The implementing period begins with a consolidation of the various levels of plans. Once your subordinate planning teams have taken the planning details of Level 1 down to Levels 2, 3, or 4, they must be reassembled to ensure plan continuity. To do this, schedule a one-day conference with representatives from each team where they present their own supporting plan and display their interpretation of the concepts. The idea is to cross-check the viability of plans across a single level, then roll the information upward to the next level. If the teams have properly followed the provided planning templates, the plans should fit together with minimum adjustment. If one subplan is out of alignment, that particular planning team must go back to adjust its targets, objectives, or goals.

If the plan fits together at Level 1, implementation begins with a communication from top management to execute tasks found in the action plan initiated according to the schedule. This leads to the most important part of implementation—the use of performance measurements.

Monitoring Your Plan to Ensure Compliance

Your plan should be monitored frequently to make sure it is being implemented in the spirit and intent of the planning conference. Some businesses in certain situations elect to monitor their progress or success on a weekly basis. This is probably appropriate for operational levels in an organization. For example, in a manufacturing environment you may choose to monitor daily and formally report weekly. Some organizations choose to report on a monthly basis. Tracking sales monthly is a common example. The minimum length of time allowed without formally checking your plan is a quarter. Reporting results on a quarterly basis is the most accepted business practice for performance measures. The framework is consistent with financial reporting, shareholder expectations, and public acceptance. I recommend this as your minimum reporting schedule (see Figure 12-2).

Figure 12-2. The implementation period is characterized by quarterly reviews. A full review and update of the plan is conducted in the fourth quarter.

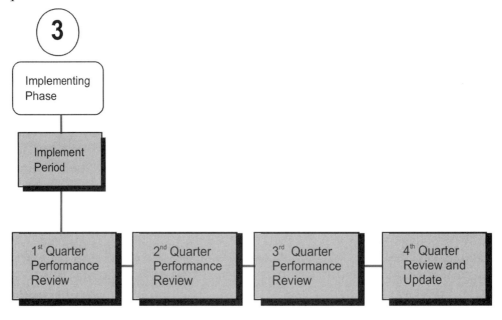

The fourth point of monitoring your plan is the annual report. At the end of the fourth quarter you need to look back at the four quarters collectively. The past year is compared with the previous year and projected out to the ten-year plan. This gives you a baseline to begin planning for the next year or repeating the one-year operational plan. The results are published in the annual report. Companies spend a lot of money and effort writing, publishing, and distributing their annual report. You may make the report simple or detailed, depending on your desire and intent.

In establishing the next operational plan, year two of the ten years, repeat the process of setting tasks as you did with the first operational plan and the related action plan list. Each year you rebuild your operational plan based on what you are trying to accomplish in the one-year period against the ten-year goals. This means your plan's time span is getting shorter each year. The common trap is to also extend the life of the business plan by one year—always keeping a ten-year time frame. This is dangerous because you fall into the trap of strategic planning creep. Allow your plan to perform or mature for a number of years before you move the ten-year goals. My clients seem to get three or four years completed on their ten-year business plan before they move the end goals. This allows them to check assumptions, qualify the accuracy of their numbers, and measure their sustained performance. The recommendation, therefore, is to let your plan run a few years before radically shifting goals. Minor adjustments are necessary and acceptable, but don't abandon your goals and plans in the first year.

Tracking the performance of your plan is easy. The numbers can be tallied. The actions can be checked off for completion. The real problem with performance is not measurement but rather accountability. What do you do when the plan is not being fulfilled? Investigate the reasons for not hitting the targets carefully before you take action. Consider these questions:

■   *Is it normal statistical deviation?* No one can accurately predict where your performance will fall on a projection chart. The plan may be off because of normal statistical deviation, or what is called the zig and zag. The issue is how far off you are from where you wanted to be. Is 5 percent deviation (i.e., a subjective percentage you set) acceptable? Can you live with 10 percent deviation? If the deviation is not in the end acceptable, you must go back into your plan to look at the data. Reexamine information such as sales projections, costs of doing business, and profit margins to find the source of plan failure. Make corrections accordingly. Remember, shortfalls are compounded. The further you get behind the further you get behind. The efforts to catch up expand exponentially.

■ *Is it a failure of the management team to implement?* This is the most common cause of plan deviation. Repeatedly I find teams not fulfilling promises made in the action plan. Once the planning session is over, business as usual prevails. The individual or team doesn't follow through with commitments. The antidote for individual failure or non-compliance is to tie the results of the plan into your performance reward program. People have a tendency to do the things for which they are rewarded. Consistent failure to perform takes on a whole different meaning that begins with coaching, progresses to performance counseling, and finally ends with termination. The sooner you legitimately get rid of nonperforming management, the greater your chance of hitting your targets.

Measuring Everyone Against a Business Performance Model

There are three levels of performance you must consider when formally tracking your business plan (see Figure 12-3). The performance is tied specifically to the annual targets of the business plan. This standard keeps each level focused on doing mission-essential work, not extraneous, fun activities. These levels are:

■ Level 1. Organizational performance (business plan track)

■ Level 2. Team performance (business plan track)

■ Level 3. Individual performance (performance review program)

Figure 12-3. There are three levels of performance that must be tracked against the business plan. They are organizational, team, and individual. All lead to the strategic goals.

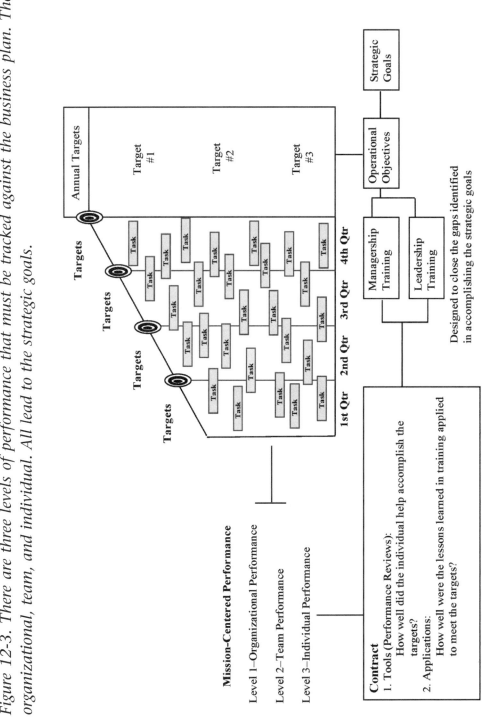

At the first level of performance measurement the company as a whole must be held accountable. This demands command responsibility. Managers are responsible for all that their units do or fail to do. Performance measurements are not complex at that level. The question is simple: Did the company hit the plan it established? If yes, the organizational performance is acceptable. If the answer is no, then excuses are not acceptable. If a company fails, then the president must be responsible and should answer to the board of directors for his or her failure to provide appropriate leadership and managership of the organization and its plan. It is that simple.

Likewise at Level 2, managers are held accountable for their teams using the same command responsibility concept. The vice president is held accountable for making the sales figures or the research and development vice president is responsible and accountable for bringing new products in on schedule. Vice presidents answer to the president in the same fashion as the president answers to the board of directors—no excuses. Their appropriate bosses likewise hold other team leaders such as plant managers accountable.

Level 3 performance is the individual measure of what is done and how well it is done. The performance review items normally found in human resources documents must accurately reflect the actual tasks the individual does each day to accomplish the annual targets. Again, no extraneous work should be allowed. The key is a fully qualified individual focused on mission-essential items. The business plan must include provisions for leadership and managership training to fill expected skills shortfalls. Don't ask people to do jobs they are not trained to do without providing them support. This training is looped back to the performance review system. How well were the lessons learned in training applied to perform the job? This criterion ties any company training activities to the business plan, prevents training for training's sake, and makes accountability for skills integral to the individual performance review.

Establishing Two Types of Standards of Performance

To successfully implement processes at the three levels, management must set and maintain its standards. This is a stabilizing factor in any organization. There are certain performance levels that must be held constant. In widely fluctuating situations it becomes difficult to know what performance factors are satisfactory and what are unsatisfactory.

Management must improve its standards. Standards are not fixed points or objectives, but rather the start points for doing a better job the next time. Once performance is fixed in place with the maintenance of standards, improvement begins.

Two types of standards exist: stabilized and evolving. Stabilized standards are the standards that tell individuals how their performance is measured. Goals and objectives usually contain standards. This helps provide stability to the work situation. As the stabilized standards are met and improvements in the workflow occur, the standards are shifted upward. These standards are said to be evolving as the system becomes fine-tuned. There can be no improvement (the ultimate goal of process mapping) if there are no standards, they are not disciplined, or they are not allowed to evolve.

Standards carry certain characteristics that help the organization form, shape, and project consistency in its story. These may be found in company documents such as the Standard Operation Procedures or policy manuals. Too few standards are a lack of discipline while too many standards could become overwhelming. Seek a working balance. The standards should have the following characteristics:

- They become the individual authorization and responsibility to carry out work.

- They are transmittal vehicles of individual experience to the next generation of employees.

- They communicate individual experience and know-how to the organization.

■ They demonstrate an accumulation of experience within the organization through their evolving nature.

■ They deploy know-how from one department to another.

■ They serve as a mark of discipline for the organization.

HOW TO SUSTAIN YOUR PLAN: THE FOUR PLAN ASSURANCE ACTIVITIES

Your plan cannot be launched without support in the background. There are at least four support areas (see Figure 12-4) for the successful implementation of your plan. They are:

1. Business Process Mapping

2. Organizational change management

3. Leadership development

4. Management development

First you must clean up any organizational inefficiency found in the processes. This is done through Business Process Mapping (BPM). Don't delay the implementation of your action plan until the process improvements are completed because they will never be finished and must be seen as ongoing initiatives. The BPM can and should run concurrent with your plan implementation.

A number of organizational change activities may also take place to support your plan. They may include activities such as restructuring the organization, an acquisition for growth, or restructuring the debt burden. Strategically realigning the resources and core competencies may be other examples of the organizational change necessary to support the future direction of your company.

Leadership and managership behavior must also be aligned with the plan. Little is accomplished by establishing a vision if leadership is remiss or by setting bold goals if the skill of managerial efforts is lacking. Actions for improving leadership functions and management behaviors necessary to match the plan requirements must be carefully programmed.

Figure 12-4. During the sustaining phase you must pay attention to four sets of activities required to keep the planning momentum.

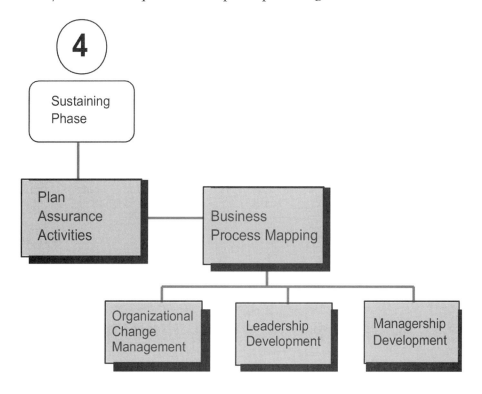

BUSINESS PROCESS MAPPING TO IMPROVE YOUR BOTTOM LINE

To ensure the healthy implementation of your business plan you must remove heat loss by conducting a series of Business Process Mapping sessions. These activities are designed specifically to remove excessive costs from your business processes through eliminating unnecessary, overlapping, and duplicate events while assigning responsibility and holding managers responsible for cost control and cost containment (see Figure 12-5).

Figure 12-5. Business Process Mapping streamlines your internal ways of doing work. That is your fastest way to increase the bottom line.

Your process looks like this.

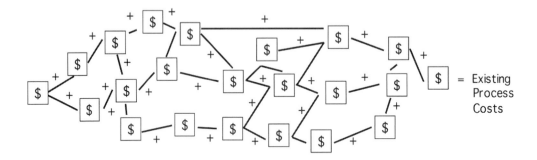

You want it to look like this.

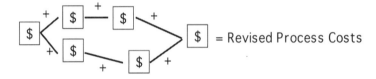

Two ways of thinking must be dovetailed for process mapping to work. First, the manager must be concerned with results. Of course results are ultimately the profit goal of any business. That doesn't mean that profit drives all actions. It simply means that profit and other cost issues must be accounted for in the thinking process. You must be results-oriented. This means a concern for profitability, cost-effectiveness, and financial goal accomplishment. The second is to think in terms of processes. This means a concern for organizational discipline and workflow effectiveness. Often the results become the focus to the exclusion of the process. The successful execution of process mapping can occur only if both process and results are integrated.

Process mapping is inherently difficult for American managers. This difficulty stems from a basic philosophy ingrained in us. We are taught to make great strides in actions by "thinking big," "stretching out," or "going for the gold." The dream of every engineer is to make a technological breakthrough in his or her field. While this is great for advancing the field of knowledge, it goes against the purpose of process mapping, which is continual, incremental improvement. This division of philosophies is so pronounced it is seen as a major difference between Japanese and American business practices. Americans pride themselves on innovation. We like to take great leaps forward by building things first. This is a successful method of moving a business forward by bounds. It is like hitting a home run in baseball. It doesn't happen in every game but when it does the results are significant. On the other hand, the Japanese pride themselves on improving existing creations. They play a steady game by opting for base hits. They see incremental improvement as the best way to win the game. This is also a successful business tool. When the two methods are compared in terms of returns on investments as business ventures, the gradual development or incremental approach historically provides the greater return.

I suggest a combination of the two approaches. You are encouraged to look for opportunities to excel. However, the real leverages in the business are in the gradual development of a fine-tuned system. This will be through process mapping and improvements of the system itself.

Levels of Processes

There are four generally accepted levels of key business processes:

1. *Level 1—Macro Business Activities.* These are functions that are the responsibility of the top management of the company. They are big picture or major activities that require high-level decision making and significantly affect the future of the company. An example may be the acquisi-

tion process. The process owners are the president and vice presidents.

2. *Level 2—Companywide Functions.* These are activities that are critical to the company but cut across functional boundaries. They are owned by a high-level executive but must be coordinated with other peer executives. Sales may be an example. While this activity is the responsibility of the vice president of sales, it must be fully coordinated with research and development, manufacturing, and shipping.

3. *Level 3—Functional or Departmental Processes.* Lower-level processes fall within the responsibility of a department and have less coordination requirements across departmental lines. For example, the process of producing a new design of wallpaper may be the primary responsibility of the creative department.

4. *Level 4—Unit/Work Group or Individual Processes.* Most processes to carry out business are found at the lowest level of the organization. Your business is a collage of many teams and individuals doing daily work. These are usually routine and often overlooked as candidates for the process mapping. Yet we know this is where some of your greatest inefficiencies occur. They may be as simple as checking in customers at the service department of an automobile dealership or conducting preventive maintenance on a piece of machinery.

The Payoffs of Process Mapping

Of all the activities that an organization can do to improve its financial position, challenge employees, and produce better performance, process mapping takes the lead. It is the fastest way I know to return the greatest amount of resources back into the system. Those resources may be dollars on the profit and loss statement, hours saved on manufacturing processes, or quality improvements in goods or services. In any case the rewards or return for process mapping should be to:

- Achieve maximum return for minimum effort.
- Achieve maximum quality with maximum efficiency.
- Eliminate unproductive hard work.
- Use resources in an effective manner.
- Make informed decisions to implement continuous improvements or reengineering.

The ability to recover inefficiencies, cut costs, and improve service is well documented in everyday examples. Many of these activities are tied to quality improvement programs. In 1992 the Rochester Institute of Technology (RIT) in Rochester, New York, teamed with *USA Today* to recognize teams that have made significant improvements in work processes. The 2000 winners and finalists include improvements such as the NCR EDI invoicing process improvement team that improved invoicing from 66.8 percent to 99.6 percent in just five months. Consider what that will do for the company's cash flow. Or consider the Team of the Future at Cordis Corporation, a medical device manufacturer in Miami Lakes, Florida, that eliminated waste in its manufacturing process. They were able to save more than $152,000 yearly by eliminating excess shrinkage in the plastics-curing process. That may not sound like much, but a little here and a little there adds up. Remember, this money goes back to the bottom line.

The Six Purposes of Process Mapping

The basic assumption of any organization is that it desires to improve its business performance. Improvement begins with looking at the way people do their work. Therefore, if a company wishes to stay a strong, viable business it must look for leverage points in its functions where improvements can be made at both the organizational and individual levels. You should use process mapping specifically to:

■ *Solve problems.* Unresolved problems are a drain on your efficiency, annoy people, and create low morale. Problem solving is usually a set of questions to be initially asked. Process mapping can be used to solve problems by helping answer three questions:

1. What is the problem? (This is called the problem statement.)
2. Why is this a problem?
3. How will you solve the problem?

■ *Define individual responsibility, authority, and accountability.* This means tasks within a company, project, or work team are assigned. It answers the questions of who is responsible for each task, what authority they have to complete the work, and how you plan to hold them accountable.

■ *Clarify work.* If we understand individual responsibilities then we must eliminate redundant tasks, eliminate repetition, and reduce effort by having a clear picture of what constitutes work.

■ *Eliminate task redundancy and duplication.* Redundant work is unnecessary, not cost-effective, and detracts from focused performance toward objectives. Often redundancy occurs when departments fail to clarify areas of responsibility and two individuals are working on the same project unknown to each other.

■ *Initiate continual improvement.* By cleaning up the specifics of workflow, improvements begin to appear in the system.

■ *Initiate reengineering if necessary.* Reengineering is an alternative choice that may develop from a process map. This decision is reached when the advantages of small changes are not sufficient to warrant the continuation of the process. If a major or bold improvement is needed, the decision becomes one to reengineer.

Process Mapping as a Motivational Tool

At the individual level, process mapping takes on a more practical tone and less of a textbook meaning. For decades management consultants have looked for the magic formula for motivating employees. The heart of the answer is to give people challenging, meaningful work. A process that is repetitive, redundant, and excessive does not meet that specification. To improve the overall sense of achievement among employees try process mapping specifically to:

- Make the job easier for the employee.
- Remove drudgery found in noncritical, boring work.
- Remove nuisances that get in the way of productivity.
- Make the job more productive overall.
- Improve the quality of the activity.
- Save time by eliminating wasted motion.
- Save costs by effectively using resources.

The Practical Applications of Process Mapping

I suggest you use Business Process Mapping to get a better picture of your organization's efforts. This accomplishes clarification of what has to be done and identifies the interdependencies of the work. If you develop a process map of divisional, departmental, and unit workflow you can eliminate redundant tasks, repetition, and unnecessary effort by having a clear picture of what constitutes work because you will know where work comes from, what work has to be done, and in what order.

The process map also establishes interdependencies for work tasks: This means you know whom you are dependent on for workflow information. It also means you are identified as a resource to someone else in the system as a dependency. It is critical to understand the connecting dependencies with other departments and divisions as well as the individual responsibilities. A process flow map shows those dependencies and provides an opportunity to clarify and agree to them. It spells out where work goes and who depends on the work.

To study tasks you must think in terms of what is done and what is implied. The implied is the most difficult. Embedded in the work maybe a hidden task. There are often many implied tasks that get overlooked. When ignored, they become the single most common reason for failure to communicate, coordinate, and act on an issue. These implied tasks should be shown on the process map.

How and Where to Start Process Mapping

Here are the steps for building a process map. Before you begin the actual work to build your process maps consider the following steps:

1. Identify all the processes you suspect need attention. This is best done with your management team and any expert advice from the employee pool.

2. Next establish which processes need to be addressed first. Your team will know where the greatest problems are because they deal with these things every day. Pick four or five to run simultaneously. You cannot do everything at once, so stay with a limited number.

3. Designate the process owners, define their responsibilities, and charge each with the authority to execute a corrected map. Tie this to the owner's performance review.

The next level of activities is to conduct the Business Process Mapping. Get your teams together in a large room with tables, long rolls of paper, and plenty of sticky notes for building the charts. You will use this manual method first because of the ongoing modifications to be made in developing the charts. When you are satisfied with the final results, the chart can be shifted to a workflow software package on your computer.

The following sequence for conducting a process mapping session has proved very effective over time and with a number of successful mapping teams:

1. Present a mini-overview of how the business process works. The participants need to know the mechanics of the process.

2. Complete the first map selected by each team. This is a flow of the "as is" activities.

3. Develop the "costs" of the map by putting a dollar figure on each action and adding the figures.

4. Develop a "wish list" of what you want each new map to do for your business.

5. Complete the second map of the process "as it could be."

6. Develop the "costs" of the map using the same criteria as you did for the first map.

7. Compare the costs of maps one and two.

8. Discuss what value each new version of the maps brings to the organization. This is where the "heat loss" or organizational inefficiency is really amplified.

9. Make decisions about how to implement the new map into the system. Make sure it is tied to individual accountability.

Connecting Individual Performance With Process Mapping

Earlier in the book I made a case for too many pitchers and only one batter: the employee having too many tasks. I strongly suggest you cut the number of individual tasks down to four or five mission-essential actions. These become the starting points for individual process mapping. Have each employee ask just two basic questions.

1. What are my tasks?

2. What is my understanding of the end product or results of doing my tasks?

To study tasks you must think in terms of what is specified in the job description and what is implied. This means your specified task is usually given to you while the implied tasks are embedded in the requirement. There are often many implied tasks that get overlooked. When ignored they become the single most common reason for failure to communicate, coordinate, and act on an issue.

The tasks you do each day can be grouped in terms of their significance to the organization. This priority listing gives clues to what is most important or what can be delayed. Tasks can be divided into four types:

1. *Ongoing Daily Work.* These are the things you do as a matter of routine. They are so frequent that they become the pattern or fabric of your daily activities.

2. *One-off Tasks.* These are unique tasks that you must attend to on an infrequent basis. They are usually small in scope and scale but require close attention before they become problem areas. You may or may not see these tasks or similar ones again for months. You may or may not choose to chart or schedule them in a formal fashion.

3. *Mini Projects.* These are tasks of a larger scope and scale than routine. You will probably choose to chart (e.g., using a Program Evaluation and Review Technique (PERT) or flowchart) or schedule these events because they require more coordination, closer attention to suspense dates, and better planning. It may be too much to carry around in your head or on a few notes in your calendar.

4. *Major Projects.* These are tasks of a very large scope and scale. They are often large enough to have a full-time project manager. The task may be so large that it overshadows your present duties. In most cases you will be required to chart or schedule this event as part of the company's historical management records. Because it requires more coordination, closer attention to suspense dates, and better resources planning, you must give this type of task

careful attention and sufficient time. You should use computers to assist you in both the development and the management of a project of this size.

Preliminary Questions Before Process Mapping

As you get ready to process map your job, there are certain questions to keep in mind. By asking these questions of yourself you may save problems later on in the actual mapping:

- What is the purpose of my job?
- When the process map is completed, what will be the outcomes?
- What problems may I expect to encounter?
- What is my authority?
- What is my responsibility?
- What items will I be held accountable for?
- What is my budget?
- What are my time restrictions?
- Who are my customers?
- Who and what are my resources?
- Who must I coordinate with to do my job?

Process Ownership and Management to Overcome Four Obstacles

The planning team must recognize and address several factors in the work environment that hinder establishment of a lean operating system. These are ingrained business phenomena that must be identified and negated. For instance:

- Business processes overlap functional boundaries yet you allow islands of power (i.e., stovepipes) to exist in the functioning of your business even though they are inefficient, disruptive, and self-serving.

■ Identified problems are usually solved within functional boundaries and often focus only on immediate problem resolution and not necessarily on the root cause. This means the solving of a problem by one staff function may actually cause problems for another agency.

■ Organizations have a tendency to seek a stage of internal equilibrium and comfort within organization boundaries. Ongoing improvement is not a natural state. Change is unnatural, feared, and resisted by most organizations.

■ The only persons who have responsibility over all aspects of a single process usually have such broad responsibilities they cannot devote adequate attention to lead the improvement process.

The best solution for the above-mentioned conditions is to assign each process to an owner. In the course of managing a process, an owner assumes responsibility for the output of the work units over which she has no direct control. This fact establishes the need for a process owner who is high enough in the organizational hierarchy to be able to get the work done. The process owner must be able to influence decisions and people outside her direct area of responsibility. The owner must have an overall perspective of her business and the environment to assess its impact on the process. Finally, there must be a reward or punishment factor for success or failure. The owner must be personally affected by the outcome of the process.

The process owner serves a critical role within the confines of the business plan. Without the support of various champions of the processes, the plan slides back to mediocre results. For the process owners to conduct meaningful business they need the authority to evaluate and approve the process as it is developed. That authority includes monitoring and rating people on how well processes are functioning. The ultimate test of a company process mapping activity is whether the results of the map are tied to the performance review system.

Using Teams in Process Improvement Activities

Successful companies know that when properly used, teams can produce significant results. They include teams in process improvement. Teamwork is defined as active participation in, and facilitation of, team effectiveness; taking actions that demonstrate consideration for the feelings and needs of others; and being aware of the effect of one's behaviors on others.

Before considering using the team approach, examine and answer these three questions:

1. *Are all functions represented?* Remember that most processes cross multiple boundaries and have an affect on other departments, units, or teams. Often these conditions are cloudy or obscure, so think carefully when putting together the cross-functional team to build the map.

2. *Are technical experts required?* Make sure you have the correct skills represented on the team to answer technical questions. This will save you time and embarrassment in the long run.

3. *Are there functions outside the process to be analyzed that need to be represented?* This means you must understand where the process fits into the bigger picture of your business functions. Little is accomplished by solving a problem in finance if it creates more problems in personnel.

THE FIVE ORGANIZATIONAL CHANGES TO SUPPORT THE BUSINESS PLAN

To carry out your plan you may need to institute change management activities. These are basic changes to the way you currently operate that will create resistance when altered or redirected. Normally these activities have long-term cultural implications and require the support of the workforce to be fully effective. A few areas frequently identified with organizational change are:

■ *Changing the Company Vision.* Any change in direction brings on concerns from the workforce along with a variety of reactions. Some employees may agree and support the vision shift while others may agree with the new direction but are fearful of the effort required. Still others will not agree with the new direction because it may be a radical shift from the very foundations of the company. This happens frequently when new management is brought into a sluggish, established company and tries to make a fresh start.

■ *Changing the Company Drivers or Focus.* A company focused on one driver attempting to shift to another focus will experience serious upheaval. For example, shifting from operational excellence to a customer-intimate focus will create confusion on the part of the employees. Just communicating the shift and describing examples of the required new behavior is time-consuming, painful, and tedious for management.

■ *Changing the Company Structure.* Just the rumor of an organizational change sends negative messages into the heart of the workforce. Structural change gets quickly translated into downsizing with the integral loss of jobs.

■ *Changing the Company's Management Behavior.* If a company is autocratic, doesn't share power, and uses centralized decision making, it is difficult to make a believable change. Perhaps new key managers take control and want to operate from a posture of collaboration, shared power, and consensus decision making. The residual effect of the old management style will be a strong influence for years on the new team.

To successfully incorporate change management and counter the above-mentioned conditions, the planning team must consider five important steps:

1. *Make sure the business plan is complete and reaches to the lowest level of the organization.* Participation of all levels in the planning model eliminates misunderstanding and dampens fears.

2. *Make sure the final plan is communicated to the operator level.* A plan that goes on the shelf or is not heard from again is designed to fail. The employees must know the final decisions and disposition of the plan.

3. *Make sure the plan is what you do every day.* If your plan requires you to do one thing but you do another on a daily basis, the plan is not believable. It is a worthless document that wasted everyone's time.

4. *Make sure the plan is monitored, measured, and accounted for in terms of results.* Let executives, managers, supervisors, and employees know you are serious about the effort put into the planning process by holding them accountable for the results.

5. *Make sure the executive team models effective managerial behavior.* The term *role model* cannot be overstated. Require every level of management and supervision to adhere to the core values and practice the philosophy of the company in day-to-day examples.

ASSURANCES FOR LEADERSHIP AND MANAGERSHIP DEVELOPMENT

So far we've covered two of the four plan assurance activities for the successful implementation of your plan. We've covered business process planning and organizational change management in some detail. The last two plan assurance activities are leadership development and managership development. They are grouped together for discussion in this section.

Leadership and managership training necessary to support the business plan is not a universal or blanket program. Rather, it is a tailored approach to focus on the shortfalls identified either in the employee satisfaction survey or during the gap analysis of your principles, values, and philosophy.

The Two Techniques for Skills Training

Two techniques to fill your skills shortfall are the spot approach and the vertical/horizontal integration approach:

1. *The Spot Approach.* Not everyone in the organization requires skill-building training. Topics should not be universally applied to the entire company body, but rather only to those who need the training. If one supervisor needs a refresher on problem solving don't make every supervisor attend. If an executive needs to polish her interpersonal skills, don't subject the whole team to the training. Using the tailored or spot approach saves the organization vast amounts of money in travel expenses, seminar fees, and lost employee productivity.

2. *The Vertical/Horizontal Approach.* This technique is used when you determine that a subject has shortfalls across all lines of manager and supervisor levels. Vertical integration means that you start with the executive level and cascade the subject downward. Do not—I repeat, do not—start with the lowest level of supervisors. A case in point could be leadership training. If you try to teach empowerment, delegation, and freedom to fail to a group of supervisors who are presently being managed by a reincarnation of Attila the Hun, you will fail. Their question will be, "Has my manager had this training?" If not, they will turn off the training as unbelievable because they know the concepts will not change upper management behavior.

   Horizontal integration means all training should lead to the next logical training piece. Training session one should show continuity to training session and subject two. This prevents the training subject from becoming a stand-alone topic with no connection to your plan or other training activities.

SUMMARY

This chapter was designed to assist you with implementing and sustaining your business plan. It included the third and fourth steps of the four-step planning process.

THE KEY QUESTIONS: IMPLEMENTING AND SUSTAINING YOUR BUSINESS PLAN

Use the following ten questions when preparing to implement your business plan.

1. Do you understand how to reassemble the plan by bringing the lower-level plans together?

2. Do you know what to do if there is a disconnect in the data of the lower-level plans and they do not add up to the Level 1 plan?

3. How do you intend to monitor progress? Weekly? Monthly? Quarterly? Annually?

4. Do you have a fully functional quarterly reporting system that is consistent with good financial reporting practices?

5. Do your performance tasks found in the action plan tie in to individual performance criteria?

6. Have you properly identified the processes necessary to map for organizational effectiveness?

7. Does each process have an owner and a team dedicated to improving the process?

8. Have the expected results of the process mapping been tied to individual performance?

9. Have you properly identified the organizational change resistance points for any changes you need to make? If yes, what actions have you taken to negate the negative influence of these resistance points?

10. Have you properly identified all the leadership and managership issues found in your surveys or in the gap analysis stages of your planning? Do you know how to fix the shortfalls?

THE PRACTICAL APPLICATIONS: IMPLEMENTING AND SUSTAINING ACTIVITIES

By following this suggested sequence of implementation you'll gain an understanding of how to establish monitoring and measuring steps at required intervals. Do the following five steps:

1. Consolidate the plan at Level 1.
2. Distribute the plan to all levels.
3. Monitor the plan on a regular time frame.
4. Make corrective actions to the plan as necessary.
5. Update the operational plan at the end of each year.

A Word From the Author

Becoming a really good planner in this new millennium is the theme of this book. We are smart people with centuries of experience trying to figure out how to make organizations work. You should be using what we already know about planning. But maybe we have been looking in the wrong direction for the last hundred years. To get a company story right you need to first get your management story together. How can you lead and manage if that story is a shambles: inconsistent, incongruent, and unbelievable?

I'm not going to start suggesting new models for the millennium for two reasons. First, there are already enough consultants trying to cash in on that. Noticed the number of new book titles that reference the twenty-first century? It seems as if we woke up on January 1, 2000, in some significantly different place.

The second reason is that many of the business models we have now are actually quite good. We know quality is a good thing. Nobody refutes taking care of the customer. It would be silly to discount high-performance work teams. Let's sort through everything we know about managing a business and throw out what doesn't work, keeping what does work, regardless of its originating school of management. The twenty-first century could be a time of great management consolidation in the known practices of successful managers, provided we don't get distracted.

Another thought is to look in a new direction. Instead of always reflecting outward, searching for new models, or tasting another flavor of the month, perhaps it is time for inward reflection. The most serious blocks to management success in the past 100 years haven't been the models, but rather the people implementing the models. Let's stop projecting our inability to lead and manage onto some intangible construct or management theory. The fault lies squarely on the shoulders of those who are in the leadership positions in every company.

Maybe this is the time to do serious reflection on how each of us carries out our leadership duties. There is no shortage of managers, but I see a serious void in leadership. Most businesses succeed in spite of their management, not because of it.

The solution I'm suggesting is for every one of you to examine your management story. Start with your vision. Where are you going? Are you just treading water or do you have some form of a vision that extends past quarterly earnings? What is your mission? Do you have purpose, or is what you do every day meaningless activity? When I was a young lieutenant my first platoon sergeant had a great saying when he caught a troop loafing: "Soldier, do you have a purpose or are you just wearing out good government boot leather and breathing our good air?" The sergeant always made his point. Are you just consuming something or are you contributing to mission-essential activity?

What are your core values? What do you stand for as a role model and businessperson? Daily I see examples of managers who don't know what they stand for in either position. They are willing to do whatever it takes to make it through the day. They tolerate horrible relationships and impossible situations, quietly hoping to just get by with some semblance of sanity.

I consider myself lucky, because I had my core values tested at an early age. Before I was thirty years old, I had twice been to war and participated at the basic level of a combat soldier. Not many people get to experience what it means to spend their day just trying to survive. It puts a whole different perspective on things, shaping and molding your leadership and managership thinking. When you live for two years out of a backpack you learn to be grateful. Everything you get in life after that experience is a bonus.

Before you start your company down a path of planning, I suggest you take a few days off to think about these things. When was the last time you had time for yourself, to reflect on your leadership and to muse about your management activities? As managers you are always taking care of other people. Who is taking care of you? Get away for a few days and give thought to what you need to do to build a story that is believable to yourself first and then to others around you. Build your story using the templates I provide throughout this book. They were designed for a company business plan, but I have helped many managers over the past few years with their own professional stories using the exact same templates. The concepts are the same; just translate them to your story as an individual. Get your managerial story together, come back strong and powerful, and plan to accomplish the great vision of which you are capable for your company.

The Full Business Planning Model

A business plan is simple on the one hand yet sophisticated on the other. You must be able to present that simplicity and complexity simultaneously. Your picture must encompass both the short- and long-term views. It must be strategic yet contain details of the daily requirements. The concept must include verification of where you are today as well as documentation of where you intend to take the business. It must serve as a reference tool for your employees and management as they conduct business.

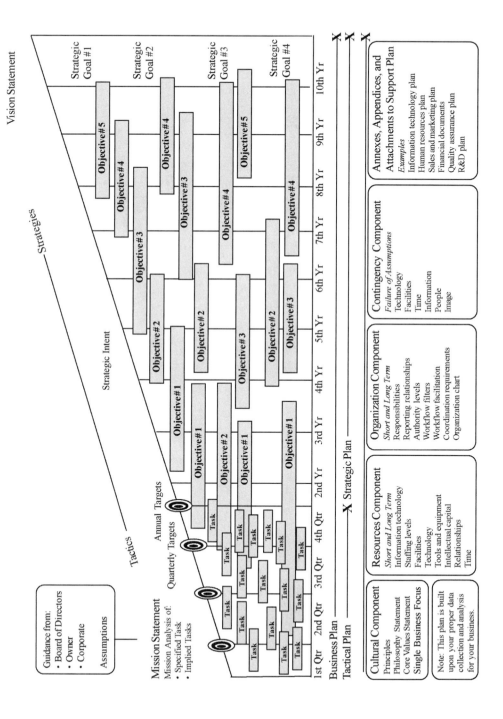

B

The 1-Page Strategic Plan

You can easily build a complete 1-Page Strategic Plan as a result of this activity. Modify this form as necessary. Use the front and back if you need more space, but keep it to one page. Do not get distracted by the order or sequencing of the blocks on this page. Arrange the elements any way they will fit.

Vision Statement

A short sentence that captures the spirit and intent of where you plan to take the company. A full vision is the sum of of all five business plans and should not be included on this page of the business plan.

Strategic Intent

A summary statement of short length of what you intend to implement and how you will do it.

Strategies

Key statements about how you will accomplish your goal. A pure planning model has only a few strategies for the complete plan.

Strategic Goals

Bold statements of what you expect to accomplish.

Objectives

Short-term or intermediate steps to accomplish the more broad strategic goals. Each goal should have four or five objectives. These must be specific, measurable, achievable, realistic, and have a specified time frame. Usually an objective has a key staff member as the champion or owner.

Focus

A description of your single driving force. This is selected from one of the six drivers identified in your operational plan (see Appendix C).

Values

What you hold important to the organization as behavioral guidelines.

Philosophy

A statement of an underlying belief of what will cause you to be successful.

Principles

Basic truths by which you lead and manage your business. These are tests of your business plan. They may or may not be restated in the actual plan.

Guidance

This is a description of any restrictions placed on you. Your plan must not exceed these boundaries.

Assumptions

Baselines on which you make your plan. If they change, your plan must change.

Mission

A one-sentence statement that defines your current business and includes a higher-order purpose.

The 1-Page Operational Plan

You can easily build a complete 1-Page Operational Plan as a result of this activity. Modify this example as necessary. Use the front and back if you need more space, but keep it to one page.

Six Drivers

This is a review of the driving forces within your system to ensure you account for each as an influencer in your business. There are six: players, processes, plans, products, properties, and payoffs. One driver should have been accounted for in the strategic component as your focus (see Appendix B).

Tactics

How you plan to accomplish the tasks.
This is the short-term action to achieve a specific goal (i.e., "how" you plan to execute your mission).

Concept of Operation

This is a short narrative of how you plan to implement actions for the next year to achieve your annual targets. Consider it a stand-alone overview of your execution of the first year of the strategic plan. This item is to briefly explain what you intend to do in the next year and how you will do it.

Coordinating Instructions

These are specific instructions to each unit for how they are to coordinate their collective implied tasks. Instructions ensure continuity of the process of providing the goods or services. Look for these in the implied tasks of the mission statement.

Mission

Restatement of the mission and an analysis of implied tasks.

Tasks (i.e., what you plan to get done)

This is a detailed list of all the items that must be accomplished. There are four sources of tasks:

1. Tasks that are derived from the formula goal, objectives, and tasks.
2. Tasks that are derived from the mission statement analysis (i.e. implied tasks).
3. Tasks that are derived from the human resources job description.
4. Tasks that you must do to provide quick hits and close the gaps found in your cultural evaluation. Gaps between what you "say" and "do" create a credibility issue. If these are not immediately addressed, your plan will be in jeopardy.

All four sets of these tasks must be combined into one inclusive document. They must be displayed at some point in a time-related chart to ensure you have not grouped all the tasks into the first quarter. The chart may look like the representation below.

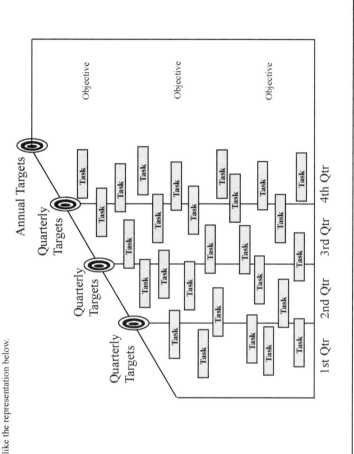

D

The 1-Page Organizational Plan

Y ou can easily build a complete 1-Page Organizational Plan as a result of this activity. Modify this example as necessary. Use the front and back if you need more space, but keep it to one page.

Soft Infrastructure

The basic command and control needed for the management of the business. This function ties directly to the culture component dealing with the organization's philosophy, values, and principles. The soft infrastructure includes:

1. Authority Levels: Is the right amount of authority pushed down to the lowest level?
2. Responsibility Levels: Does this match with the authority level?
3. Accountability Methods: How and how often are people being held accountable for measurable results?

It also maps:

1. The information flow through the system
2. The flow of decision making
3. The informal channels of leadership
4. The levels of power and influence by groups and individuals

Organization Charting

A traditional wiring diagram illustrates two dimensions:

1. Reporting relationships
2. Groups to accomplish work

For illustration purposes this organizational chart has been reduced in scope and scale.

Filters

Is there:
Fragmentation of tasks?
Duplication of work?

Is:
Work being done by the right person?
All work being done that should be done?
Unnecessary work being done?

Facilitation

Does the structure:

1. Use the talents of all people and resources?
2. Aid coordination among the critical staff sections?
3. Make communications between and among work units easy?
4. Facilitate the development, motivation, and retention of key people?
5. Achieve minimum costs?
6. Provide for logical growth and succession of the management team?
7. Facilitate coordination of special project teams?

Hard Infrastructure

The basic facilities, equipment, services, and installations needed for the growth and functioning of the business. This might include:

1. *Facilities Utilization Plan (Annex)*. This ties directly to and must be coordinated with the resources component (see Appendix E).

2. *Equipment Utilization Plan (Annex)* This includes items such as local area networks and computer installations that support the basic business functions.

Functions

A review of the mission statement for each work unit ensures all organizational functions are covered. Examples are:

Operational division is to————.
Principal Staff
HR is to————.
Marketing is to————.
Operations is to————.
Administration and logistics is to————.
Special Staff
Financial
IT
Legal

Note: Functions, filters, and facilitation are elements to test your business plan.

E

The 1-Page Resources Plan

You can easily build a complete 1-Page Resources Plan as a result of this activity. Modify this form as necessary. Use the front and back if you need more space, but keep it to one page.

Time

Timelines included for the acquisition of the needed resources must be tied to the budget and the financial plan.

Information Requirements

Defined as:
1. Volume
2. Type
3. Usage
4. Speed of acquisition
5. Transferability
6. Accuracy

Staffing Levels

Define the following for both the short term and the long term:
1. Skills needed
2. When they are needed
3. Lead time to train
4. Key positions to fill
5. Succession planning

Image

Define the following:
1. Reputation
2. Market value of image
3. Strength of management

Facilities

Describe what is needed and the acquisition plan both short term and long term in terms of:
1. Space
2. Design and special features

Tools and Equipment

Describe what is needed and the acquisition plan both for the short term and the long term.

Technology

Describe what is needed and the acquisition plan both for the short term and for the long term. Caution: Do not build a long-term plan on technology that has not been invented.

Financial

May include all or some of the following:
1. Assorted long-range financial documents
2. Annual budget
3. Capital investments

Financials must be closely coordinated with the other resource requirements. This is especially sensitive when Level 2 details are developed. Costing of resources is especially difficult and must be given careful consideration when building a business plan. The financial staff must work in conjunction with the operating units and other functional staff to ensure the resources and financial resources support each other.

Relationships

Define in context as:
1. Strategic Alliances
2. Partnerships
3. Outsources
4. Virtual Teams
5. Internal Customers
6. External Customers

Intellectual Capital

Describe what will be done in the short term and the long term to increase the use of human potential in terms of:
1. Organizational development
2. Education
3. Knowledge
4. Training
5. Skills building

Annual Target(s) --> Strategic Goal(s)

APPENDIX

F

The 1-Page Contingency Plan

You can easily build a complete 1-Page Contingency Plan as a result of this activity. Modify this form as necessary. Use the front and back if you need more space, but keep it to one page.

Assumptions

Contingency plans are triggered when a single assumption found in your strategic plan fails. This plan calls for you to have alternatives ready to implement at the earliest decision.

People

Defined by answering these questions:
1. How to shift staffing resources if there is a loss of people?
2. How to fill losses for the long term?
3. How to shift expertise on a needed basis?
4. How to sustain ongoing activities with given staffing levels?

Leadership and Managership

Effective management control is needed even more in a contingency situation. Sustained upswings or unprogrammed surges in business growth can have serious impact on the morale of employees. Likewise, downturns in business can have devastating results. The key is to demonstrate by role modeling effective behavior.
1. Consider how to demonstrate more leadership in a crisis situation.
2. Weigh the timing of decisions made during critical periods.
3. Anticipate how employees will react to the situation.
4. Act as role models. How you act under pressure (good or bad) will be remembered long after the crisis.

Facilities

1. In case of a disaster contingency, describe what is needed in terms of:
   ■ Alternate sites
   ■ Restoration of endangered systems
   ■ Location of the management team during the crisis
2. In case of an unexpected rapid growth situation, describe what is needed in terms of:
   ■ Additional space
   ■ Additional supporting infrastructure

Information

Describe what is needed pertaining to:
1. Accurate information about the crisis or situation
2. Reestablishment of information channels
3. Policies for communications with the media

Tools and Equipment

Describe what is needed in terms of:
1. Special tools
2. Special equipment
3. Where and when the tools and equipment will be required

Time and Timing

1. When is the critical point reached for your decision?
2. How much time is remaining before the situation becomes even more damaging?
3. What is the "timing" of a decision and its effect?

Technology

1. For your present technology define:
   ■ Substitute techniques
   ■ Substitute equipment
   ■ Alternate methods
2. What is your plan to negate known competitive disruptions?
3. How do you plan to counter or offset "disruptive technology"?

Image

Consider:
1. Dangers from slow or no reaction. What messages are being sent?
2. Overreaction. What could the long-term effect be if you react too soon?
3. Community (i.e., public and business image).
   ■ How is the image affected?
   ■ How much damage control will be required?

Annual Target(s) --> Strategic Goal(s)

G

Preconference Assignment

Please answer the following questions to the best of your ability. Bring your work to the planning conference. Be prepared to discuss your responses in detail.

GUIDANCE

This is a description of restrictions placed on you. Your plan must not exceed these boundaries.

1. What is your guidance?

2. Are you now operating outside of your guidance?

3. What do you think your guidance might look like?

VISION

Describe what the company could look like at some long-term date.

1. What do you want to be in five to ten years, as a company?

2. What would that business look like? Please describe.

3. What should your vision statement be? Attempt a draft.

FOCUS

This is a description of your single driving force.

1. What is your single focus? Pick from one of the following:

   - Customer intimate—The customer is in the center of your business for problem solving.

   - Plans driven—There is a need for high compliance for success.

   - Operationally excellent—There is no wasted motion in the system.

   - Products driven—There is a steady flow of new or continuously improved products.

   - Properties driven—There is maximum focus in keeping the physical or intellectual properties in use every day.

   - Payoff driven—There is a clear understanding of why customers buy or use your products, which is usually perceived status.

2. What problems will occur when you move to a single focus?

ASSUMPTIONS

You make your plan using baselines. If they change, your plan must change.

1. What assumptions can you make for your industry?
2. What assumptions can you make for your company?

MISSION

Your mission is a definition of what business you are in today. What is your single-sentence mission statement? Attempt a draft now. Be prepared to conduct a detailed mission analysis at the planning conference.

Related to the mission are a specified task and implied tasks.

■   *Specified Task.* This identifies the single thing you must do to make money and stay viable. To identify a specified task, ask:

    1. What business are you in?
    2. Does everyone agree to this single element?

■   *Implied Tasks.* These identify all the things that must be accomplished for your mission to succeed.

    1. What are your implied tasks?
    2. How well are these tasks understood?

PHILOSOPHY

The crux here is how you plan to run your business.

1. Write your philosophy statement.
2. Is there a gap between what you say and what you do?
3. How do you propose to close the gap?

VALUES

Your values are those things you hold important to the organization as behavioral guidelines.

1. List your core values—that is, those deep-seated convictions that are important to you.
2. Define in action terms what they mean.
3. Is there a gap between what you say and what you do?
4. How do you propose to close the gap?

PRINCIPLES

These are the basic truths by which you lead and manage your business.

1. List the principles by which you intend to run your business.
2. Is there a gap between what you say and what you do?
3. How do you propose to close the gap?

STRATEGIC GOALS

Use bold statements to describe what you expect to accomplish.

1. What are the four or five bold goals you need to accomplish?
2. What will prevent you from accomplishing these goals?

OBJECTIVES

Intermediate steps are necessary to accomplish each of the more broad, strategic goals.

1. What are the four or five objectives for each goal?
2. Please write your specific objectives.

TASKS

Create a detailed list of all the items that must be accomplished. The focus is on the short term for the coming year. Tasks are assigned to specific persons with time limits set.

1. What are all the tasks that must be completed for the next year?
2. How many of these tasks will be assigned to you?

STRATEGIES

As important as your goals is how you plan to move forward. Strategies bridge the present to the future attainment of your goals.

1. What are your strategies?
2. Please list and describe each strategy.

TACTICS

A tactic is any short-term action to achieve a specific goal (i.e., "how" you plan to execute your mission).

1. What are your tactics?
2. Please list and describe various tactics to achieve specific goals.

STRATEGIC INTENT

This is a recapitulation of what you intend to implement in the future and how you intend to do it.

1. What is your strategic intent?
2. Be prepared to state this intent in public.

PROCESSES

Tasks are usually grouped in processes. These processes can be sources of great inefficiencies.

1. Name your major processes.
2. Which process do you suspect of being inefficient?
3. Who should be involved with each process?

ANNUAL TARGETS

These are the specific performance measures you will work toward meeting.

1. What do you wish to achieve next year?
2. Are these targets realistic and attainable?

3. What are your key success factors or key performance indicators?

MILESTONES

Milestones are progress markers. Ask yourself:

1. What milestones will ensure that work is being completed toward the goals?

2. Are these milestones significant or important enough to be progress markers?

AUTHORITY LEVELS

Clearly define who has specific power.

1. What are your current authority levels?

2. How are they communicated?

3. How are they measured or enforced?

4. How is accountability used in your organization?

COORDINATING INSTRUCTIONS

These are specific instructions to work units of how they are to coordinate their collective implied tasks. Instructions ensure continuity of the process of providing the goods or services.

1. Is your plan uncoordinated? If so, what are the causes?

2. Who needs to coordinate with whom?

CURRENT ASSESSMENT

Do a present-day analysis of the following items:

❑   Target Markets

1. Who is and isn't your principal market? Be very disciplined in this identification.

2. Who are your customers?

3. How profitable is each market segment or account?

4. Where do your customers come from?

5. How do you know where they come from?

❑   Management Team

1. What are your strengths and weaknesses as a business team today?

2. Historically, where have you succeeded and where have you failed?

3. What is your management's track record so far?

4. Do you believe this management team can succeed? If not, why?

❑   Customer Satisfaction

1. When was the last time you completed a customer satisfaction survey?

2. What shortfalls were identified in your last survey?

3. What has been done to date to complete the actions to correct issues?

❑   Employee Satisfaction

1. When was the last time you completed an employee satisfaction survey?

2. What shortfalls were identified in your last survey?

3. What has been done to date to complete the actions to correct issues?

❏   Business Development

1.   Where are you on the growth line? Is your organization entrepreneurial, professionally managed, or bureaucratic?

2.   Are you "stuck" or flat in growth?

3.   How do you plan to get unstuck?

❏   Other Data

1.   What other information is available that would be useful in the planning process?

2.   Have you interpreted the data wisely?

STRUCTURE

Structure refers to how you plan to organize to accomplish your business plan.

1.   Does your organizational structure use the talents of all people and resources?

2.   Does it control business drivers?

3.   Does it aid coordination among critical staff sections?

4.   Does it facilitate the development, motivation, and retention of key people?

5.   Does it help achieve minimum costs?

6.   Is there duplication of work?

7.   Is the right person doing work?

8.   Is there fragmentation of work being created by your structure?

9.   Is all work that should be done being attempted?

10. What work should not be done?

RESOURCES

You need facilities, tools, equipment, time, and human resources to accomplish your business plan.

1. What technology do you need?
2. What skill sets and numbers of people do you need?
3. Are you using your intellectual capital to its full advantage?
4. What relationships need to be developed?
5. What impact does time have on your plan?
6. What type and kind of facilities do you need?
7. What information and information systems do you need?

CONTINGENCY: "WHAT IF" SITUATIONS

1. What is the worst situation that can happen in your business?
2. What alternative plans have you made for adverse situations?

Plan Continuity

Your plan must reach down from the top to the lowest level of the organization. This includes all teams and individuals. The number of levels will differ from organization to organization, but all levels must be included or the plan will not have continuity.

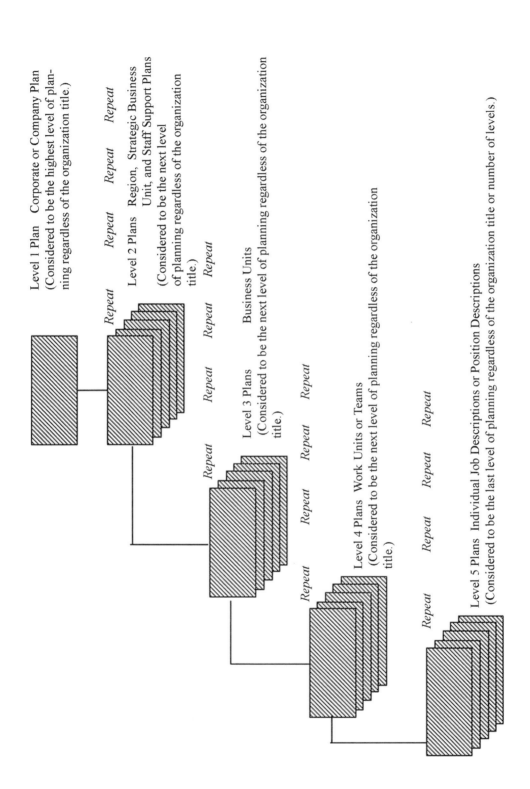

Level 1 Plan   Corporate or Company Plan
(Considered to be the highest level of planning regardless of the organization title.)

Level 2 Plans   Region, Strategic Business
Unit, and Staff Support Plans
(Considered to be the next level
of planning regardless of the organization
title.)

Level 3 Plans   Business Units
(Considered to be the next level of planning regardless of the organization
title.)

Level 4 Plans   Work Units or Teams
(Considered to be the next level of planning regardless of the organization
title.)

Level 5 Plans   Individual Job Descriptions or Position Descriptions
(Considered to be the last level of planning regardless of the organization title or number of levels.)

Repeat   Repeat   Repeat

Repeat   Repeat   Repeat

Repeat   Repeat   Repeat

Repeat   Repeat   Repeat

Repeat   Repeat   Repeat

BUSINESS UNIT SUPPORT OF COMPANY PLAN

Development Plan
Describe the education, skills, and training required to support your plan. State the schedule to complete development.

Intent
Describe your intentions for your business unit. Describe how you plan to communicate the company business plan and the business unit plan to all staff members.

Structure
Examine your structure in view of the plan. Describe long- and short-term change requirements.

Cost Reduction
Identify the major areas where costs containment and control can be practiced. State your schedule to conduct formal work on these efforts. Tie the results to the measurements in the company plan. Tie individual performance management to the cost-reduction activities.

Contingency Plan
Describe how you plan to support the company's catastrophic contingency plan. Describe how you plan to deal with more local or routine blocks to your business unit plan. Describe what you will do if a major assumption in the company business plan fails.

Resource Requirements
What resources are required for the one-year tactical plan? What resources are required for the long-term strategic plan?

Operational Tasks
What specific tasks must be completed for the next year? (These are the nuts and bolts of daily operations.)

Principles
Check to make sure you have not violated any of the business principles.

Business Unit Goal(s)
What are the goals for your business unit?

Operational Targets
What are your total annual business unit targets? What are your quarterly milestones? What are your performance measures? Have these been tied to annual performance reviews?

Business Unit Objectives
What objectives do you have to support your goals?

Philosophy
State how you plan to support the company's philosophy.

Focus
A description of your unit's single driving force. Is your focus consistent with the company's driving forces? Is it consistent with other units? How will differences be played out operationally? What must you do to resolve any operational disconnects at both levels? How will you maintain acceptable performance levels on the other five drivers?

Assumptions
What assumption do you need to make for your specific business unit?

Values
How do you plan to reinforce the company values? How do you plan to close any identified gaps?

Guidance
This is a description of restrictions placed on you by the company plan. Your business unit plan must not exceed these boundaries.

Mission
Specified Task: Identifies what purpose your business unit serves for the company.
Implied Tasks: Identifies implied functions you must perform. Implied tasks are key to effective coordination of the company's overall plan.

STAFF SUPPORT OF COMPANY PLAN

Development Plan
Describe the education, skills, and training required to support your plan. State the schedule to complete development.

Contingency Plan
Describe how you plan to support the company's catastrophic contingency plan. Describe how you plan to deal with more local or routine blocks to your staff support plan. Describe what you will do if a major assumption in the company business plan or your staff plan fails.

Intent
Describe your intentions for your staff function. Describe how you plan to communicate the company business plan and the staff unit plan to all staff members.

Structure
Examine your structure in view of the plan. Describe long- and short-term change requirements.

Cost Reduction
Identify the major areas where costs containment and control can be practiced. State your schedule to conduct formal work on these efforts. Tie the results to the measurements in the company plan. Tie the individual performance management to the cost-reduction activities.

Operational Targets
What are your total annual staff targets? What are your quarterly milestones? What are your performance measures? Have these been tied to annual performance reviews?

Resource Requirements
What resources are required for the one-year tactical plan? What resources are required for the long-term strategic plan?

Operational Tasks
What specific tasks must be completed for the next year? (These are the nuts and bolts of daily operations.)

Staff Goals
What are the goals for your staff?

Philosophy
State how you plan to reinforce and support the company philosophy statement.

Staff Objectives
What objectives support your goals or the company's strategic goals?

Principles
State the principles of your staff function that underpin your building of this plan.

Focus
A description of your staff's single driving force. Is your staff focus consistent with the company's driving forces? Is it consistent with other staff sections? How will differences be played out operationally? What must you do to resolve any operational disconnects at both levels? How will you maintain acceptable performance levels on the other five drivers?

Values
How do you plan to reinforce the company values? How do you plan to close any identified gaps?

Guidance
This is a description of restrictions placed on you by the company plan. Your staff support must not exceed these boundaries.

Assumptions
What assumptions can you make about your staff function to support the company plan?

Mission
Specified Task: Identifies what purpose your staff function serves for the company.
Implied Tasks: Identifies implied functions you must perform. Implied tasks are key to effective staff coordination.

INDIVIDUAL SUPPORT OF COMPANY PLAN

An individual performance plan consists of the answers to three questions:

- *What am I supposed to do today to support the company goals (i.e., my mission)?* This "individual plan" consists of four or five tasks that help the organization accomplish its vision and mission.

- *How will I be measured?* Know what your company's performance measurement plan involves.

- *How will I be rewarded?* Know what kind of pay, compensation, bonus, and other rewards your company or business unit offers.

Master Action Plan Worksheet

This is a place to design your action items. It allows you to start with the strategic goals and work backward to the detailed tasks list necessary to ensure you have accounted for all planned work. The tasks must be cut over to your calendar.

Master Action Plan Worksheet

Mission

Vision

This section answers the question "what is to be accomplished."

				Strategic Goal
	Tasks	**Objectives**		1.
Specified Task	**Implied Tasks**	1.		
1.	1.	2.		
	2.	3		
	3.	4		
	4.			
	5.			
	6.			

This section answers the question of "how it will be accomplished."

—————— **Strategies** ——————
1.
2.

Tactics
1.
2.

This section answers the question "what is to be measured."

Weekly Targets	**Monthly Targets**	**Quarterly Targets**	**Annual Targets**
1.	1.	1.	1.
2.	2.	2.	2.
3.	3.	3.	3.

Note: The numbers vary for each category. Here are general numbers as "rules of thumb."
1. You will probably have no more than 4 strategic goals
2. Each strategic goal will have no more that 4 to 5 objectives
3. Each objective will have 5 to 6 tasks
4. You will probably have 1–2 strategies per strategic goal
5. You will probably have 2–3 tactics per strategic goal
6. Implied tasks from the mission statement must match with the tasks supporting the objectives
7. The numbers of monthly, quarterly, and annual targets may vary but must include all functions in the business

Note: Each strategic goal, objective, and task must have the following:
1. A time condition such as a completion date
2. A resources requirements list
3. A person identified for accountability and responsibility
4. A coordination work plan relating to other persons and tasks

Copyright 2000, Al Coke
All rights reserved.

Short-Term or "Quick Fix" Action Plan Worksheet

This is a place to capture all the "to do" items you identified during the planning process.

They are quick hits or actions to:
      a. Prevent embarassment
      b. Trigger short immediate action results
      c. Instill confidence in the plan

These actions should cut over to your calendar.

Short-Term or "Quick Fix" Action Plan Worksheet

Action Source	Person/Agency	Task Description	Measurement Indicators	Date Completed	Resources Required
Assessment Issues (All issues needing attention found in the preplanning interviews)					
Cultural Issues (All gap issues found during planning)					
1. Gap analysis of philosophy 2. Gap analysis of values 3. Gap analysis of principles 4. Gap analysis from single business focus					

Copyright 2000, Al Coke
All rights reserved.

NOTES

CHAPTER 1

1. Howard Gardner, *Leading Minds: An Anatomy of Leadership* (Basic Books, 1995), p. 43.
2. Margaret J. Wheatley, *Leadership and the New Science* (San Francisco: Berrett-Koehler Publishers Inc., 1992), p. 55.
3. Ichak Adizes, *Corporate Lifecycles: How and Why Corporations Grow and Die and What to Do About It* (New Jersey: Prentice Hall, 1988), p. 93.
4. Thomas J. Peters, *The Circle of Innovation* (New York: Alfred A. Knopf Inc., 1997), p. 372.

CHAPTER 2

1. *Violence and Theft in the Workplace,* U.S. Department of Justice, Bureau of Justice, Statistics Crime Data Brief NCJ-148199 (July 1994).

CHAPTER 3

1. Danah Zohar and Ian Marshall, *Quantum Society: Mind, Physics, and a New Social Vision* (New York: William Morrow and Company Inc., 1994), p. 23.

2. Frances Hesselbein, Marshall Goldsmith, and Richard Beckhard, eds., *The Organization of the Future* (San Francisco: Jossey-Bass Publishers, 1997), pp. 215–342.
3. Peter M. Senge, *The Fifth Discipline: The Art and Practice of the Learning Organization* (New York: Doubleday Currency, 1990), p. 22.
4. Alan Downs, *Beyond the Looking Glass: Overcoming the Seductive Culture of Corporate Narcissism* (New York: AMACOM, 1997), p. 80.

CHAPTER 4

1. Howard Gardner, *Leading Minds: An Anatomy of Leadership* (New York: Basic Books, 1995), pp. 42–43.
2. Frances Hesselbein, Marshall Goldsmith, and Richard Beckhard, eds., *The Organization of the Future* (San Francisco: Jossey-Bass Publishers, 1997), p. 347.
3. Bruce A. Pasternack and Albert J. Viscio, *The Centerless Corporation: A New Model for Transforming Your Organization for Growth and Prosperity* (New York: Simon & Schuster, 1998), p. 272.
4. Peter M. Senge, *The Fifth Discipline: The Art and Practice of the Learning Organization* (New York: Doubleday Currency, 1990), p. 212.

CHAPTER 5

1. Henry Ford Museum, Dearborn, Mich. (on a plaque inside the museum).
2. Frances Hesselbein, Marshall Goldsmith, and Richard Beckhard, eds., *The Organization of the Future* (San Francisco: Jossey-Bass Publishers, 1997), p. 215.
3. Sam Walton with John Huey, *Sam Walton Made in America, My Story* (New York: Doubleday, 1992).
4. James C. Collins and Jerry I. Porras, *Built to Last: Successful Habits of Visionary Companies* (New York: HarperBusiness, 1994), p. 9.
5. Thor Valdmanis, "AHP-Monsanto Merger Dies From Culture Clash." *USA Today*, October 14, 1998.
6. Peter Elkind, "Cendant: A Merger Made in Hell," *Fortune* (November 9, 1998), p. 134.
7. Gordon R. Sullivan and Michael V. Harper, *Hope Is Not a Method: What Business Leaders Can Learn From America's Army* (New York: Times Business, Random House, 1996), p. 98; pp.134–135.

CHAPTER 6

1. Michael Treacy and Fred Wiersema, *The Discipline of Market Leaders* (Reading, Mass.: Addison-Wesley Publishing Company, 1995), p. xiv.
2. Robert W. Keidel, *Corporate Players: Designs for Working and Winning Together* (New York: John Wiley & Sons, 1988), p. xviii.
3. Hal Rosenbluth, *The Customer Comes Second, and Other Secrets of Exceptional Service,* (New York: Quil, 1994).
4. Sam Walton with John Huey, *Sam Walton Made in America: My Story* (New York: Doubleday, 1992), p. 50.
5. Laura Goldstein, "Dressing Up an Old Brand," *Fortune* (November 9, 1998), p. 154.
6. Charles Fombrun, *Reputation: Realizing Value From the Corporate Image* (Boston: Harvard Business School Press, 1996), p. 5.

CHAPTER 7

1. James C. Collins and Jerry I. Porras, *Built to Last: Successful Habits of Visionary Companies* (New York: HarperBusiness, 1994), p. 73.
2. Michael Lewis, *Liar's Poker, Rising Through the Wreckage on Wall Street* (New York: W. W. Norton & Company, 1989), p. 167.
3. John Micklethwait and Adrian Wooldridge, *The Witch Doctors: Making Sense Out of Management Gurus* (New York: Times Books, 1996), p. 142.
4. Ibid., p. 118
5. Gordon R. Sullivan and Michael V. Harper, *Hope Is Not a Method: What Business Leaders Can Learn From America's Army* (New York: Times Business, Random House, 1996), p. 134.

CHAPTER 8

1. Garrett Hardin, "The Tragedy of the Commons," *Science* (December 13, 1968), p. 295.

CHAPTER 9

1. James P. Womack, Daniel T. Jones, and Daniel Roos, *The Machine That Changed the World: The Story of Lean Production* (New York: Harper Perennial, 1990), p. 138.
2. This story comes from a 1986 six-hour BBC television series produced by Gordon Menzies, *The Celts: Rich Traditions and Ancient Myths*, presented by Frank Delaney, segment produced by Tony McAuley, directed by David Richardson.
3. Dr. T. O. Jacobs, *Social Exchange in Formal Organizations* (Alexandria, Va.: Human Resources Research Organization, 1970), p. 44.
4. Danah Zohar and Ian Marshall, *Quantum Society: Mind, Physics, and a New Social Vision* (New York: William Morrow and Company Inc., 1994), p. 29.

CHAPTER 10

1. Thomas J. Peters and Robert H. Waterman Jr., *In Search of Excellence: Lessons From America's Best-Run Companies* (New York: Harper & Row Publishers,1982), p 119.
2. Gordon R. Sullivan and Michael V. Harper, *Hope Is Not a Method: What Business Leaders Can Learn From America's Army* (New York: Times Business, Random House, 1996), pp. xv-xxii.
3. Donald G. Shomette, *Shipwrecks on the Chesapeake: Maritime Disasters on Chesapeake Bay and Its Tributaries, 1608–1978* (Centreville, Md.: Tidewater Publishers, 1982), p. 129.
4. George Labovitz and Victor Rosansky, *The Power of Alignment: How Great Companies Stay Centered and Accomplish Extraordinary Things* (New York: John Wiley & Sons, Inc., 1997), p. 4.
5. James R. Lucas, *Fatal Illusions: Shredding a Dozen Unrealities That Can Keep Your Organization From Success* (New York: AMACOM, 1997), p. 59.
6. James P. Womack, Daniel T. Jones, and Daniel Roos, *The Machine That Changed the World: The Story of Lean Production* (New York: Harper Perennial, 1990), p. 26.

7. Robert Friedman, ed., *The Life Millennium: The 100 Most Important Events and People of the Past 1,000 Years* (Life Books Time Inc., 1998), p. 139.
8. Mary Walton, *The Deming Management Method* (New York: The Putnam Publishing Group, 1986), p. 10.
9. Masaaki Imai, *Kaizen: The Key to Japan's Competitive Success*, 5th Edition (New York: McGraw Hill Publishing Company, 1986), p. xx.
10. Philip Crosby, *Quality Is Free* (Cambridge: McGraw-Hill, 1979), p. 101.
11. Phillip R. Thomas, *Competitiveness Through Total Cycle Time: An Overview for CEOs* (New York: McGraw-Hill Publishing Company, 1990), inside flap of jacket cover.
12. Charles J. Fombrun, *Reputation: Realizing Values From the Corporate Image* (Boston: Harvard Business School Press, 1996), p. 81.

CHAPTER 11

1. General H. Norman Schwarzkopf with Peter Petre, *The Autobiography: It Doesn't Take a Hero* (New York: Bantam Books, 1992), p. 502.
2. Philip B. Crosby, *Completeness: Quality for the 21st Century* (New York: Penguin Group, 1992), p. 214.
3. George A. Steiner, *Strategic Planning: What Every Manager Must Know* (New York: Simon & Schuster, 1979), p. 230.
4. Ibid.
5. Peter M. Senge, *The Fifth Discipline, The Art and Practice of the Learning Organization* (New York: Doubleday, 1990), p. 8–9.
6. Lee Iacocca with William Novak, *Iacocca, an Autobiography* (New York: Bantam Books, 1984), p. 189.
7. Donald Shomette, *Shipwrecks on the Chesapeake: Maritime Disasters on Chesapeake Bay and Its Tributaries, 1608–1978* (Centreville, Md.: Tidewater Publishers, 1982), p. xii.
8. Larry Barton, Ph.D., *Crisis: When Disaster Strikes*, video. Produced by Zaretsky and Assocs., (702) 898-0711, available by calling (800) 328-0500.

BOOKS

A

Adams, John D., gen. ed. *Transforming Work*, 2nd ed. Alexandria, Va.: Miles River Press, 1998.

Adizes, Ichak. *Corporate Lifecycles, How and Why Corporations Grow and Die and What to Do About It*. New Jersey: Prentice Hall, 1988.

B

Barker, Joel Arthur. *Discovering the Future: The Business of Paradigms*. St. Paul, Minn.: ILI Press, 1985.

Bridges, William. *Managing Transitions: Making the Most of Change*. Reading, Mass.: Addison-Wesley Publishing Company, 1991.

Brill, Peter L. and Richard Worth. *The Four Levers of Corporate Change*. New York: AMACOM, 1997.

Violence and Theft in the Workplace. U.S. Department of Justice, Bureau of Justice, Statistics Crime Data Brief NCJ-148199, July 1994.

C

Carr, Clay. *Choice, Change, and Organizational Change: Practical Insights From Evolution for Business Leaders & Thinkers*. New York: AMACOM, 1996.

Celente, Gerald. *Trends 2000: How to Prepare for and Profit From the Changes of the 21st Century*. New York: Warner Books, Inc., 1997.

Cohen, Jack and Ian Stewart. *The Collapse of Chaos: Discovering Simplicity in a Complex World*. New York: Viking, 1994.

Collins, James C., and Jerry I. Porras. *Built to Last: Successful Habits of Visionary Companies,* New York: HarperBusiness, 1994.

Crosby, Philip B. *Completeness: Quality for the 21st Century*. New York: Penguin Group, 1992.

Crosby, Philip. *Quality Is Free*. Cambridge: McGraw-Hill, 1979.

D

Davidow, William H. and Michael S. Malone. *The Virtual Corporation: Structuring and Revitalizing the Corporation for the 21st Century*. New York: Harper Collins Publishers, 1992.

Davis, Stan and Bill Davidson. *2020 Vision: Transform Your Business Today to Succeed in Tomorrow's Economy*. New York: Fireside, 1991.

Deal, Terrence E. and Allen A. Kennedy. *Corporate Cultures: The Rites and Rituals of Corporate Life*. Reading, Mass.: Addison-Wesley Publishing Company, 1982.

Downs, Alan. *Beyond the Looking Glass: Overcoming the Seductive Culture of Corporate Narcissism*. New York: AMACOM, 1997.

Drucker, Peter F. *Managing in a Time of Great Change*. New York: Truman Talley Books/Dutton, 1995.

E

Enrico, Roger and Jesse Kornbluth. *The Other Guy Blinked: How Pepsi Won the Cola Wars*. New York: Bantam Books, 1986.

F

Fombrun, Charles J. *Reputation, Realizing Value from the Corporate Image.* Boston: Harvard Business School Press, 1996.

Friedman, Robert, ed. *The* Life *Millennium: The 100 Most Important Events and People of the Past 1,000 Years.* Life Books Time Inc., 1998.

G

Gardner, Howard. *Leading Minds: An Anatomy of Leadership.* New York: BasicBooks, 1995.

Gibson, Rowan, ed. *Rethinking the Future.* London: Nicholas Brealey Publishing, 1997.

Gleick, James. *Chaos: Making a New Science.* New York: Penguin Books, 1987.

Goldratt, Eliyahu M. and Jeff Cox. *The Goal: A Process of Ongoing Improvement.* Great Barrington, Mass.: North River Press, Inc., 1984.

Goleman, Daniel, *Working With Emotional Intelligence,* New York: Bantam Books, 1998.

H

Hamel, Gary and C. K. Prahalad. *Competing for the Future.* Boston: Harvard Business School Press, 1994.

Hammer, Michael. *Beyond Reengineering.* New York: Harper Collins Publishers, 1996.

Hammer, Michael and James Champy. *Reengineering the Corporation: A Manifesto for Business Revolution.* New York: Harper Business, 1993.

Henry, Robert Selph. *First With the Most: Nathan Bedford Forrest.* New York: Mallard Press, 1991.

Hersey, Paul and Ken Blanchard. *Management of Organizational Behavior: Utilizing Human Resources,* 4th ed. Englewood Cliffs, N.J.: Prentice-Hall, 1982.

Hesselbein, Frances, Marshall Goldsmith and Richard Beckhard, eds. *The Organization of the Future.* San Francisco: Jossey-Bass Publishers, 1997.

Hickman, Craig R. and Michael A. Silva. *Creating Excellence: Managing Corporate Culture, Strategy, and Change in the New Age.* New York: NAL Books, 1984.

I

Iacocca, Lee with William Novak. *Iacocca: An Autobiography.* New York: Bantam Books, 1984.

Imai, Masaaki. *Kaizen: The Key to Japan's Competitive Success*, 5th ed. New York: McGraw Hill, 1986.

J

Jacobs, Dr. T. O. *Social Exchange in Formal Organizations.* Alexandra, Va.: Human Resources Research Organization, 1970.

K

Kanter, Rosabeth Moss. *The Change Masters: Innovation for Productivity in the American Corporation.* New York: Simon & Schuster, 1983.

Kaplan, Robert S. and David P. Norton. *Balanced Scorecard.* Boston: Harvard Business School Press, 1996.

Keidel, Robert W. *Corporate Players: Designs for Working and Winning Together.* New York: John Wiley & Sons, 1988.

Kotter, John P. *Leading Change.* Boston: Harvard Business School Press, 1996.

Kouzes, James M. and Barry Z. Posner. *Credibility: How Leaders Gain and Lose It, Why People Demand It.* San Francisco: Jossey-Bass Publishers, 1993.

L

Labovitz, George and Victor Rosansky. *The Power of Alignment: How Great Companies Stay Centered and Accomplish Extraordinary Things.* New York: John Wiley & Sons, 1997.

Lewis, Michael. *Liar's Poker: Rising Through the Wreckage on Wall Street.* New York: W. W. Norton & Company, 1989.

Liebig, James E. *Merchants of Vision: People Bringing New Purpose and Values to Business.* San Francisco: Berrett-Koehler Publishers Inc., 1994.

Lucas, James R. *Fatal Illusions: Shredding a Dozen Unrealities That Can Keep Your Organization From Success.* New York: AMACOM, 1997.

M

Marks, Mitchell Lee and Philip H. Mirvis. *Joining Forces: Making One Plus One Equal Three in Mergers, Acquisitions, and Alliances.* San Francisco: Jossey-Bass Publishers, 1998.

Matejka, Ken and Richard J. Dunsing. *A Manager's Guide to the Millennium.* New York: AMACOM, 1995.

McNeilly, Mark. *Sun-Tzu and the Art of Business: Six Strategic Principles for Managers.* Oxford: Oxford University Press, 1996.

Micklethwait, John and Adrian Wooldridge. *The Witch Doctors: Making Sense of the Management Gurus.* New York: Random House, Inc., 1996.

Miles, Robert H. *Leading Corporate Transformation: A Blueprint for Business Renewal.* San Francisco: Jossey-Bass Publishers, 1997.

Miner, Margaret and Hugh Rawson. *The New International Dictionary of Quotations*, 2nd ed. New York: Penguin Books, 1994.

N

Naisbitt, John. *Global Paradox: The Bigger the World Economy, the More Powerful Its Smallest Players.* New York: William Morrow and Company, Inc., 1994.

Naisbitt, John and Patricia Aburdene. *Megatrends 2000.* New York: William Morrow and Company, Inc., 1990.

Nolan, Richard L. and David C. Croson. *Creative Destruction: A Six-Stage Process for Transforming the Organization.* Boston: Harvard Business School Press, 1995.

O

O'Toole, James. *Leading Change.* San Francisco: Jossey-Bass Inc. 1995.

P

Pasternack, Bruce A. and Albert J. Viscio. *The Centerless Corporation: A New Model for Transforming Your Organization for Growth and Prosperity.* New York: Simon & Schuster, 1998.

Peppers, Don and Martha Rogers, Ph.D. *The One to One Future: Building Relationships One Customer at a Time.* New York: Doubleday Currency, 1993.

Peters, Thomas J. *The Tom Peters Seminar: Crazy Times Call for Crazy Organizations.* New York: Vintage Books, 1994.

Peters, Thomas J. *The Circle of Innovation.* New York: Alfred A. Knopf Inc., 1997.

Peters, Thomas, J. and Robert H. Waterman Jr. *In Search of Excellence: Lessons From America's Best-Run Companies.* New York: Harper & Row Publishers, 1982.

Prigogine, Ilya. *Order Out of Chaos.* New York: Bantam Books, 1970.

R

Robert, Michel. *Strategy Pure & Simple: How Winning CEOs Outthink Their Competition.* New York: McGraw-Hill, Inc., 1993.

Rosenbluth, Hal. *The Customer Comes Second, and Other Secrets of Exceptional Service.* New York: Quil, 1994.

S

Sanders, T. Irene. *Strategic Thinking and the New Science: Planning in the Midst of Chaos, Complexity, and Change.* New York: The Free Press, 1998.

Schwartz, Peter. *The Art of the Long View.* New York: Doubleday Currency, 1991.

Schwarzkopf, General H. Norman, with Peter Petre. *The Autobiography: It Doesn't Take a Hero.* New York: Bantam Books, 1992.

Scott-Morgan, Peter. *The Unwritten Rules of the Game.* New York: McGraw-Hill, Inc., 1994.

Senge, Peter M. *The Fifth Discipline: The Art and Practice of the Learning Organization.* New York: Doubleday Currency, 1990.

Sherman, Andrew J. *Mergers and Acquisitions From A to Z: Strategic and Practical Guidelines for Small- and Middle-Market Buyers and Sellers.* New York: AMACOM, 1998.

Shomette, Donald G. *Shipwrecks on the Chesapeake: Maritime Disasters on Chesapeake Bay and Its Tributaries, 1608–1978.* Centreville, Md.: Tidewater Publishers, 1982.

Silver, A. David. *Quantum Companies: 100 Companies That Will Change the Face of Tomorrow's Business.* Princeton, N.J.: Peterson's/Pacesetter Books, 1995.

Simon, Hermann. *Hidden Champions: Lessons Learned From 500 of the World's Best Unknown Companies.* Boston: Harvard Business School Press, 1996.

Slywotzky, Adrian J. *Values Migration: How to Think Several Moves Ahead of the Competition.* Boston: Harvard Business School Press, 1996.

Stack, Jack. *The Great Game of Business.* New York: Doubleday, 1992.

Steiner, George A. *Strategic Planning: What Every Manager Must Know.* New York: Simon & Schuster, 1979.

Stine, G. Harry. *The Corporate Survivors.* New York: AMACOM, 1986.

Sullivan, Gordon R. and Michael V. Harper. *Hope Is Not a Method: What Business Leaders Can Learn From America's Army.* New York: Times Business, Random House, 1996.

T

Talbot, Michael. *The Holographic Universe.* New York: Harper Collins Publishers, 1991.

Tapscott, Don and Art Caston. *Paradigm Shift: The New Promise of Information Technology.* New York: McGraw-Hill, 1993.

Thomas, Phillip R. *Competitiveness Through Total Cycle Time: An Overview for CEOs.* New York: McGraw-Hill, 1990.

Tobin, Daniel R. *Re-Educating the Corporation: Foundations for the Learning Organization.* Essex Junction, Vt.: Oliver Wight Publications, Inc., 1993.

Tomasko, Robert M. *Rethinking the Corporation: The Architecture of Change.* New York: AMACOM, 1993.

Treacy, Michael and Fred Wiersema. *The Discipline of Market Leaders.* Reading, Mass.: Addison-Wesley Publishing Company, 1995.

U

Ulrich, Dave and Dale Lake. *Organizational Capability: Competing From the Inside Out.* New York: John Wiley & Sons, 1990.

W

Waldrop, M. Mitchell. *Complexity: The Emerging Science at the Edge of Order and Chaos.* New York: Simon & Schuster, 1992.

Walton, Mary. *The Deming Management Method.* New York: The Putnam Publishing Group, 1986.

Walton, Sam, with John Huey. *Sam Walton Made in America, My Story.* New York: Doubleday, 1992.

Waterman, Robert H., Jr. *The Renewal Factor: How the Best Get and Keep the Competitive Edge.* New York: Bantam Books, 1987.

Welsh, Douglas. *The Complete Military History of the Civil War.* Greenwich, Conn.: Dorset Press, 1990.

Wheatley, Margaret J. *Leadership and the New Science.* San Francisco: Berrett-Koehler Publishers Inc., 1992.

Wick, Calhoun W. and Lu Stanton Leon. *The Learning Edge: How Smart Managers and Smart Companies Stay Ahead.* New York: McGraw-Hill, Inc., 1993.

Womack, James P., Daniel T. Jones, and Daniel Roos. *The Machine That Changed the World: The Story of Lean Production*, New York: Harper Perennial, 1990.

Wurman, Richard Saul. *Information Anxiety.* New York: Doubleday, 1989.

Z

Zey, Michael G., Ph.D. *Seizing the Future.* New York: Simon & Schuster, 1994.

Zohar, Danah and Ian Marshall. *Quantum Society: Mind, Physics, and a New Social Vision.* New York: William Morrow and Company Inc., 1994.

MAGAZINES AND NEWSPAPERS

Elkind, Peter. "A Merger Made in Hell." *Fortune* (November 9, 1998).

Goldstein, Laura. "Dressing Up an Old Brand." *Fortune* (November 9, 1998).

Hardin, Garrett. "The Tragedy of the Commons." *Science* (December 13, 1968).

RESEARCH STUDIES

American Competitiveness Study: Characteristics of Success. Ernst & Young (1990).

Business Goals and Strategies: The Human Resources Perspective. The American Management Association. New York: AMA Research, 1995.

Change Management: A Survey of Major U.S. Corporations. American Management Association and Deloitte & Touche LLP. New York: AMA Research, 1995.

INSTITUTIONS

The Henry Ford Museum, Dearborn, Mich.

VIDEOS

Barton, Larry, Ph.D. *Crisis: When Disaster Strikes.* Produced by Zaretsky and Associates, (702) 898-0711, available by calling (800) 328-0500.

The Celts: Rich Traditions and Ancient Myths. BBC program, presented by Frank Delaney, series produced by Gordon Menzies, segment produced by Tony McAuley, directed by David Richardson. (1986).

INDEX